CRESTLINE

GIANT
EARTHMOVERS

KEITH HADDOCK

MBI Publishing Company

First published in 1998 by MBI Publishing Company, 729 Prospect Avenue, PO Box 1, Osceola, WI 54020-0001 USA

MBI Publishing Company books are also available at discounts in bulk quantity for industrial or sales-promotional use. For details write to Special Sales Manager at Motorbooks International Publishers & Wholesalers, 729 Prospect Avenue, PO Box 1, Osceola, WI 54020-0001 USA.

Printed in the United States of America

Library of Congress Cataloging-in-Publication Data
Haddock, Keith.
    Giant earthmovers : an illustrated history/
    Keith Haddock.
      p. cm. – (Crestline series)
    Includes index.
    ISBN 0-7603-0369-X (paperback : alk. paper)
    1. Earthmoving machinery–History. I. Title. II. Series.
TA725.H33   1998
624.1'52–dc21   98-3692

On the front cover: The immense scale of this Bucyrus-Erie 1650-B stripping shovel is put into perspective by the two men standing inside its 55-yard dipper. Most passenger cars and trucks could fit inside with room to spare. This is the first 1650-B delivered to the River Queen Mine. Later the 1650-Bs had their dipper capacity increased to 70 cubic yards. *Bucyrus International*

On the back cover: **Top photo:** Colossal. Titanic. Mammoth. Even these adjectives understate the size of bucket wheel excavators. As a class, the bucket wheel excavators are the largest excavators in existence, and they are the largest mobile land machines on the planet. The W4 Kolbe wheel, a cross-pit bucket wheel machine built by the Freeman-United Coal Mining Company, has the capacity to excavate at the rate of 2 million cubic yards of overburden per month. **Bottom photo:** Caterpillar, commonly known as Cat, is one of the most recognizable names in the earthmoving business. This particular species is a hydraulic mining shovel. This model, the 5230, is the largest hydraulic excavator made by Caterpillar. Powered by a Caterpillar 1,470-horsepower engine, it weighs just under 350 tons.

CONTENTS

ACKNOWLEDGMENTS

I am indebted to the many individuals and organizations who responded to my requests for information, photographs, and literature. To those listed below and others too numerous to mention, I thank you for your help in making this book the "bible" of earthmoving equipment. Whether you provided a vast amount of information, and photographs, or just one single but vital piece of information, I really appreciate your time and effort. Without your help, this major book project could not have turned out to be as comprehensive and accurate as I believe it to be. To all those who have helped in a greater or lesser degree, I thank each one of you.

Steen Ahlberg, O&K Orenstein & Koppel, Inc. Canada; Peter Ahrenkiel, O&K Orenstein & Koppel, Inc. U.S.A.; P. Aydin, Cleveland Trencher Co.; William Barlow/Champion Road Machinery Ltd.; Peter Bence, Tiger Engineering, Australia; Tom Berry, Historical Construction Equipment Association; Mike Borodawka, C.R.C. Evans Ltd.; The Canadian Institute of Mining; Matt Cloutier, Badger Construction Equipment Co.; Stuart Davis, Rimpull Corporation; Lynne Dunstan, Banister Equipment; Dennis Fearon, Svedala Bulk Materials Handling; Don Frantz, Historical Construction Equipment Association; The Galion Historical Society; Denis Gaspe, Fording Coal Ltd.; Ad Gevers, Son en Breugel, Netherlands; Al Gilbert, Trencor, Inc.; Peter Gilewicz, Marion Power Shovel Co.; Edie Gillette, Trencor, Inc.; Karen Greer, LeTourneau University; Peter Grimshaw, PNG Communications; Lee Haak, Komatsu America International Co.; Ian Hamilton, Terex Equipment Ltd. Scotland; Arthur Henuset, Henuset Pipeline Services Ltd.; Mike Holland, Holland Construction Co.; Pete Holman, Caterpillar, Inc.; Lutz Holthaus, O&K Orenstein & Koppel, AG, Germany; Merilee Hunt, Liebherr Mining Equipment Co.; Russell Hutchison, Milwaukee, Wisconsin; Bob Jelinek, Bucyrus International, Inc.; Russell Jones, Hurley, England; Wayne Kabert, Cline Truck Manufacturing Co.; Harold Kammerzell, Jr., Atlas Copco Wagner; Ron Ketron, Indianapolis, Indiana; Bruce Knight, Transwest Dynequip; Cindy Knight, State Historical Society of Wisconsin; Leigh Knudson, Costa Mesa, California; Edward Kress, Kress Corporation; Dave Lang, Bucyrus International, Inc.; Mike Larson, Manitowoc Cranes, Inc.; John Leach, Hitachi Construction Machinery Canada Ltd.; Yvon LeCadre, Trignac, France; Joyce Luster, Caterpillar, Inc.; Frank Mancini, Mancini and Associates; Darin McCoy, CMI Corporation; Chris Metzger, Shelby, Ohio; Chris Meurer, Fiat-Allis North America; Vern Miles, Taylor Machine Works, Inc.; Tim Miller, Komatsu America International Co.; Aidan Mitchell, Krupp Canada; Gordon Morris, Wajax Industries Ltd.; Carlos Moser, Marion Power Shovel Co.; Bob Myers, Berrien County Historical Association; Bill Nelson, Payhauler Corporation; Randall Nelson, John Deere & Company; Alvin E. Nus, Volvo Construction Equipment; Eric Orlemann, ECO Communications; Bob Pierce, Unit Rig, Div. Terex; Francis Pierre, ATM, Malakoff, France; Ed Prodor, Prodor Construction Co. Ltd.; Max Richler, Maxter Industries Ltd.; David Rogers, Case Corporation; Jim Rosso, Bucyrus International, Inc.; Ferdinand Sattler, Voest-Alpine, Austria; Anna-May Schwaderer, Edward Huber Memorial Association; Bob Seidler, Kukla Trenchers; Bill Senior, Ardrossan, Alberta; Dave Sharples, Komatsu America International Co.; Tony Shelling, Coast Crane; Melanie Shope, Huber Construction Equipment; John Sproule, Pennsylvania; Jaydee Stoner, Rahco International; Darrel Taftlinger, Volvo Construction Equipment; Thomas Tautges, Parsons Trenchers; G.W. von Alten, O&K Orenstein & Koppel, AG, Germany; Michael VonFlattern, Innovative Mining & Equipment, Inc.; Paulette Weiser, Hancock Historical Museum; Bill Williams, P&H Mining Equipment; Al Wilson, Case Corporation; Peter Winkel, Liebherr France; Dave Wootton, Hednesford, England; Ulrich Wulfert, Demag Komatsu GmbH, Germany; Larry Yarc, Komatsu America International Co.; Zeke Yargici, MinnPar, Inc.

Very special thanks must go to the following individuals from the list above, who made extra special efforts "beyond the call of duty" to fulfill my requests for information and material:

William Barlow/Champion Road Machinery Ltd.; Don Frantz, Historical Construction Equipment Association; Lee Haak, Komatsu America International Co.; Bob Jelinek, Bucyrus International, Inc.; Alvin E. Nus, Volvo Construction Equipment; Bob Pierce, Unit Rig, Div. Terex; Jim Rosso, Bucyrus International, Inc.; Bill Williams, P&H Mining Equipment; Zeke Yargici, MinnPar, Inc.

Last but not least, a special thank you to my friend and acclaimed author Eric Orlemann. Eric, without your help and encouragement this book would not have been possible. Above all, I thank my dear wife, Barbara, for her patience and understanding during the past 14 months of intense research and writing. I literally spent all my spare time on the book, while being fully employed in a demanding engineering position. She has meticulously edited all my text, and supported me all the way.

INTRODUCTION

Welcome to the ultimate guide to giant earthmoving equipment! If it is large and has moved earth, you should find it between these breathtaking pages. Consider this exhaustive work to be the bible of earthmoving books. This pictorial history accompanied by detailed text is the result of over 25 years of collecting data, photographs, and literature by the author, followed by 14 months of intensive research and writing. The manufacturers' histories have been brought up to date as far as possible. The author has consulted with manufacturers, equipment literature, and a multitude of individuals to ensure accuracy. Every effort has been made to deliver the most accurate information. Reference to current means the 1997/1998 model year.

The manufacturers covered are those companies that have achieved some innovation during their history, or attained a world record for size in any particular machine category. The book has also attempted to cover the current products of companies making the giant earthmovers of today.

Although it was the author's intent to cover all significant types of giant earthmoving equipment as well as the manufacturers and models, it wasn't possible to include every earthmover that roamed the face of the planet. The vast amount of information available on such a wide range of machine types and manufacturers meant that information had to be condensed. All uncredited photos appearing in the text have been personally taken by the author or are from his archive collection.

The photographs are as stunning as they are rare. They provide a spectacular look inside the world of earthmoving equipment. Final selection of the photos was a daunting task because there were so many wonderful images to choose from.

About the Author

The author, J. Keith Haddock, P. Eng., C. Eng., M.I.C.E., F.C.I.M., was born and educated in Sheffield, England. He became a chartered engineer (C. Eng.) and full member of the London-based Institution of Civil Engineers (M.I.C.E.) in 1970. A lifelong passion and involvement with earthmoving and heavy equipment started in England took him to Scotland and then to Canada in 1975, where he resides today. Haddock has been employed in a variety of engineering positions with the Luscar group of companies. He became a registered Professional Engineer (P. Eng.) when he attained membership in the Association of Professional Engineers, Geologists, and Geophysicists of Alberta, also in 1975. Currently, he is manager of engineering with responsibility of all engineering functions for two of the company's surface mines in Alberta.

Haddock co-founded the Historical Construction Equipment Association (HCEA) based in Grand Rapids, Ohio. The HCEA has a growing worldwide membership, currently numbering over 3,500. He is a regular contributing writer to the HCEA's official magazine *Equipment Echoes* and has been involved with or initiated several antique equipment preservation projects in Canada. In addition, he has written and contributed over 200 photographs to several trade magazines. He has also been involved with several book projects, including "Marion Power Shovel 1884-1984."

An active member of the Canadian Institute of Mining & Metallurgy (CIM), Haddock is currently the chairman of the CIM Heritage Committee. In 1998, he received the CIM's "Fellowship Award" (F.C.I.M.). He has also presented several papers to learned societies on surface mining and heavy equipment.

Specifications

The machine specifications used throughout this book are in standard U.S. (English) weights and measures. Reference to a machine weight in tons is calculated at 2,000 pounds (lbs) per short ton. The industry standards used to compare sizes of different machine types are as follows:

Bulldozer/crawler tractor: horsepower (hp)
Front-end loader: bucket capacity (cubic yards)
Scraper: bowl capacity (cubic yards)
Grader: weight (tons or pounds)
Truck: carrying capacity (tons)
Cable excavators including stripping shovels: bucket capacity (cubic yards)
Draglines: bucket capacity (cubic yards), and boom length (feet)
Hydraulic excavators: bucket capacity (cubic yards), and weight (tons)

Where gross horsepower is stated, it refers to the output of the engine as installed in the machine without the major accessories connected. Flywheel horsepower, also referred to as net horsepower, is the actual engine power output with all accessories including the fan, air compressor, generator, and hydraulic pump, etc. Where trucks are identified with 4x4, 6x4, etc. nomenclature, the first number indicates the total number of wheels and the second number indicates the number of *driven* wheels.

Chapter One

FROM MAN TO MACHINERY

Since the dawn of civilization, the human race has found it necessary to move and reshape the earth. Great construction projects, such as the pyramids of Egypt, the Great Wall of China, and the Roman network of highways across Europe involved vast amounts of earthworks. In 1681, the Languedoc Canal in Europe required massive amounts of earth to be moved, which demonstrated the need for earthmoving equipment. These and other early earthmoving projects used manual labor. Thousands of men, sometimes assisted by animals, but without the help of machines of any sort, completed these immense undertakings.

As centuries passed, the need for moving material by mechanized equipment increased. Just as today's science-fiction writers create future gadgetry and automation far beyond current technology, in the fifteenth and sixteenth centuries, such creative thinkers as Leonardo da Vinci sketched many types of earthmoving machines and other mechanical contrivances. Still, it would be several centuries before technology allowed them to be constructed.

Mechanized earthmoving equipment is largely a twentieth-century phenomenon. The Industrial Revolution and the steam age of the eighteenth century produced a greater need to move large quantities of material. The desire to move people and materials from place to place spawned the earliest forms of mechanized equipment. Ships were one of the first means of transportation over long distances, and it was only natural that the first self-powered earthmoving machines were dredges. (Chapter 10) The earliest forms of water-borne machines excavated harbors and deepened waterways to make them usable by ships.

Next the railways developed, and the land excavator was born. The 1835 steam shovel designed by William S. Otis is the earliest known single-bucket excavator used on land. Otis was a partner in a firm of contractors that used its own machines for railroad construction. Just after Otis received a patent for his machine in 1839, he unfortunately died of typhoid

When man discovered that economic progress depended on moving earth, there were no mechanical means available. Hand labor, assisted by animal power, had to be employed. Here, a typical Irish "navvy" is ready for work on one of the many vast projects completed by hand in the nineteenth century. *JKH collection*

fever at the age of 26. Although Otis did not live to see the fruits of his invention, his family's contracting business maintained the steam shovel patent for over 40 years and benefited from its advantage. Due to Otis patents and inexpensive labor, mechanized excavation evolved very slowly. In fact, few Otis shovels were ever built. Manufacture of the Otis shovels was continued by John Souther & Company until about 1913, surprisingly without major design changes.

When the Otis patents finally expired in the 1870s, several other companies began building steam shovels in the United States. The leading manufacturers were the Osgood Dredge Company, Troy, New York (1875); Bucyrus Foundry & Manufacturing Company, Bucyrus, Ohio (1882); Vulcan Iron Works Company, Toledo, Ohio (1882); and Marion Steam Shovel Company, Marion, Ohio (1884). These companies are the ancestors of the American excavator industry, which produced the giant shovels and draglines of the 1960s—the largest machines ever to move on the earth. Parallel development occurred in Europe, with companies such as Ruston Proctor & Company of England (1874), Menck &

Although the steam shovel was invented in 1835, hand labor and animal power constructed most of the railways of Europe up to the early part of the twentieth century. Hand labor was plentiful and cheap, so mechanized methods were slow to catch on. *JKH collection*

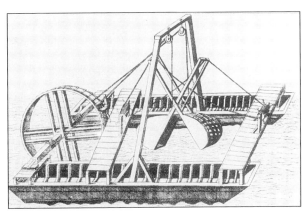

An early floating clamshell excavator from an illustration in a book by Verantius in 1591. Various drawings of excavating machines appeared in certain ancient documents, but there is no evidence that they were built, or indication of how reliable they might have been. *JKH collection*

Hambrock of Germany (1899), and Carlshutte of Germany (1900) entering the shovel industry.

While mechanized excavation slowly progressed, most of the world's railways were built using hand labor, even after the invention of the steam excavator. Probably the earliest major mechanized earthmoving project was the Manchester Ship Canal in England, starting in 1887. Here, 58 Ruston steam shovels, 18 Priestman clamshell excavators, and numerous other excavators worked with 173 steam locomotives and 6,300 rail wagons to move material at rates up to 1.2 million cubic yards per month. In all, 54 million yards were excavated over a six-year

A horse-drawn rail wagon transports excavated earth from an early steam shovel. This was the only means to transport material over long distances in the early days of railroad construction. *JKH collection*

period. This project was followed by the much larger Panama Canal, in which 77 Bucyrus, a Thew, and 24 Marion steam shovels moved 255 million cubic yards from 1904 to 1914.

As the twentieth-century projects got steadily larger, so did the machines. But at the other end of the scale, smaller and smaller machines also became as economical as hand labor. Machines were made in ever increasing varieties, and the distinctive types, such as graders, scrapers, loaders, and bulldozers, evolved.

Benefit to Mankind

Modern civilization, with the high standard of living we enjoy today, is largely a product of earthmoving machines. The list of applications for these machines is endless. From the quarrying of building materials, the mining of precious metals and coal, to the construction of roads, dams, power stations, irrigation canals, railways, factories, and docks, excavating machines provided the basis for industry and trade. Almost every activity involves some form of earthmoving. The saying, "everything we use must be either grown or mined" certainly holds true.

Earthmoving equipment has been an essential part of military operations. Winston Churchill developed the idea of the tank when he saw a crawler tractor demonstration during World War I. In World War II, thousands of airfields were built around the world in the shortest possible time using fleets of the latest equipment. During times of war, earthmoving equipment manufacturers were required to turn over a large portion of their production, sometimes their entire production, to the war effort. The triumphs of the Seabees with their large fleets of mobile earth-

The first mechanical excavator was the steam shovel invented by William S. Otis in 1835. The earliest illustration of an Otis machine was this drawing made in 1841 by S. Rufus Mason. Eastwick and Harrison of Philadelphia, Pennsylvania, built the machine. *JKH collection*

movers are legendary. After World War II, the ravaged cities of Europe needed rebuilding. Their rapid recovery was due in no small part to the employment of earthmover fleets.

The surface mining industry has been responsible for the creation of the largest earthmoving machines. The vast open pit mines for the extraction of ore, such as copper and gold, have constantly demanded larger and larger machines to move enormous quantities of overburden to expose the ore. Annual production of coal, over half coming from surface mines, is on the increase and forecast to be in even greater demand in the future. Surface coal mines, especially those in the midwestern United States during the 1950s and 1960s, fostered mammoth excavating machines. (Chapters 8 and 9)

The earthmoving industry has changed with the times. Much is said today about harm to the environment brought on by the use of our earthmoving machines. However, it is not the machines that cause the problem. It is how they are used. Earthmoving

One of the earliest photographs of a steam shovel in action. Taken in 1872, the picture shows an Otis shovel working on the Midland Railroad at Paterson, New Jersey. As can be seen, the early shovels attracted considerable public attention, and manual labor was still very much in evidence. *JKH collection*

The earliest major earthmoving project involving large fleets of steam shovels was the Manchester Ship Canal in England. Over 80 steam excavators moved 54 million cubic yards of material over a six-year period commencing in 1887. A Ruston Dunbar shovel is shown here loading a horse-drawn wagon. *JKH collection*

machines are far more likely to be seen cleaning up and beautifying an area than causing environmental damage. In today's surface mining industry, enormous amounts of valuable minerals can be extracted from a site. Afterward, the mine is reclaimed to such a degree that it becomes hard to tell where it existed. Certainly, some of the early strip mines destroyed land. But the problem arose because the land was improperly managed, and reclamation was not carried out. Today, the public is more than willing to pay the extra cost to reclaim the land and to protect the environment. The actual earthmoving operation may change the landscape temporarily, but the completed project will benefit the people who use the facility, and will contribute to a higher standard of living.

Some of the greatest advancements in machine design have been in the area of health and safety. In the early machines, a place for the operator appears nonexistent. The large machines with nonpower-assist levers needed musclemen for their operation. But the present-day air conditioned, heated, and radio-equipped cabs with power-assisted controls are designed with the operator's welfare in mind. Machines can't damage the hearing of those who operate them or the peace of those nearby. Rollover protection is mandatory, and even the paint finish must meet nontoxic standards.

Unfortunately, earthmoving machines are seldom acknowledged for the work they do. The machines just get on with the job at hand, then move on to the next project. The giant machines in the surface mines are rarely seen by the public, even though most mines will welcome visitors with prior notice.

Elsewhere, earthmovers work largely unnoticed by the public and news media, until traffic hold-ups during road construction draw attention to the industry. One of the objectives of this book is to give the public a true appreciation of these fantastic, larger-than-life machines, which are an integral part of our industrial heritage and essential for our modern lifestyle.

Mergers and Takeovers

The earthmoving equipment industry has had more than its fair share of corporate mergers and takeovers. The last 15 years have been particularly prolific in bankruptcies and mergers, to the extent that keeping track of the companies has become a major task for historians. Today, it is sometimes difficult to detect "who makes what," or who owns which company, or where a machine is manufactured. The major manufacturers are now truly global. "Badge engineered" is a term being used frequently in the modern-day global interchange of manufacturing. Manufacturers are making machines under contract for other companies. There are many cases where a certain machine made in one plant is sold under two, or even three different brand names even though the machines have identical specifications!

Chapter Two

BULLDOZERS

The idea of mounting a vehicle on crawler tracks to improve traction and decrease ground pressure dates back more than two centuries. In England during 1770, Richard Edgeworth patented a track that clearly employed the principles of the modern crawler, but no records exist to prove that it was ever put into practice.

The needs of agriculture at the turn of the twentieth century sparked the development of the crawler tractor. The vast areas of rich California soil needed big, powerful tractors, but only wheel tractors were available, and these had severe problems with flotation. Due to their high ground pressure, any degree of moisture caused the machine to bog down or get stuck in the rich soil. The problem was tackled by the Holt Manufacturing Company of Stockton, California, which had been building wheeled steam traction engines since 1890. Holt fitted larger and larger wheels, and more of them, on his tractors trying to overcome the problem. Some of these multiwheel behemoths measured over 45 feet wide and had wheels up to 12 feet in diameter. They were extremely cumbersome to maneuver.

The crawler track principle eventually solved the flotation problem. In 1904, Holt tested the idea by removing the driving wheels from one of his three-wheeled steam traction engines and replacing them with a pair of crawler tracks. The front steering, or tiller, wheel was retained. After further tests, the first production steam crawler was sold in 1906.

Simultaneous development of the crawler track was also taking place in England. David Roberts, chief engineer with R. Hornsby & Sons of Grantham, patented a crawler track design in 1904. The following year, a Roberts "chain track" was fitted to a Hornsby oil tractor built in 1896. Several Hornsby steam- and oil-powered tractors were completed with crawler tracks. Despite significant promotion, including the first film ever made for commercial purposes (1908) and demonstrations for high-ranking military personnel, the idea did not catch on.

Having received only one civilian order, for a tractor to be used for hauling coal in northern Canada, the Hornsby

The crawler tractor that started an industry! The first Holt crawler machine appeared in 1904. The steam tractor was on a test and had its wheels replaced by a pair of crawler tracks. The 9-foot-long tracks were made of 3x4-inch wooden slats, 42 inches wide. *Caterpillar archives*

In an almost simultaneous development to Holt, R. Hornsby & Sons of England replaced the wheels of a Hornsby steam tractor with a pair of crawler tracks. This was the "chain track," first tested in 1905. Hornsby sold its patent rights for the "chain track" to Holt in 1914. *Ray Hooley collection*

The early Holt tractors utilized a "tiller wheel" at the front to assist steering. Introduced in 1913, the Holt 75 was able to tackle the heaviest jobs. It was a very successful tractor, and thousands were built before the model was discontinued in 1924. *JKH collection*

The Best Sixty tractor, unveiled in 1919, was one of only two models from the former Best line to be adopted by the Caterpillar Tractor Company, when it was formed in 1925 by the merger of the Holt and Best companies. It lasted in the Caterpillar line until 1931. The machine shown here is owned by Junior Christian, and was on display at the H.C.E.A. show at Bowling Green, Ohio.

company became disillusioned. It sold the patent rights to the "chain track" to the Holt Manufacturing Company in 1914 for $8,000. The crawler tractor gave Winston Churchill the idea of building the tank, when the British army needed a new fighting machine in World War I. Unfortunately, designers had to start from scratch to construct a suitable track-laying machine, when just a year earlier Hornsby had sold what they needed to Holt. As an added irony, when the British army needed crawler tractors for the war effort in 1914, it purchased Holt.

Like other companies, Caterpillar went through many mergers and acquisitions. A 70-year-old Daniel Best had weathered years of competitive battles with Holt. In 1905, he had sued Holt for patent infringement. Before a decision was handed down, Best and Holt chose to settle the lawsuit out of court. Best looked to retirement and eventually reached an agreement to sell the company to Holt in 1908. This sale was contingent on Holt's son, Clarence Leo Best, being installed as the new president of Holt Manufacturing Company.

Clarence Best became president of Holt; however, he was unhappy with the situation and left to form his own company in 1910–The C.L. Best Gas Traction Company. In 1913, the Best 75 was the first crawler tractor to roll out of the Elmhurst, California, factory and others soon followed. The famous Best Sixty, unveiled in 1919, was the standard of large tractors of its day, and it was the first to bear the "Caterpillar" name.

In 1909, Holt acquired a plant in Peoria, Illinois, and the first Peoria tractor was assembled in that year. Farming applications led the market by a large margin, and most machines were sold as "bare" tractors. The Holt company prospered. Employment increased from 300 in 1909 to 1,000 in 1914. But the year 1925 is fixed in most tractor historians' minds as the date of one of the greatest mergers in equipment history. In that year, Holt Manufacturing Company merged with the C.L. Best Gas Traction Company to form Caterpillar Tractor Company. Caterpillar had been a trade name previously used by Holt; it had gained significant popularity. The legend was born.

The models adopted from the two companies to form the first product line of the new Caterpillar Tractor Company were the Best Sixty and Thirty, and the Holt 2-Ton, 5-Ton, and 10-Ton tractors. Holt and Best did not have the crawler tractor market entirely to themselves; dozens of companies ventured into the business during the early twentieth century. Many, however, were very short-lived and made only a few machines. Some of those enjoying a much longer life, or that continued under

Horsepower applied to a bulldozer blade. This picture was taken from a 1917 Russell catalog. *Caterpillar archives*

A very early application of a bulldozer blade on a crawler tractor. The hand wheel operates the blade on this Holt 10-Ton tractor working near Soldier Field, Chicago, 1924. *Caterpillar archives*

This Caterpillar Thirty tractor is equipped with a LaPlant-Choate Manufacturing Company dozer blade, one of the first hydraulically powered types. A single cylinder acts on the rear of the pivoting frame to which the blade is attached. *JKH collection*

other names following mergers, were Bates, Monarch, Cleveland (Cletrac), and McCormick-Deering (IHC).

By the early 1930s, the tractor manufacturing industry stabilized under a number of smaller companies. Although crawler tractors continued to serve farming applications, the earthmoving industry started to evolve. Bulldozer blades were being mounted on crawler tractors to move earth. Rippers and loader buckets made tractors even more versatile. The tractor companies that survived through World War II have become leaders in today's market and are described in this chapter.

Bulldozer History

The bulldozer had its origins in crude, horse-pushed contraptions in the nineteenth century. As crawler tractors became more robust and reliable, they were found to be ideal for carrying a bulldozer blade. The early tractor-mounted blades, however, did not have power control. It was left to the operator (or an assistant) to crank the blade up and down by means of tiresome, wrist-wrenching hand wheels.

An early innovator of the power-operated dozer blade was the LaPlant-Choate Manufacturing Company of Cedar Rapids, Iowa. Founded in 1911, LaPlant-Choate came out with a hydraulically-operated dozer blade in 1925. The blade was mounted on a rectangular frame, pivoted on the crawler frames, and operated by a hydraulic cylinder at the rear of the tractor.

A reliable cable-operated Power Control Unit (PCU) was invented in 1928 by earthmoving pioneer R.G. LeTourneau. Driven from the tractor's power take-off, the PCU was available with up to four winches, controlled by individual clutches and brakes. The PCU operated not only a dozer blade but also pull-type scrapers, rippers, and other attachments. The PCU was regarded as a major breakthrough in crawler tractor development. A description of the LeTourneau company is included in Chapter 4.

Bulldozer blades were initially supplied by manufacturers other than those building the tractors. As time went on, the major builders of tractor attachments aligned themselves with particular tractor manufacturers. Notable examples were Baker with Allis-Chalmers, Bucyrus-Erie with International, and LeTourneau with Caterpillar. The main tractor builders started to make their own blades and other equipment in the 1940s. However, there was still a good market for even more

When big blades were needed, and tractors didn't have enough power, two tractors were run together. The 24-foot blade shown here takes two of Caterpillar's tractors in the early 1970s to reclaim spoils at this Kentucky mine. The model is the SxS D9H. The advent of the Caterpillar D10 in 1977 made these twin tractor outfits instantly obsolete. *Eric Orlemann*

One of the pioneers of the crawler loader was the Trackson Company. The early example shown here, attached to a D4 tractor, is digging a Pennsylvania basement in 1940. The earliest crawler loaders were cable operated, having the draw works over the top of the engine hood and tending to make the machine unstable. The bucket had no power tilt and was dumped by a spring release. *Caterpillar archives*

specialist tractor attachments, and the industry spawned many new entrants over the years. One example was Balderson Inc., established in 1949 and known for its giant dozer blades, designed to push light materials, such as coal or wood chippings.

The contributions the bulldozer made to the World War II effort is well documented. Thousands of crawler tractors, most carrying LeTourneau blades or pulling LeTourneau scrapers, made their way overseas to prepare the ground for fighting forces. Bulldozers helped build the Alaska Highway, as well as chains of bases across the Aleutian Islands and the South Pacific. Admiral William F. Halsey stated, "The four machines that won the war in the Pacific were the submarine, radar, the airplane, and the bulldozer."

By the mid-1950s, bulldozers were no longer a tractor with an attachment. They had become an integrated unit, designed for production from the ground up. In the mid-1950s, the leading makes of crawler tractors competed equally with each other to create the largest machines of the day. They were seen with equal frequency on every big job. The "big red teams" of International TD-24s, and the fleets of "Persian" orange Allis-Chalmers HD-21s, worked alongside the latest bright yellow Caterpillar models, including the just-launched D9s. And then the "Euclid green" TC-12, largest crawler tractor in the world, gave the long-time tractor makers even more competition.

As impressive as these 1950s giants were, they pale in comparison with the enormous tractors of today. Spearheaded by Caterpillar's "high drive" D10 in the 1970s, the

push for larger tractors has continued. The current largest is Komatsu's D575A-2, boasting almost three times the power of the largest crawler built in the 1950s.

The demand for large bulldozers exceeded the capability of engines and transmissions in the 1960s. In a transitional phase, before the super dozer era, the largest tractors were doubled up and run by one operator. Initially, this was tried in the 1950s with Allis-Chalmers HD-19s and Caterpillar D8s. Caterpillar continued the concept with the DD9G (one tractor behind the other) for push-loading scrapers and the SxS D9G (two tractors side-by-side with a 24-foot-wide dozer blade). The combined horsepower of the "twin" D9G outfits is equivalent to the 770 horsepower of Caterpillar's D11R bulldozer. The D9G models were upgraded to the D9H models in 1974, and the twin dozers continued until they were eclipsed by the D10 in 1978.

Crawler Loaders

Another machine originating as an attachment to a tractor and developing into an integrated production machine is the crawler loader. The very first models consisted of a bucket mounted on a simple pivoting beam, raised and lowered by a cable winch driven by the tractor power take-off. When digging, a full bucket depended on the momentum of the machine entering the bank or earth pile. To dump, the bucket was released by a simple latch mechanism.

The modern-day manufacturer realizes that the crawler loader must be designed from the ground up. It is not sufficient simply to mount the loader arms and bucket on a standard crawler tractor. It must be designed with the correct balance and a strong frame to withstand the rigors of heavy excavating.

One of the first loading shovels, developed by the Trackson Company, was designed for mounting on standard Caterpillar tractors. Organized in 1922, the Milwaukee firm started making tractor equipment for Caterpillar in 1936, and in the following year its high-lift shovel appeared. By 1950, hydraulics had been incorporated into the Trackson loaders, the first being mounted on a modified D4, and known as the model HT4. The following year, Caterpillar purchased the Trackson Company and gave its name to Caterpillar's line of "Traxcavators." Caterpillar's first integrated crawler loader was the No. 6 Traxcavator, built from 1953 to 1955.

The introduction of the Caterpillar 955 in 1955 heralded a new line of Traxcavators from Caterpillar. By the end of that year, the 933 and 977 were added, giving the company a three-machine range from 1 to 2 1/4 cubic yards. Caterpillar's largest crawler loader, the Model 983, came out in 1969 with a bucket rated at 5 cubic yards. Caterpillar introduced hydrostatic drive and rear engine

After Caterpillar purchased the Trackson Company in 1951, it expanded the "Traxcavator" line to include a full line of crawler loaders. The largest was the 983, introduced in 1969, with a 5-cubic yard bucket.

The Tractomotive Corporation was the first company to develop a hydraulically powered bucket tilt on a loader in 1946. The first model was fitted to an Allis-Chalmers HD-5 tractor, as shown here. Allis-Chalmers purchased Tractomotive in 1959.

The Bucyrus-Erie tractor loader was one of a long line of tractor attachments from the company "tailor-made" for International tractors. Mounted on an International TD-6 tractor and looking very cumbersome, this outfit is definitely short on visibility. Note the nonpowered bucket release. *JKH collection*

Another type of crawler loader was the "overshot" loader, which dumped its load to the rear after hoisting it right over the top of the operator. This Athey loader is fitted to a Caterpillar D4 tractor of 1940s vintage. Cab protection was mandatory on this type of loader, long before standard cabs, ROPS, and FOPS were even dreamed of!

mounting when the 943 came out in 1980. Currently, the range consists of five sizes from the 933 to the 973.

Another early all-hydraulic loader mechanism was developed by the Tractomotive Corporation in 1946. Designed to fit the Allis-Chalmers HD-5 tractor, the loader was the first to include a hydraulically-powered bucket, permitting bucket roll-back during digging and controlled dumping.

In the 1950s, Tractomotive became a major supplier to Allis-Chalmers while manufacturing its own line of wheel loaders. When the HD-19G crawler loader came out in 1950, the 4-yard machine held the world record size for many years. In a move similar to that made by its competitors, Allis-Chalmers purchased its main supplier of tractor equipment, Tractomotive Corporation, in 1959.

Renowned excavator manufacturer Bucyrus-Erie Company manufactured tractor equipment from 1938 to 1954, and during the 1940s made a line of shovel attachments that were hydraulically hoisted and gravity dumped. Bucyrus-Erie tractor products were sold exclusively through International Harvester dealers, and therefore, most of their loaders and dozer attachments found their way onto International tractors.

The Athey Corporation had a cable-operated rig designed to fit Caterpillar D4 and D6 tractors. This was one of many "overshot" loaders available in the 1940s. In this type of loader, the bucket was hoisted over the top of the cab and dumped at the rear. The main advantage was that the tractor did not have to turn to dump its load, but visibility was restricted due to the heavy protective frame required over the operator.

In 1950, an agreement was reached between International Harvester Company and the Drott Manufacturing Company to sell crawler tractor shovels under the International-Drott name. Drott, which had previously supplied tractor attachments, was the pioneer of the four-in-one or multipurpose bucket. The additional bucket motion enabled it to be used for loader, scraper, dozer, or clamshell duties. From the Drott line, International developed its own line of crawler loaders. One of its largest was designed for the TD-20 tractor, and boasted a bucket of 3 cubic yards. The Model 250 replaced it, in the same size class, and survived with upgrades through the 250E into the 1990s. In 1988, under the Dresser name, the modern hydrostatically driven, rear-engined, 2 1/2-yard Model 200, was announced. However, this was only built until 1991. Today, just one crawler loader, the 2-yard Model 175C, remains in the Dresser line.

Another crawler loader, of advanced design for its day, was marketed from 1955 to 1960 by the Frank G. Hough Company, known primarily for its wheel loaders. Ahead of its time, the Hough H-12 had its engine in the rear, a design not adopted by others until two decades later.

Although Komatsu had a few models of its crawler tractors fitted with loaders in the 1950s, it rapidly expanded its line of crawler loaders in the 1960s. By 1972, five sizes of crawler loaders were offered with buckets ranging from the 0.5-yard D20S to the 2.6-yard D75S. The larger D95S was added in 1974 with a bucket size of 4.2 cubic yards. This was followed by the massive 350-horsepower, 5.9-yard D155S, which was the largest crawler loader ever built.

Fiat-Allis/Allis-Chalmers Crawler Tractors

The industrial giant, Allis-Chalmers Manufacturing Company, expanded its tractor division in 1928, when it purchased Monarch Tractor Corporation of Springfield, Illinois. In 1913, Monarch Tractor Company was originally founded in Watertown, Wisconsin, to build crawler tractors. Before the purchase, the farm tractor and equipment division of Allis-Chalmers represented 6.8 percent of the company's business. By 1930, with the addition of Monarch, the tractor division accounted for almost 30 percent of Allis-Chalmers' total business.

The 6-ton Monarch Model H and 10-ton Model F were renumbered the Model 50 and 75 and manufactured by Allis-Chalmers while still bearing the Monarch name. In 1931, Allis-Chalmers came out with the first of its own new line: the 75-horsepower Model L, a large tractor for its day. The "letter" series of tractors was expanded throughout the 1930s, and the gasoline Models L, K, and M proved to be the most popular. The oil-powered LO and KO models introduced in 1935 weren't as popular, but at 80 horsepower, the LO was the largest tractor in the line.

Allis-Chalmers started developing its diesel-powered tractor line in 1938, using Detroit Diesel engines. Three models were put in production in 1940 to replace the previous oil tractors: the HD-7, HD-10, and HD-14. The HD-14 produced 132 horsepower and was the most powerful crawler tractor available on the market at that time. In 1946, the HD-14 was the first crawler tractor offered with a torque converter. In the same year, Allis-Chalmers added the smaller HD-5 to the line-up.

In 1947, Allis-Chalmers upped the ante again with the 163-horsepower HD-19, which took the world crawler tractor size record. It was also equipped with torque converter drive. Other "HD" models followed in the 1950s. In 1951, the HD-19 was upgraded to the 175-horsepower HD-20. The HD-20 was then replaced by the 204-horsepower HD-21 in 1954. The HD-21 was so successful, it remained in production for almost two decades.

Allis-Chalmers made headlines with the massive HD-41 at the 1963 Road Show in Chicago, Illinois. With an operating weight of 70 tons and a 524-horsepower engine, it broke the world crawler tractor size record. A lengthy

Sporting a 3-yard bucket, International's largest crawler loader was the Model 250. International loaders were developed from the Drott Corporation, with whom International formed a marketing agreement in 1950. Drott loaders were of the clamshell-type. Known as the "four-in-one" bucket, they could perform as a dozer, loader, clamshell, or scraper. *JKH collection*

The Hough Model 12 crawler loader was ahead of its time and had a rear-mounted engine, giving full visibility for the operator. Made from 1955 to 1960, it carried a 1 3/4-cubic yard bucket and a 90-horsepower International engine.

testing program with prototypes followed, and customers had to wait until 1970 before it was put into production.

In 1974, Fiat S.p.A. of Italy purchased a majority interest in Allis-Chalmers, and the Fiat-Allis joint venture was born. Crawler tractor production continued but the "HD" prefix was dropped, and the former Allis-Chalmers models were upgraded to the B- and C-series machines through the 1970s. In 1980, the upgraded FD-series was introduced, and the top-of-the-line 41-B was renamed as the FD-50. Market conditions softened in the 1980s for Fiat-Allis, and in 1989 the company announced it was ceasing manufacture of its earthmoving products in North America. Although its plants closed, Fiat-Allis has maintained a sales organization to market machines imported from Italy. The current line includes six crawler tractors from 107 to 349 horsepower, and two crawler loaders in the 2- to 2 3/4-yard class.

Caterpillar Crawler Tractors

The merger of the two leading tractor companies, Holt and C. L. Best, created the legendary Caterpillar Tractor Company in 1925. Of the five tractors carried over from the former companies, only the two Best machines continued into the 1930s: the Sixty until 1931 and the Thirty until 1932.

A full line of gasoline crawlers was introduced in the years up to 1934. The Ten, Fifteen, Twenty, Twenty-Two, Twenty-Five, Twenty-Eight, Thirty-Five, Forty, Fifty, and Sixty-Five ranged from 15 to 73 horsepower. By early 1933, every model had been redesigned, and the former gray with red trim was replaced with the now-famous "highway" yellow in 1932.

When Caterpillar's first diesel tractor, the Model Sixty-Five, went to work in 1931, it featured Caterpillar's own diesel engine. This was a major contributor to the company's phenomenal growth and its dominance today. By 1937, U.S. manufacturers had produced two million horsepower of diesel engines, and Caterpillar had produced one-third of that total. In addition, the crawler had become the largest user of diesel power, and Caterpillar was the largest manufacturer.

The 83-horsepower Diesel Seventy-Five tractor was made from 1933 to 1935. Then it grew into the first Caterpillar D8, the 1H series. The D8 would become one of the most famous number designations on any earthmoving machine, and would form the basic nomenclature of Caterpillar's full line of crawler tractors up to the present day, over 60 years later.

The world's largest crawler loader was the Komatsu D155S, lifting a bucket of just under 6 cubic yards. Powered by a 350-horsepower Komatsu engine, this giant weighed in at 46 tons. *Komatsu Mining Systems*

The 60-horsepower Monarch Model F crawler tractor was renumbered the 75 when Allis-Chalmers took over the Monarch Tractor Corporation in 1928. It remained in the Allis-Chalmers line until 1931. This fine restored example is owned by Bill Senior of Ardrossan, Alberta. *Bill Senior*

This unusual combination brings together a 50-horsepower Allis-Chalmers Model K tractor and a Bucyrus-Erie "Bullgrader," normally found on International tractors. B-E used the latter term to identify its angle dozer line. *JKH collection*

Another rare dozer blade is this Buckeye cable rig mounted on an Allis-Chalmers HD-7 tractor. Note the tube arrangement to bring the cable from the rear-mounted winch to the twin sheaves at the front. The HD-7 was a 60-horsepower tractor.

The D8 changed throughout the years until reaching the current D8R. Each major change was accompanied by a suffix letter, usually signifying increased horsepower. The same model designation system was used for Caterpillar's entire line of crawlers, which expanded from the D2 through to the current D11R.

The 286-horsepower D9 was released in 1955, offered with either torque converter or direct drive. As the series progressed through D9D, D9E, D9G, and D9H, power and weight increased until the D9H produced 410 horsepower. In 1978, Caterpillar made a big breakthrough with the production of the "high-drive" tractor—the first D10.

High-sprocket design had an extensive development period, going back as far as 1969. Many ideas and concepts were tested before the first prototype was built in 1973. Uneven ground shocks were absorbed by a cushioned undercarriage instead of the drive axle, and the drivetrain was much higher to keep it out of the mud. When the D10 went into full production, it was a daring move on Caterpillar's part. This totally new concept was about to change its entire line of large tractors, the company's big moneymakers. The 700-horsepower D10, weighing 88 tons with blade, was by far Caterpillar's heaviest and most powerful tractor built up to that time.

The gamble paid off handsomely for Caterpillar. Nearly 1,000 D10s were sold until the 770-horsepower D11N replaced it in 1986. By that time, the high-drive design had expanded to all tractors down to the D6H size. Since then, high-drive versions of the D5 and D4 models have joined the line. Caterpillar's current crawler line includes "M" and "R" series tractors, spanning power ratings from 70 to 850 horsepower. The largest is the D11R CD (Carrydozer), which has a special 22-foot-wide curved blade, enabling it to carry more material than a standard blade. It takes considerably less power to carry a load than to push it, and the Carrydozer moves 20 to 30 percent more material than the standard D11R.

Cletrac Crawler Tractors

Cletracs were made by the Cleveland Tractor Company, which was organized in 1916. Initially, the company built lightweight tractors for farming, but during the 1930s, tractors were utilized for construction work. Cletrac made some vital contributions to crawler tractor development, although it did not break any size records. Cletrac was one of the first makers to build a high-sprocket-drive tractor, with the Model F introduced in 1920. This design is similar to the Caterpillar system developed some 55 years later. Cletrac also pioneered differential steering, which maintains power to both tracks at all times. This patented system was based on a planetary arrangement, in which either track could be slowed through braking action.

The top-of-the-line HD-14 was one of the range of powerful crawler tractors offered by Allis-Chalmers in 1940. At 132 horsepower, it was the most powerful tractor available at that time.

The Allis-Chalmers HD-19 came out in 1947. With a torque converter and Detroit Diesel 6-71 engine developing 163 horsepower, it claimed the title of the world's largest crawler tractor. *Ron Ketron collection*

In 1954, Allis-Chalmers' big tractor was the HD-21, at 204 horsepower. It grew out of the previous HD-20 and HD-19 models which had relatively short lives. The "21," however, with its various upgrades, lasted in the line for almost three decades. *Ron Ketron collection*

The Caterpillar Diesel Seventy-Five was made from 1933 to 1935. This early diesel tractor was the forerunner of the famous Caterpillar D8 series tractors, which first appeared in 1935. The machine shown here is making full use of the LeTourneau cable-operated blade, controlled from a rear-mounted winch. *R.G LeTourneau Inc.*

The first series Caterpillar D9 is shown under test. The machine had 286 horsepower when first put on the market in 1955, but was upgraded to 320 horsepower the following year. *Caterpillar Inc.*

Making its first appearance in prototype form at Conexpo 1963, the HD-41 again gave Allis-Chalmers the title to the world's largest crawler tractor. However, customers had to wait until 1970 before the 524-horsepower giant was put into production.

In 1933, five models were offered from the small Model 20 at 22 horsepower to the 84-horsepower Model 80, a popular model often seen hauling wagons and scrapers on construction jobs. By 1940, the largest Cletrac was the 100-horsepower Model FDLC. It was clear that Cletrac intended to compete with the large tractor companies of the day.

In 1944, the Cleveland Tractor Company was acquired by the Oliver Corporation, a farm tractor and equipment builder with roots going back to the 1850s. After the takeover, the machines acquired the Oliver name. Beginning in the mid-1950s, Oliver crawlers were updated and renumbered with OC as a prefix signifying their Cletrac connections. The largest tractor in this series was the 161-horsepower OC-18. It retained the Cletrac tradition of differential steering.

The White Motor Corporation purchased the Oliver Corporation in 1960. After 1960, the crawler machines were sold only in limited numbers, and most models were discontinued by 1964. The last crawler machine built was the OC-96 crawler loader released in 1959. It remained in production until 1965.

Dresser/International Crawler Tractors

International Harvester Company (IHC) entered the crawler tractor industry in 1929 and eventually established itself as an industry leader in earthmoving. At the time, IHC was one of the leading builders of trucks and farm equipment. The earthmoving equipment line would eventually include crawler and wheeled loaders, off-highway trucks, scrapers, and hydraulic excavators. Its first crawler tractor was the 10-20, which was based on the McCormick-Deering wheeled 10-20.

The 45-horsepower TD-40 was the first diesel crawler, produced from 1933 to 1939. This was the largest of several T-series (gasoline) and TD-series (diesel) crawlers of the mid-1930s known as "TracTracTors." A new line of redesigned and renumbered crawlers led by the 88-horsepower TD-18 replaced them, starting in 1938. This family included the T-6, TD-6, TD-9, and TD-14.

The much larger TD-24 came out in 1947 and became the world's largest crawler. At 180 horsepower, it clipped the title from the 163-horsepower Allis-Chalmers

The Caterpillar D9-series tractors has continued to the present day, with letter designations reaching "D9R" on the elevated sprocket model. This 385-horsepower D9G of early 1970s vintage is shown at work with a Kelley Ripper.

With the D10 model shown here, Caterpillar took the bold step of launching its revolutionary elevated sprocket design. The first production models of this 700-horsepower super tractor appeared in 1978.

An example of Caterpillar's current large bulldozer lineup is this D8R, shown with ripper and dozer blade. The D8R weighs 41 tons and has a Caterpillar diesel engine developing 305 horsepower.

The current largest Caterpillar bulldozer is the D11R, here shown in its CD (Carrydozer) version. At 850 horsepower and 120 tons operating weight, this giant comes with a specially curved blade, which enables it to carry more material than a standard dozer blade.

This is the Cletrac Model F tractor introduced in 1920 by the Cleveland Tractor Company. Note that it utilizes an early form of elevated sprocket drive. This model was one of many light-duty crawlers marketed in the 1920s by Cleveland.

The 84-horsepower Cletrac Model 80 is put to good use here, hauling rock for contractor Ralph Mills on a road construction job near Frankfort, Kentucky. The Cletrac 80 was built from 1930 to 1936. A Lima 601 shovel is loading the Euclid tracked trailer. *H.C.E.A. archives*

When the Oliver Corporation took over the Cleveland Tractor Company in 1944, the Cletrac crawlers were continued. The 80-horsepower Model DDH of 1949 vintage shown here easily fills this LeTourneau Model D Carryall. The equipment is owned by Bill Graham, who periodically carries out county road jobs in central Alberta, Canada, using only his collection of vintage equipment.

HD-19, which had come out earlier the same year. The TD-24 model remained in production until 1959 and was seen on many of the biggest earthmoving jobs of the 1950s. An even larger tractor, the TD-30, was introduced in 1962. This heavyweight 320-horsepower tractor competed with Caterpillar's D9, but only remained in production for five years. Other TD-series crawlers were introduced or upgraded through the 1970s and 1980s.

In 1982, Dresser Industries Inc. purchased the Construction Machinery Division of International Harvester and the tractors were absorbed into the International Hough Division of Dresser. In 1985, the biggest "International" crawler tractor, the TD-40, was marketed to the industry, although a prototype was tested as early as 1978. Initially built at the Libertyville, Illinois, plant, it weighed over 67 tons outfitted for dozer work, and was powered by a 460-horsepower Cummins engine. Now built in Poland, the TD-40 series of tractors was upgraded to the TD-40B series in 1989 and to TD-40C in 1997.

In 1988, Dresser formed a joint venture with Komatsu of Japan to form Komatsu Dresser Company (KDC). Later, Komatsu purchased all of KDC. Currently, the Dresser crawler tractors, from the 70-horsepower TD7H to the TD-40C, are marketed under Komatsu America International Company.

Komatsu Crawler Tractors

Komatsu built their its crawler tractors in 1931 for farming applications. The following year the Model G25 appeared, looking very much like a Caterpillar 2-ton. Komatsu debuted the D50 bulldozer in 1944, and by 1962, production had exceeded 10,000 units. With this stable base established, Komatsu expanded its crawler line throughout the 1960s. By the 1970s, Komatsu boasted 12 models of crawler tractors, including four low ground pressure "swamp bulldozers." These ranged from 35 to 300 horsepower. The top-of-the-line 300-horsepower machines were the D155A with torque converter and the direct drive D150A.

In the 1950s, the Cletrac tractors were upgraded to the "OC" (Oliver-Cletrac) series. The largest in this series was the 161-horsepower OC-18, which continued the Cletrac tradition of differential steering, providing power to both crawlers during turns.

The last of the Oliver-Cletrac machines was the OC-96, introduced in 1959. It remained in production until 1965, after White Motor Corporation had purchased Oliver Corporation in 1960.

The small International T-20 gasoline tractor illustrated here came out in 1931, and was listed at 18 drawbar horsepower. It was developed from International's first crawler tractor, the McCormick-Deering wheeled Model 10-20. The early International crawlers were known as "TracTracTors."

The 53-ton D355A and 82-ton D455A tractors were introduced in 1974 and 1977 to compete with the largest tractors on the market. The 1977 crawler lineup consisted of an amazing 31 models, including "swamp bulldozers" and a radio-controlled model.

At the Conexpo '81 exhibition in Houston, Texas, Komatsu showed the world it was serious about large crawler tractors. It displayed the D555A bulldozer, boasting 1,000 horsepower. With an operating weight of 133 tons, it easily took the title of the world's largest crawler tractor. Although this machine never reached the production stage, its successor, the D575A-2 SR (Super Ripper), took over the "largest ever" title in 1991. It produced 1,050 horsepower and weighed 145 tons when equipped with dozer and ripper. In 1995, this machine was joined by the 1,150-horsepower D575A-2 SD (Super Dozer) which was designed for dozer applications. With a weight of 157 tons, and equipped with a blade measuring over 24 feet wide, it is the largest bulldozer currently available.

The large bulldozers in Komatsu's lineup, comprising the 525-horsepower D375A-3, the 770-horsepower D475A-2, and the two D575A models, are marketed today by Komatsu Mining Systems, Inc., formed in 1997. Bulldozers smaller than these models are marketed by Komatsu America International Company.

Euclid/Terex Crawler Tractors

In 1955, the Euclid Division of General Motors entered the crawler tractor industry with the world's most powerful crawler tractor—the TC-12. Euclid started the development on the giant crawler, which continued after General Motors (GM) took over in 1953. The new tractor followed the twin-power concept already used on Euclid's large trucks and scrapers. It was powered by twin GM 6-71 engines that produced 402 net combined horsepower. They were mounted on each side of a split frame, enabling the TC-12 to oscillate independently over uneven ground. Since each engine drove one track through its own power-shift transmission, the 40-ton tractor was remarkably nimble. It could be steered by simply adjusting the speed or direction of one track. Spin turns were possible by putting one track in forward and the other in reverse.

After the launch of the TC-12, Euclid went straight to work on designing another tractor exactly half the power of the TC-12, with a single GM 6-71 engine. This

RIGHT: The big red International TD-24 came out in 1947, and was the biggest tractor of the day, with its 180-horsepower engine. The "hard nose" version shown here carries a cable-operated blade, controlled from a front-mounted winch. The machine is leveling spoils on a British opencast coal site.

The International TD-18A diesel tractor, introduced in 1949, was an upgrade from the earlier TD-18. This TD-18A pushing a full load of dirt in front of its Bucyrus-Erie dozer blade has a 107-horsepower engine. *The State Historical Society of Wisconsin*

Although sold under the Dresser name, the TD-40B tractor is a direct descendent from the International TD-40, marketed since 1985. At 520 horsepower, and weighing just under 70 tons, it is the largest tractor ever produced by the company. Currently built in Poland, the TD-40 was elevated to a "C" series in 1997. *Komatsu America International Company*

Komatsu's first crawler tractor was built in 1931. The Model G25, which came out in 1932, is shown here. It is preserved at the factory in Japan. *Komatsu America International Company*

Typical of the large crawler tractors sold worldwide in the 1970s was this D155A fitted with a Komatsu "Giant" ripper. This tractor has a 300-horsepower engine, and is cutting down an old slag pile on a reclamation project in England.

was the C-6, introduced to the market in 1958, following a test period lasting almost three years. In 1966 Euclid renumbered its models: The C-6 became the 82-30, and the TC-12, now rated at 425 horsepower, became the 82-80. That same year, an intermediate-sized crawler was introduced, the 275-horsepower 82-40. The big 82-80 survived in production until 1974.

In 1968 Euclid truck manufacture passed into the hands of the White Motor Corporation in North America. The Justice Department ruled that GM must discontinue making off-highway trucks in the United States for five years, and divest itself of the Euclid name. At the same time, the Terex name was born to represent the remaining GM earthmoving products. Terex was acquired by German equipment group IBH in 1980, and the Terex crawler line was combined with the German Hanomag crawlers. When IBH failed in 1983, GM came to the rescue and bought Terex back. Three years later, Terex was sold again to Northwest Engineering Company, and at that time the Terex crawler tractors were discontinued. The last Terex crawler tractor built was a Model D800 in 1986.

John Deere Crawler Tractors

The purchase of Lindeman Power Equipment Company by John Deere in 1947 brought crawler tractors to the well-established Deere line of wheeled tractors. Starting out as Holt tractor dealers in 1922, and later selling Cletracs, Lindeman began building crawler conversions for John Deere tractors. These sold extremely well and prompted Deere to purchase the family business. The first fully John Deere-designed crawler was the MC, which came out in 1949.

John Deere has served the smaller end of the crawler tractor market ever since its first machine. However, Deere made a major mark on the industry at the Conexpo '75 show in Chicago, when it announced nine new machines in five equipment categories. Most of these machines were larger than any previously built by Deere, including two crawler tractors, the JD750 and JD850 of 110 and 140 horsepower. Crawler loader versions were also offered in the JD755 and JD855. Not only were these the largest crawlers built by Deere, they were equipped with hydrostatic drive, a bold concept at that time. These hydrostatic tractors remain in the John Deere line today, after going through B-series and C-series upgrades.

The Komatsu D575A-2 Super Dozer is the largest and most powerful bulldozer on the market today by big margin. This giant machine has 1,150 horsepower under the hood, and can muster its 157-ton weight behind a 24-foot dozer blade. *Komatsu America International Company*

The Komatsu D475A is a large, powerful 770-horsepower bulldozer that is popular with surface mining companies. It is shown equipped with dozer and ripper.

John Deere's smaller crawler tractors (under 100 horsepower) are offered with a choice of torque converter or direct drive, and have now reached the G-series, in models 450, 550, and 650.

Case Crawler Tractors

In 1951, the American Tractor Corporation (Ateco) commenced making a range of small crawler tractors known as "Terratracs." The first machine was the GT-25 at 20 horsepower. When J.I. Case purchased Ateco in 1957, the company was offering eight different models. Although Case retained some of these for a short time, the entire line was redesigned and expanded almost immediately. In 1957, Case launched a line consisting of seven sizes, from the 40-horsepower Model 310 up to 100-horsepower Model 1000.

Like John Deere, Case has concentrated on the small end of the crawler tractor market. The 100-horsepower barrier was broken in 1972 by the Model 1150B at 105 horsepower, an upgrade of the 1150 introduced in 1965. The larger 130-horsepower Model 1450 came out in 1973, and was upgraded to the 1450B in 1980. In 1987 the 1450B was replaced by the 150-horsepower hydrostatic drive Model 1550, which was marketed until 1993. In 1994, Case launched the G-series crawler tractors consisting of the 550G, 650G, 850G, and 1150G, ranging from 67 to 118 horsepower.

Other Large Crawler Tractors

The largest crawler tractors ever built were non-production units built by private contractors for a special purpose. In 1962, Alberta Coal Ltd. (now Manalta Coal Ltd.) of Calgary, Alberta, built the XDE 80, the largest crawler tractor up to that time. Designed by Vice President Chuck Doerr, the machine only reached the experimental stage, but it did some good work for the surface coal mining company that built it. Based on two Euclid TC-12 tractors converted to electric drive, the four-crawler machine was powered by twin Cummins NVH-525-B engines totaling 1,050 horsepower. Two 500-horsepower generators provided power to an electric motor in each crawler assembly while another motor operated the blade. Working weight was estimated to be 90 tons.

The largest crawler tractor of all time was built in the early 1980s by Italian contractor Umberto ACCO for an earthmoving contract in Libya. With two engines mounted side-by-side under the hood, for a total of 1,300 horsepower, the giant dozer is two stories high and measures almost 40 feet from blade to ripper. Equipped with Caterpillar engines and transmissions, the machine weighs 183 tons.

Euclid's entry into the crawler tractor market in 1955 featured a unique design that was never again repeated. The Model TC-12 featured a split pivoting frame, with an engine and transmission on each half. When introduced, its 40-ton weight and 402 horsepower gave it the title of the world's largest tractor.

The C-6 was Euclid's second crawler, which came out in 1958. It was basically half a TC-12, powered with a single GM 6-71 engine. The machine illustrated carries a cable-operated dozer blade with hydraulic power tilt.

Large Wheel Dozers

Rubber-tired tractors fitted with dozer blades or push blocks are known as wheel dozers and represent some of the very largest bulldozer-type machines ever constructed. They are used as cleanup machines under large shovels in stockpile work on coal and other minerals, heavy bulldozing such as reclamation work, or in push-loading scrapers. They have found particular favor in large surface mines where their high-speed mobility is important for traveling between different assignments.

Many large wheel dozers were developed from wheel loaders by fitting a dozer blade in place of the loader arms and bucket. However, manufacturers of today's wheel dozers recognize that purpose-built machines with proper transmissions, gear ratios, and strong frames for mounting the dozer arms are essential for maximum reliability.

Caterpillar's first wheel dozers rolled the earth in 1963. Models 824 and 834 generated 300 and 400 horsepower. Compactor versions, on which the rubber tires are replaced with steel tamping-foot wheels, were available in the late 1960s. The smaller 170-horsepower Model 814 came out in 1970. In 1997, after several upgrades, Caterpillar offered the models 814F, 824G, and 834B wheel dozers, ranging up to 450 horsepower, as well as compactor versions of the same models.

Caterpillar further expanded its wheel loader line late in 1997, when it purchased the rights to manufacture two rubber-tired dozers from Tiger Engineering Ltd. of Australia. The two models are the 844 and 854G, of 625 and 800 horsepower.

In 1962 Allis-Chalmers released one of the largest wheel dozers ever built, the Model 555, which incorporated an unusual concept. It was developed from the Allis-Chalmers 562 twin-engined scraper concept, in which engine and drive modules were mixed and matched with scraper bowls. The 555 was simply a two-wheel prime mover coupled through an articulated joint to a rear-powered push unit. In effect, it was a twin-powered scraper without its bowl. Front and rear engines were identical A-C 25000 diesels, providing 870 maximum horsepower. The 555 had a short production life, but the Allis-Chalmers 184-horsepower D-30 and 310-horsepower D-40 dozers, which came out in 1963 and 1964, were more successful. They were modified from the TL series of wheel loaders.

When International decided to build its first wheel dozer, it started at the top. The D-500 was developed as a purpose-built, 600-horsepower wheel dozer with a 64-ton operating weight, a prototype of which appeared as early as 1959. When it was unveiled in 1961, it was claimed to be the first articulated wheel dozer and certainly was the largest ever built by International. The H-400 loader, in the 10-yard class, was released in 1964 and was based on the D-500. That same year, the dozer line was expanded downward with the models D-100 and D-120.

FWD-Wagner, Inc., of Portland, Oregon, made some large articulated wheel dozers in the 1960s. The top-of-the-line Model WI-30 featured two Cummins 350-horsepower diesel engines and dual controls, and was advertised as "Either direction is forward." It could be fitted with a dozer blade on one end and a push block for scrapers on the other.

In 1970, the Multi-Wheel 70, a large dozer by CF & I Engineers Inc. of Denver, Colorado, was offered. It consisted of a rigid frame and four inline driving wheels on each side, connected by chains. The machine was equipped

In 1966, the Euclid crawlers were renumbered, and the TC-12 became the 82-80. By this time, it had also received several upgrades and increased power to 425 horsepower. This 82-80 push-loads scrapers on a British opencast coal site, utilizing a special cushion (spring-mounted) blade, designed for the purpose.

When two of the big Euclid TC-12 tractors are required to push together to load scrapers, a rear push-block is required. This picture shows the arrangement of the spring-mounted twin blocks.

When IBH acquired Terex in 1980, the Hanomag and former Euclid/Terex tractors were combined into one line. The former 82-series Terex models took on the D100-series Hanomag nomenclature. The 350-horsepower Terex D800 shown here was the last crawler tractor model to be built by Terex (1986). *JKH collection*

The XDE is a giant one-of-a-kind bulldozer, designed and built by Alberta Coal Ltd. in 1962. Until the advent of the recent giant Komatsu dozers, this diesel-electric monster was by far the largest crawler bulldozer built! It housed twin Cummins engines that spun out 1,050 horsepower, and its working weight was 90 tons. Its long frame pivoted only in the vertical plane. *JKH collection*

An early John Deere crawler tractor showing its Lindeman heritage. The Lindeman Power Equipment Company was purchased by John Deere in 1947, bringing crawler tractors to the well-established line of John Deere wheel tractors.

The Model MC was the first John Deere-designed crawler tractor. The small machine could muster up 19 horsepower, and was the first of a long line of John Deere crawler tractors.

with two 335-horsepower engines. Each engine powered one side through its own transmission, so that the operator could steer by varying the speed of one side or the other. It was also possible to turn the machine within its own length by putting one transmission into forward and the other in reverse. The 70-ton machine featured a swivel seat so the operator always faced in the direction he was going. Appropriately, this machine, which utilizes the skid-steer principle, was acquired by Melroe of Bobcat Loader fame. Melroe Multi-Wheel was established and sold 10 of the models M-870 and M-880 from 1978 to 1982. After this, the Multi-Wheel dozer laid dormant until 1996, when a new company, Innovative Mining & Equipment of Gillette, Wyoming, started to rebuild the original machines and today offers an upgraded M-880 dozer with twin 425-horsepower engines.

Another large wheel dozer was the V-Con dozer designed by the Peerless Manufacturing Company of Dallas, Texas. This was a diesel-electric machine with planetary wheel motors in each wheel and a power unit of 1,500 horsepower. Designed as a reclamation dozer for surface mining operations, its operating weight was 150 tons. In 1973, the V-Con dozer was adopted by the Marion Power Shovel Company, which marketed it for a few years through their Vehicle Constructors Division.

R.G. LeTourneau Wheel Dozers

The first large rubber-tired dozers were those produced by R.G. LeTourneau, beginning in 1947. Four sizes were developed, known as the Models A, B, C, and D Tournadozers. The huge 750-horsepower Model A Tournadozer didn't progress past the experimental stage. The 300-horsepower Model B and 143-horsepower Model D had only limited success, but the Model C was a different story. Initially, it was fitted with a 160-horsepower Buda engine and later with a 218-horsepower GM 6-71 engine. The C survived as the Super C until 1972, by which time it was part of the LeTourneau-Westinghouse (Wabco) line. All the Tournadozers had mechanical drive, electrically operated blade controls and utilized the skid-steer principle for steering.

Some world record-beating wheel dozers were also built by R.G. LeTourneau after he sold his earthmoving equipment business to Wabco in 1953. These were all diesel-electric machines with electric motors in each wheel hub. The two 600-horsepower "Crash Pushers" built in 1955 for the U.S. Air Force were developed from the earlier "Tree Crasher" of similar six-wheel design. In 1960, the K-series dozers were launched. The K-53 and K-54 were fitted with 420-horsepower engines while the Models K-103 and K-104 were fitted with 840-horsepower engines, and the K-205 contained three 420-horsepower Cummins engines. The last digit in the model numbers signified the number

The John Deere 750 crawler tractor first appeared at the 1975 Conexpo equipment show in Chicago. The 110-horsepower model featured hydrostatic drive, a bold concept for that time. *JKH collection*

John Deere also offered loader versions of its industrial crawler tractors. Here a JD 755 shows off its dumping reach. Like the dozer versions, the loaders also featured hydrostatic drive. *JKH collection*

Case purchased the American Tractor Corporation and its line of Terratrac crawler tractors in 1957. That same year Case introduced seven new models, including this top-of-the-line Model 1000 at 100 horsepower. *Case Corporation*

A Case 1000 crawler loader of 1960s vintage. This model remained in the Case line until 1965, after receiving "C" and "D" upgrades.

of wheels. The colossal five-wheeled K-205 weighed 160 tons when ballasted for traction. It was primarily designed to push-load scrapers. Literature published at the time boasted, "How to swap three tractors for one and still load 45 scrapers an hour." The immense power of the K-205 can be fully comprehended when the three tractors mentioned are identified as Euclid TC-12s, the largest crawlers available at that time, and those scrapers were 40-yard outfits!

Western 2000 Push Tractor

The largest wheel dozer ever built roamed the earth over 35 years ago. In 1961, Western Contracting Corporation decided it needed a mammoth rubber-tired rig to give a super boost to the largest scrapers available. Such a rig was not offered by any manufacturer, so with the help of C. W. Jones Engineering Company, a totally new tractor was designed and built over a two-year period. The outfit was built by Intercontinental Engineering & Manufacturing Corporation in Parkville, Missouri, and first used on the 17-million-yard Milford Dam job near Junction City, Kansas.

The largest crawler dozer ever built by Case was this Model 1550. This 150-horsepower model was in production from 1987 to 1993. *Case Corporation*

This is one of many crawler tractors built in the former Soviet Union. It is a Model A-384 of 300 horsepower and operating weight of 34 tons.

The most powerful and heaviest crawler tractor of all time was this ACCO made by Italian contractor Umberto ACCO in 1980. The two-story-high tractor housed two engines that produced a total of 1,300 horsepower. Its operating weight was 183 tons. *Yvon LeCadre*

At 1,850 horsepower, this machine is still the most powerful wheel or crawler dozer of all time. The main engine was a 16-cylinder GM 16-278A diesel, which put out 1,650 horsepower at only 720 rpm. The engine was connected to a 1,400-kilowatt DC generator providing power to a 400-horsepower electric motor in each of its four wheels. A second engine, a GM 6-71 at 200 horsepower, ran a 75-kilowatt AC generator. The 15.5-foot-wide, 47-foot-long Western 2000 had an operating weight of 170 tons and was articulated at both ends, giving the unit a 37 1/2-foot turning radius. Tires were 44.5x45, the largest made at that time. The machine was a great success for Western Contracting Corporation and served it well from 1963 until it was scrapped in 1981.

Tiger Wheel Dozers

A relative newcomer to the big dozer scene is Tiger Engineering Pty. Ltd. of Australia. Tiger dozers have found a niche in the larger size market of earthmoving and surface mining. The machines are based on stan-

dard Caterpillar wheel loaders but with modified drivetrains and custom frames, strengthened appropriately for dozing applications.

The first Tiger 690 wheel dozer was developed in 1981 at the request of BHP Iron Ore, for use at its Mount Whaleback Mine in Western Australia. Further units were sold around Australia for use in various coal mines, and in 1987, the first unit was exported to the United States. The machines were based on the Caterpillar 992C loader with 690 flywheel-horsepower Caterpillar 3412 engine. In 1994, Tiger released the Model 590, which was based on the Caterpillar 990 loader. In 1997, the 790G dozer, based on the Caterpillar 992G loader equipped with a Caterpillar 800-horsepower 3508B engine, hit the market.

From the outset, Tiger products were made under Caterpillar Inc. approval. In 1997, however, Caterpillar purchased the designs and manufacturing rights for two of Tiger's dozers, the 590 and 790G. These became the 625-horsepower 844 and the 800-horsepower 854G, and are sold as Caterpillar machines.

The first Caterpillar wheel dozers were the 824 and 834, launched in 1963. Here a 300-horsepower 824 cleans up around electric mining shovels on an opencast coal site in Wales.

Currently, Caterpillar offers the 450-horsepower Model 834B wheel dozer. Because of its high-speed mobility, it is a popular utility machine in large surface mines.

The famous D-500 Paydozer from International was the first recognized articulated wheel dozer ever built. With its 64-ton operating weight and 600 horsepower, it was also International's largest wheel dozer. The first D500, built in 1959, spawned other smaller wheel dozers and wheel loaders from International in subsequent years. *State Historical Society of Wisconsin*

From 1973, the V-Con dozer was marketed by the Vehicle Constructors Division of Marion Power Shovel Company. This Model V220 featured diesel-electric drive and was equipped with a Detroit Diesel 16V-149T engine of 1,500 gross horsepower. The machine toured the major surface mines of the Midwest in the late 1970s under a demonstration program. *Eric Orlemann collection*

One of the first series of the Melroe Multi-Wheel dozers undergoes testing. The Model M870 dozer was powered by two 335-horsepower engines, each with its own transmission. This arrangement allowed skid steering and spin turns by varying the speed and direction of the wheels on each side of the rigid frame. *JKH collection*

A new company, Innovative Mining & Equipment, now markets the Melroe Multi-Wheel dozer as the Model M-880. The current machines are offered with 850 horsepower from two engines and operating weight of 112 tons. With its skid-steer and a three-way adjustable blade, this dozer is nimble and versatile for its size. *Innovative Mining & Equipment Inc.*

The LeTourneau Model A Tournadozer, which only reached the experimental stage, is shown here under test. The 750-horsepower dozer weighed 50 tons and was equipped with a cable-operated blade. *JKH collection*

This is the Model C Tournadozer. Much more successful than its sister Models A, B, and D, the C was in production from 1947 to 1972, and went through several upgrades and horsepower increases. The last version, as a Wabco machine, was fitted with a 218-horsepower GM 6-71 engine. *JKH collection*

This is the Tiger 790G wheel dozer, made by the specialist dozer manufacturer, Tiger Engineering Pty. Ltd. of Australia. It is based on the 800-horsepower Caterpillar 992G loader. In 1997, Caterpillar purchased the engineering rights to the Tiger dozers, and two models continued as Caterpillar products. The 790G became the Caterpillar 854G. *Tiger Engineering*

This giant LeTourneau Model K-205 dozer ran on five electrically driven wheels, and was powered by no less than three 420-horsepower engines. This monster could do some serious pushing when it came out in early 1961. *JKH collection*

This is the largest, most powerful dozer ever built! It was made specially for Western Contracting Corporation in 1963 and designed to push-load the largest scrapers in the shortest time. Known as the Western 2000, this king of all pushers weighed 170 tons and measured 15.5 feet wide by 47 feet long. *JKH collection*

Chapter Three

WHEEL LOADERS

The simple idea of mounting a shovel attachment on a tractor is a surprisingly recent invention when compared to other types of earthmoving equipment. The wheel loader, also known as the front-end loader or tractor shovel, originated in the 1920s, when certain small agricultural-type tractors were fitted with a shovel mechanism and bucket. Primarily designed as a rehandling shovel for light materials, the loader has gradually developed into a heavier machine for earthmoving applications. One of the greatest uses for the wheel loader has been in the sand and gravel industry. Currently, most gravel pits rely on wheel loaders for the majority of their output. The loaders have taken over the work previously done by crawler-mounted draglines or shovels, most popular in the 1950s.

There are still many makes of small, versatile wheel loaders, which are attachments to agricultural tractors. Today's front-end loader, as used in construction, earthmoving, and mining, is designed specifically as a digging and loading machine, not an attachment to a tractor. Although not designed as "rock shovels," the midrange and largest loaders have found increasing use as the main production tools on earthmoving projects and in surface mining. Its scope has further expanded as it is used to assist the loader by blasting rocky material or ripping with large dozers. Currently, the largest loaders are performing duties that only a few years ago were thought to be exclusively the domain of the rope excavator.

There are hundreds of wheel loader manufacturers worldwide, ranging from those that make the smallest agricultural attachments and popular skid-steer loaders to those making the world's largest mining front-end loader with buckets of over 45 cubic yards. This chapter concentrates on the development of world record-breaking machines, as well as notable innovations and advances achieved by well-known North American manufacturers.

Wheel Loader Development Highlights

The earliest wheel loaders were cable machines with hoisting action derived from a clutch-operated winch.

This is a typical example of an early wheeled loader. It is cable-operated from a winch above the driver's head, and the bucket is dumped by a spring latch mechanism. The early wheel loaders were intended only to rehandle stockpiled material, rather than perform excavation duties. The loader is mounted on a Fordson tractor. *JKH collection*

Bucket dumping was actuated by gravity through a trip release mechanism. When the bucket returned to the ground, it locked in a fixed position and consequently could not be crowded or tilted to obtain a load. A full bucket could only be obtained by the wheel traction or momentum of the machine running into the bank. Cable-operated loader attachments on agricultural tractors first appeared in the 1920s. E. Boydell & Company

The first Hough loader demonstrates its capability in tight places. Launched in 1939, the Model HS was one of the first machines built specifically as a wheel loader, and not as an attachment to a tractor. *State Historical Society of Wisconsin*

The Hough HM was the first four-wheel-drive hydraulic loader. Built in 1947, it carried a 1 1/2-cubic yard bucket. This machine is gasoline-powered and dates from 1949.

of Manchester, England, was one of the first recorded makers of this type with its Muir-Hill loader in 1929. It had a 1/2-yard cable-controlled bucket mounted on a 28-horsepower Fordson tractor.

Other small wheel loaders began to appear by the late 1930s, including the Hough Model HS in 1939, one of the first integrated machines built specifically as a wheel loader. After World War II, established manufacturers produced wheel loaders in larger sizes, and several new manufacturers entered the market to specialize in this type of machine. Hydraulic systems were proven on loaders in the 1940s, making the cable types totally obsolete by the end of the decade.

A common safety hazard on the larger wheel loaders of the 1950s was the location of the loader-arm pivot behind the operator. This meant that as the arms were raised they moved perilously close to the operator. Not only was the operator at risk of being hit by the moving arms, but side visibility was dangerously blocked when the arms were in the raised position. Toward the end of the 1950s, manufacturers began working with the U.S. National Safety Council to relocate the arm pivot in front of the operator. One of the first manufacturers to adopt the new and safer design was Hough, with its model HO. Soon all manufacturers followed suit, including Allis-Chalmers in 1961 and Michigan in 1962. Case and Caterpillar both adopted the front-mounted arm pivot on their first wheel loaders introduced in 1958 and 1959 respectively.

The next significant step in the development of the wheel loader was the introduction of the articulated frame. The concept was pioneered by Mixermobile Manufacturers of Portland, Oregon, in their Scoopmobile Model LD-5 in 1953. Like so many other brilliant innovations, articulation wasn't immediately appreciated by the industry. Eventually, its greater maneuverability, enabling a shorter travel distance and resulting in a shorter cycle time, was recognized by the entire loader industry. The leading manufacturers introduced articulated models into their lines: Caterpillar in 1963, International Hough in 1964, Michigan and Allis-Chalmers in 1965, and Trojan in 1966.

UPPER LEFT: The Hough H-series of loaders is represented by the 1 3/4-cubic yard H-60 (pictured). The H-60 and the subsequent H-60E were produced from 1961 to 1975. Although the Hough company merged into International Harvester Company in 1952, the Hough name was retained for many years to identify the loaders.

The International Hough H-400 first came out in 1964 as a 10-yard loader. Developed from the D-500 dozer, it was International's largest loader at the time and the company's first articulated loader.

The massive 580 Payloader was the largest of International's 500-series loaders. First displayed at the American Mining Congress in Las Vegas in 1970, it was the world's largest at the time. Initially billed as 18 yards in capacity, it was later boosted to 22 cubic yards. Power came from a 1,200-horsepower Detroit diesel.

The "Haulpak" 4000 evolved from the original International 580 Payloader, which survived in the Payloader line through the Dresser and Komatsu acquisitions. The 1,350-horsepower 4000 Payloader, first of which was sold in 1992, was produced under the Haulpak Division of Komatsu Dresser Company until 1996.

Currently the largest Komatsu loader is this WA-900 introduced in 1996. It carries a standard bucket of 17 cubic yards and a diesel engine of 873 maximum horsepower. *Komatsu Mining Systems*

Today, all large wheel loaders and most of the small units have articulated frames.

Manufacturers are divided as to the best location for the operator's cab. Some choose the front section in line with the bucket, while others choose the rear section. Those from the "front-mounted" school stress the advantage of better visibility, and point to long-established cable shovels whose operators always face the work. Those locating the cab on the rear section insist the operator has a great advantage in being able to "steer" the bucket. He always knows the positions of the rear section relative to the front, and he is positioned further away from any material falling from the back of the raised bucket.

Throughout the 1960s, there was a progression toward larger and larger wheel loaders. Following Caterpillar's introduction of the 6-cubic yard Model 988 in 1963, industry surveys showed that there was a need for even larger loaders. The Hough Division of International Harvester responded with an extensive design program to build a 10-cubic yard class machine. The company had already produced the large articulated D-500 wheel dozer of similar size, and many of the features of the basic D-500 tractor were transposed into the new loader, which surfaced as the H-400 in 1964. Other loaders in the 10-yard class soon followed—the Michigan 475 in 1965, the Scoopmobile 1200 in 1967, and the Caterpillar 992 in 1968.

Pushing the size trend even further was International Hough's 18-yard 580 Payloader and Clark-Michigan's massive 675 loader with a 24-yard capacity. Both these machines were developed in the early 1970s and displayed at Conexpo '75 as production machines.

Japan's Surface Mining Equipment for Coal Technology Research Association (SMEC) developed the world's largest wheel loader, built by Kawasaki Heavy Industries Ltd. in Japan in 1986. SMEC is an organization consisting of 11 major construction equipment manufacturers, under the guidance of the Ministry of International Trade and Industry. The super wheel loader was developed through three years of intensive research, and it ranked as the world's largest in terms of bucket size (25 yards), rated engine power (1,360 horsepower), and operating weight (200 tons). A pair of 680 horsepower Cummins diesels provided its power.

At present in the loader industry, we see giant loaders in sizes thought impossible a few short years ago. By the early 1990s International-Dresser, LeTourneau, and Caterpillar all followed the lead set by Clark-Michigan and came out with loaders exceeding 24 cubic yards in capacity. Today, LeTourneau is out in front with the record-breaking L-1800, boasting a standard capacity of no less than 33 cubic yards.

The 1-yard Tractomotive TL-10 is one of the loaders that established Allis-Chalmers in the loader business. It was launched in 1950, and nine years later, Allis-Chalmers purchased the Tractomotive Corporation and expanded the loader line. *JKH collection*

In the early 1960s, Allis-Chalmers loaders rapidly increased in size. Here is a TL-30 with 4-yard bucket at a surface coal mine in Ohio.

In 1965, Allis-Chalmers introduced its first articulated loader, the 3-yard Model 645. This machine spawned a full line of "45" series loaders, which soon replaced the former rigid-frame models.

The top-of-the-line Allis-Chalmers loader was the 945-B, which carried a standard 6-cubic yard bucket and had an operating weight of 34 tons. *JKH collection*

The famous Scoopmobile Model HP demonstrates its handiness. With the transmission in neutral, it could be towed from job to job behind a utility truck. The HP, introduced in 1957, remained in production for 32 years. In later years, it was built by Eagle Crusher Company up to 1989. *Tom Berry*

The Scoopmobile LD-8A, built from 1956 to 1962, was rated at 3 1/2 cubic yards. Scoopmobile was the originator of the articulated loader.

Case Wheel Loaders

Although Case is primarily recognized for its farm equipment, Case wheel loaders made a significant impact in the construction industry. Many Case farm tractors had been fitted with small loaders during the 1950s. In 1958, the W-9 loader introduced the first integrated four-wheel-drive loader from Case. It was followed closely by the W-10 and W-12, both four-wheel-drive models. The W-5 was also a front-wheel-drive model. These first Case loaders formed the basis from which the subsequent Case line has evolved into the present-day range.

The W-series loaders expanded throughout the 1960s and 1970s. The W26, with a 3-yard standard bucket, was the largest to date when introduced in 1968. This was replaced with the larger 4-yard W36 in 1977. The W-series loaders featured their cabs mounted on the front half of the machine.

Since 1987 with the introduction of the Model 621, the entire Case loader line has graduated into the 21-series, a modern line featuring rear-mounted operator's cab. Currently, Case offers four sizes of loaders. The largest is the 921B, carrying a 4 3/4-cubic yard standard bucket. It has been Case policy to produce efficient machines to serve the smaller end of the wheel loader market.

Caterpillar Wheel Loaders

When Caterpillar introduced the 944 in 1959, it was the first wheel loader to be marketed by the established tractor builder. The following year it was joined by the 922 and 966 series A machines. Buckets of these three models spanned from 1 1/4 to 2 3/4 cubic yards, and engines ranged from 80 to 140 flywheel horsepower. The loaders featured four-wheel drive with power shift transmission and torque converter. The front-mounted bucket arm pivot allowed an unobstructed operator's compartment with "walk-through" design. These three loaders, along with the up-rated 922B in 1962, were the only rigid-frame loaders ever built by Caterpillar. The 944 and 922B survived in the line until 1968.

Caterpillar's first articulated loader, the Model 988 in 1963, was also its largest loader up to that time. It carried a 6-yard standard bucket and 325 horsepower engine. With upgrades denoted by suffix letters, the 988, as well as the 966, have reached the G-series and remain in Caterpillar's loader line. Caterpillar has filled out its loader line with many new models introduced over the past three decades. A big jump in size was achieved in 1968 with the introduction of the 10-yard 992, followed by the 992B in 1973 and then the 12 1/2-yard, 690 flywheel horsepower 992C in 1977.

Caterpillar's flagship loader today is the giant 994, one of the biggest loaders currently in the field. First available in 1991, the 994 has a standard bucket of 23 cubic yards and an operating weight of 196 tons. It is powered by a single Caterpillar 3516 engine with 1,250 flywheel horsepower.

Dart Wheel Loaders

The Dart Truck Company's entire contribution to the wheel loader industry was confined to one size class. But it was a big one—45,000 pounds carrying capacity or 15 cubic yards! First appearing in 1966 after some earlier prototypes, the D600 was the largest production loader available up to that time. Initially a rigid-frame machine, it was converted to an articulated type very early in its development.

The huge mechanical-drive D600, with its isolated cab overhanging one side, had a distinctive appearance and boasted several unique features. The standard engine was a Cummins VT12 at 700 maximum horsepower, but the brochure says, "How Dart engineers get 840 horses out of a 700-horsepower engine." It was achieved by what Dart called a balanced boom. Two cylinders filled with nitrogen pulled with enough force to counterbalance the weight of the boom and empty bucket. With the engine providing power only to raise the payload, 120 horsepower was saved. Another 20 horsepower was saved by using a "de-clutch" fan, working on the thermal delay principle. The fan automatically disconnected during the digging and hoisting part of the cycle where most power is needed. When the loader backed away from the digging face, the fan restarted in time to catch up with the increase in engine temperature caused by thermal delay.

The DE620, an electric-drive version, utilized the same Dart mechanical axles and planetary reductions as on the straight mechanical loader. Each axle was driven by one DC motor powered from a diesel-driven generator.

The D600 proved to be a very popular machine with mining and earthmoving contractors, and hundreds were sold. Upgrades through the D600B and 600C models occurred over the years, and engines up to 875 horsepower were offered. Dart was purchased by Unit Rig in 1984, and production was moved to the Unit Rig plant at Tulsa, Oklahoma. Four years later, Unit Rig was purchased by Terex Corporation. The Dart trade name remained on the loader until 1995, when the last Dart loader left the factory.

John Deere Wheel Loaders

The most recent of the "big name" construction equipment manufacturers to enter into four-wheel-drive wheel loader production is John Deere. In 1967, they launched the first of their wheel loader line—the JD-544. The articulated, four-wheel-drive machine had a 94-horsepower engine and buckets up to 3 cubic yards. The larger JD-644 was introduced the following year.

The Model 1200, the giant of all Scoopmobiles, was the largest loader ever built when it was introduced in 1965. It led the way for other manufacturers to follow with even larger units. The 1200 could be fitted with buckets from 10 to 20 yards; it was powered by a 525-horsepower Cummins diesel. *Eric Orlemann collection*

One of many sizes of rigid-frame loaders introduced by Yale in the 1960s was this 2-yard Model 134A. Sold under the trade name Trojan, these machines were very popular with municipalities. *O&K Orenstein & Koppel Inc.*

The largest Yale Trojan rigid-frame loader was the 404, which had a production run from 1958 to 1968. It could carry buckets up to 6 cubic yards. *O&K Orenstein & Koppel Inc.*

The unique double-articulated Yale Trojan loader, the Model 8000, came out in 1966. Not only was it Yale's first articulated loader, it was the largest ever built by the company. Buckets up to 9 cubic yards could be attached to this 52-ton giant. *O&K Orenstein & Koppel Inc.*

A Yale Trojan 4000 articulated loader of 1980s vintage. The 4000 carried a 5-yard bucket and a 230-horsepower engine. *O&K Orenstein & Koppel Inc.*

Clark Equipment Company launched into the loader business in 1954 with three loader models. The 75A with a 1-yard bucket was the smallest, but it was later upgraded to 1 1/4 yards. The example shown here is owned by the Historical Construction Equipment Association at Bowling Green, Ohio.

Normally carrying a 1 3/4-yard bucket, the Michigan 125A shown here is fitted with a tree transplanting attachment. This rigid-frame machine is of 1960s vintage. *JKH collection*

A 262-horsepower Michigan 280 wheel dozer gives a boost to a Terex TS-14 scraper on a British opencast coal site in 1968. This is one of the early rigid-frame versions, introduced in 1957. Later versions featured an articulated frame design.

As early as 1965, Michigan announced a 12-yard loader, which materialized a year later as the Model 475A. Seen here is one of the very first Michigan 475s at work near Owingsville, Kentucky, on the construction of a section of Interstate 64. Its operating weight was 60 tons. *JKH collection*

In 1971, two models were introduced as a refined A-series. Further refinements brought the B-series in 1974. To fill a niche at the smaller end of the line, the JD-444 was introduced in 1976. A 5-yard loader, the JD-844 introduced in 1979, featured a newly developed V-8 John Deere diesel engine. Further upgrades brought the C-series in 1981, the D-series in 1985, the E-series in 1987, and the G-series in 1993.

Most recently, John Deere announced the H-series loaders in 1997, comprising seven models from 1- to 5-cubic yard capacity.

Dresser/International/Hough Loaders

The Frank G. Hough Company was one of the first manufacturers to market a wheel loader, with its model HS in 1939. With a bucket capacity of about 1/3 cubic yard, it was dumped by gravity through a latch mechanism. An improved, larger model, the HL was released in 1941. Even though it still had gravity dump and only rear-wheel drive, the HL was a milestone in loader development, because it featured the first hydraulically operated loader arms.

In 1944, the first hydraulically actuated bucket tilt was introduced on a Hough model. This not only allowed controlled dumping, but it let the operator approach the bank in low gear and obtain a full bucket by tilting the bucket back during loading. Of course, all loaders today incorporate this feature.

Advancing further, in 1947, Hough came out with the model HM, which can be termed the forerunner of the modern wheel loader. This was the world's first four-wheel-drive hydraulic loader. Bucket size was 1 1/2 cubic yards, and power came from a 76-horsepower gasoline or diesel engine. A much larger machine, the HW, with a 4-cubic yard bucket, was on the market by 1950. This was the first wheel loader to have planetary axles, a torque converter, and power shift transmission.

In 1952, the Frank G. Hough Company was merged with International Harvester Company. The merger allowed the Hough Payloaders to be marketed through the already established International Harvester network of dealers. International rapidly expanded the Payloader line bringing out new models, which gradually increased in size and sophistication. The H-120 Payloader came out in 1958 as the first of the now-famous H-series, which continued until the end of the 1970s. The last model, the H-90E, actually continued until 1983.

In 1970, the 560 was launched as the first of the 500-series Payloaders. The following year saw the giant 580 Payloader appear at the American Mining Congress in Las Vegas, Nevada. At 18 cubic yards, the 580 was the world's largest loader at the time, almost double the size of the previous largest Payloader H-400B.

The massive Michigan 675 carried a bucket of 24 cubic yards! This 1970 prototype machine was equipped with two GM 635-horsepower engines, making it the world's largest wheel loader ever built up to that time. The 675 was exactly double the size of Michigan's previous largest loader, the 475, which was powered by one of the same GM 635-horsepower engines used on the 675. *Volvo Construction Machinery*

Another loader in the L-series from Volvo, this L-160 shows its distinctive Volvo heritage. The L-160 fits into the 4 1/2-yard class.

One of the Michigan 675 production machines at work in a western Pennsylvania surface coal mine in 1979. It didn't take many 24-yard buckets to bury this Euclid R-85 truck! The 14 Model 675 production models built from 1973 to 1976 were powered with twin 635-horsepower Cummins engines.

This L320 was one from the new line of Michigan L-series loaders introduced after Clark-Michigan became a subsidiary of the VME group in 1985. The former Michigan models were combined with the Volvo loader line, resulting in the upgraded L-series. The L320, showing its Michigan heritage, worked with a standard 8-yard bucket, and was current in the early 1990s.

The 580 featured a constant-speed engine and power-modulated control, allowing the operator infinite power adjustment between the hydraulic system and drivetrain.

In 1982, Dresser Industries acquired International Harvester's Payline Division and the trade name Dresser was adopted for the loaders. New machines were introduced to complement the existing 500-series loader line. The 520B, 545, 550, and 560B were added in the period 1982 to 1984, and the 555 in 1988.

Yet another change took place in 1988 when Japan's Komatsu Ltd. and Dresser Industries, Inc., began a joint venture, resulting in the establishment of the Komatsu Dresser Company (KDC), to market both companies' lines. The 500-series loaders were continued, but several of the existing Komatsu loaders were rechristened to fit into the Dresser numbering system for sale in certain parts of the world. For example, the Komatsu WA-320, WA-380, and WA-420 were renumbered the 532, 538, and 542 respectively. Today, Komatsu owns 100 percent

Caterpillar's first wheel loader was the 100-horsepower 944 with 2-cubic-yard capacity. Unveiled in 1959, it was followed the next year by Models 922 and 966. These first three Caterpillar loaders were of rigid-frame design. *Caterpillar Inc.*

of KDC, and the Komatsu WA-series loaders are gradually replacing the Dresser 500-series.

The top-of-the-line 580 Payloader, already upgraded to 22-yard capacity by 1975, stayed in the line as a Dresser machine until the KDC joint venture took over. It was then produced and marketed by Dresser's Haulpak Division at Peoria, Illinois, and grew into the 24-yard Haulpak 4000, the first of which was sold in 1992. The giant 1,350-horsepower loader was produced under the Haulpak Division of KDC until discontinued in 1996.

The current top-of-the-line Komatsu loader is the WA-900, introduced at the Minexpo equipment show in Las Vegas in 1996. It comes with a standard bucket of 17 cubic yards and a Komatsu engine of 873 maximum horsepower.

Fiat-Allis/Allis-Chalmers/Tractomotive Loaders

An early competitor to the Hough company was the Tractomotive Corporation of Findlay, Ohio, founded in 1945. It developed an all-hydraulic loader mechanism in 1948, designed to mount on the Allis-Chalmers HD-5 crawler tractor. That same year, Tractomotive mounted the loader on the back of a farm

tractor which, when driven in reverse, put the load on the drive wheels, thus increasing traction. In 1950, the 1-yard TL-10 was introduced which had torque converter drive. It was Tractomotive's first self-contained unit, designed specifically as a wheel loader.

Also in 1950, Tractomotive built a new plant at Deerfield, Illinois, and signed an agreement allowing Tractomotive products to be sold through the approved Allis-Chalmers dealers. The first four-wheel-drive loader from Tractomotive, the TL-12, hit the market in 1954. Power shift with single-lever control was introduced on the two-yard Model TL-20 in 1957.

In 1959, the Tractomotive Corporation was purchased by Allis-Chalmers Manufacturing Company. This came as no surprise, since both companies had worked closely together, sharing the same distributors for many years. The range of Allis-Chalmers loaders was expanded through the early 1960s with the two largest models, the TL-30 and TL-40, coming out in 1961 and 1962. The largest at the time, the TL-40, had a standard excavating bucket of 5 cubic yards and an A-C 21000 engine rated at 310 horsepower.

45

One of the world's largest wheel loaders is the Caterpillar 994. Running on 12-foot tires, and carrying 23 yards in its bucket, it is powered by a single Caterpillar 3516 engine developing 1,250 horsepower.

Allis-Chalmers began articulated loader design with the Model 645 in 1965. This model heralded the 45-series loader range, which was expanded to smaller and larger machines through the 1970s. The Model 945 was Allis-Chalmers' largest-ever wheel loader, with an operating weight of 34 tons, 450-horsepower A-C engine, and 6-cubic yard general purpose bucket.

Fiat S.p.A. of Italy purchased the majority of Allis-Chalmers shares in 1974, and the Fiat-Allis joint venture was born. The wheel loader line continued under the Fiat-Allis name. Fiat-Allis gradually replaced the loader models with the upgraded FR-series, beginning in 1980 with the FR-20 to replace the 745-C. In 1989, Fiat-Allis ceased manufacturing its earthmoving products in North America. The FR-series loaders are still available from Italy, consisting of 10 models from the FR-70 at 1 3/8 yards to the FR-220 at 5 1/2 yards capacity.

LeTourneau Wheel Loaders

In keeping with its long tradition of building record-breaking machines, today's LeTourneau line includes the largest wheel loader ever built. Still made in the Longview, Texas, plant, established by its founder, R.G. LeTourneau, the four-model loader line starts with the L-1000 having a standard (rock) bucket of 17 cubic yards, and goes up from there. The top-of-the-line L-1800, announced in

This Caterpillar 922B loader is equipped with a side-dumping bucket. The 922B came out in 1962 as an upgrade from the original 922. It was the last of only four models of rigid-frame loaders ever produced by Caterpillar. *JKH collection*

1992, comes with a standard bucket of 33 cubic yards, or can carry buckets up to 45 yards for coal loading. Used in surface mining for coal loading or overburden removal, the behemoth L-1800 rides on four 12-foot diameter tires—the largest in the industry. The intermediate 22-yard L-1100 and 28-yard L-1400 loaders complete the line.

LeTourneau loaders feature diesel-electric drive with DC electric motors in each wheel, the principle developed

The 988, introduced in 1963, was Caterpillar's first articulated wheel loader. Working with a standard bucket of 6 cubic yards, it was also the company's largest wheel loader built to that time.

A big jump in size came with the introduction of the 992 series. This wheel loader, the first Caterpillar loader to reach the 10-yard class, carried a 550-horsepower engine.

The 992 was upgraded to the "C" model in 1977. It was a huge jump in size from the previous 992B. Engine power increased to 690 horsepower, and bucket size grew a whopping 25 percent to 12 1/2 cubic yards. On a special sample test in a Canadian coal mine, the operator of this 992C took care not to bury the GMC truck!

Euclid started small when it entered the loader field with this L-7 model in 1957. This 49-horsepower rigid-frame model was the only Euclid loader on the market until the first Euclid articulated models appeared in 1962.

The first Euclid series L-20 loader was one of the earliest articulated loaders in the industry and was one of two articulated models introduced by Euclid to the market in 1962.

by R.G. LeTourneau many years earlier. LeTourneau produced some very big electric loaders in the early 1960s, with power to the hoist and bucket tilt transmitted through a rack-and-pinion drive. One example was the Model SL-10 with a bucket of 10 cubic yards, an unheard-of size in 1960 when it appeared. Another record-beater came in 1965. Nicknamed "The Monster," it was the SL-40 with a 19-yard rock bucket and twin GM engines totaling 950 horsepower. Although these LeTourneau loaders were articulated, the advantage of articulated steering was lost due to their great length, the SL-40 measuring over 52 feet long.

The large rack-and-pinion drive LeTourneau loaders were not a commercial success, and few were built. However, they did work, as records show that some had a working life of over 20 years.

LeTourneau's present-day loader line is derived from the original L-700 electric-drive model made available in 1968. The L-700 was the forerunner to a series of successful loaders produced in large numbers, still continuing today after many updates and improvements. The L-series models have hydraulically operated bucket action, bringing them in line with the rest of the industry, and departing from the LeTourneau tradition of rack and pinion. The electric drive to the wheels, however, has been retained.

After R.G. LeTourneau's death in 1969, the company was sold to Marathon Manufacturing Company the next year, and became the Marathon-LeTourneau Company. In 1994, Rowan Industries purchased the company, and today's LeTourneau Inc. was born. Through these changes, the loader line was improved and developed into the present-day lineup. LeTourneau has also maintained its strong position in the offshore oil rig and lumber industries.

O&K/Trojan/Yale Loaders

The Yale & Towne Manufacturing Company of Batavia, New York, came into the loader field in 1950 with the Yale Model LM-75 wheel loader. During the 1950s, Yale established a line of rigid-frame loaders, and offered front-wheel or all-wheel drive. The loaders were known by the trade names "Yale" or "Trojan."

The rigid-frame loader line was expanded in the 1960s, with models like the 114, 124, 134, and 204 becoming very popular in the 3/4- to 2 1/4-cubic yard class. These rigid machines had a very long production life, lasting into the early 1970s. The largest rigid loader was the Model 404, which carried buckets up to 6 yards, weighed 24 tons in operating condition, and had a production run from 1958 to 1968.

The later version of Euclid L-20 loader of mid-1960s vintage. The L-20 carried a standard bucket of 3 cubic yards.

In 1968, the Euclid loaders became Terex loaders. The following year, the top-of-the-line Terex 72-81 came out, with a 9-yard capacity. The 72-81 turned out to be the largest loader ever built by the company.

The forerunner of Dart's big 15-yard loader was this rigid-frame model, shown on test in the early 1960s. While it was being developed, the industry turned to articulated designs, so Dart returned to the drawing board. It redesigned its machine with articulation, and launched into the loader business with the D600 in 1966. *Unit Rig, Div. Terex Corp.*

The Yale company was later than most to introduce articulated wheel loaders, but when it eventually did, it was in grand style. The huge Trojan 8000, unveiled in 1966, was not only the largest wheel loader Yale has ever built, it was articulated in two places instead of one. It carried buckets up to 9 yards and had an operating weight of 52 tons. Power was provided by a GM 12V71N at 530 maximum horsepower. The unique machine placed the operator on the center section, with the articulated sections working together in front and behind him. The advantage of the double articulation, claimed Yale, was that the center section acted as a laterally moving counterweight for greater stability, shifting its bulk to the outside of every turn. However, the 8000 had a production life of only three years.

Two much more successful articulated loaders also came out in 1966, the 3000 and 4000 models in the 3- to 5-yard class. These machines, with their upgrades, stayed in production until 1974. Gradually, other articulated loaders were introduced, until all the rigid models were replaced. Yale models in the 1970s and 1980s ranged

The giant Dart D600 loader features an offset cab that is prominently shown in this photograph. The operator had a good view of all that was going on, but it took a little time to get used to being on one side. The machine shown is in a load-and-carry operation at a coal mine in New Mexico, carrying a good 15 cubic yards of rock and dirt.

Another view of the 15-yard Dart D600 loader. With engines up to 875 horsepower, the model was upgraded through the "B" and "C" models until 1995, when the last one left the factory.

from the Model 1500 to the Model 7500, covering bucket requirements from 1 1/2 to 8 1/2 cubic yards.

In 1982, Faun A.G. from Germany merged the Trojan line into the Faun line of wheel loaders, which were derived from the German Frisch line a few years earlier. In 1986, Orenstein & Koppel (O&K) from Germany took over the Faun company along with the wheel loaders and continued their production under the O&K name in the original Batavia plant. The former Yale/Trojan models were gradually phased out until the Batavia plant was closed in 1992. The O&K loaders built today in Germany comprise models derived from the Faun range, as well as from the original line of O&K loaders.

Euclid/Terex Wheel Loaders

The General Motors Euclid Division entered the wheel loader field in 1957 with a small rigid-frame unit known as the L-7. Although some experimental models came out in the intervening years, the 49-horsepower L-7 remained the only loader in production from the Euclid stable until 1962, when the L-20 and L-30 articulated loaders entered the market. As Euclid was one of the first U.S. companies to build articulated loaders, these 2- to 3-yard capacity machines attracted much attention when they first came out. With the operator's cab on the rear frame, the advertisements said, "You steer the bucket."

The L-series had expanded to four models (L-15, L-20, L-25, L-30) by 1967, when the entire line was

LeTourneau's smallest loader from the current line is the L-1000, featuring a standard 17-yard bucket! The special 26-yard bucket on this L-1000 works at a western Canadian coal mine. In keeping with the long-term tradition, LeTourneau wheel loaders feature diesel-electric drive and articulated design.

The flagship of the loader industry today is the LeTourneau L-1800. This monster machine wields a 33-yard standard bucket, but for coal loading duties, its capacity can go up to 45 cubic yards. Featuring a 1,800-horsepower engine, the L-1800 offers power and mobility for the modern-day surface miner. *Eric C. Orlemann*

revamped and the 72-series came out. The four initial models, the 72-21, 72-31, 72-41, and 72-51, spanned sizes up to 3 1/2 cubic yards.

Just as the new line was getting established in 1968, a change in name took place. The Euclid Division of General Motors was forced to drop the Euclid name because of anti-trust laws, and sell off its haul truck business. (See Chapter 6 to learn about the Euclid/Terex story.) However, the loader line was not affected, except that the new name "Terex" was adopted. The much-larger 72-81 brought Terex into the big league when it was announced in 1969, with its 9-yard bucket and 438-horsepower GM 12V-71T engine. It turned out to be the largest loader Terex ever built.

Terex passed into the hands of the German IBH Group in 1981, and shortly afterward, the Terex loader line was merged into the Hanomag loader line from Germany, another company acquired by IBH. The combined line consisted of eight models from the 2-yard 40C to a new, top-of-the-line model, the 90C, which replaced the 72-81. The 90C was rated at 7 1/2 cubic yards, slightly less than the former 72-81.

After the failure of IBH in 1983, Terex returned to General Motors. However, only the original GM-designed loaders were retained as Terex machines. (The Hanomag-designed loaders were adopted by a new company in Germany, and continued under the Hanomag name.)

The novel 10-yard LeTourneau was the world record holder loader, featuring rack-and-pinion drive for all its motions. This is one of the first loaders built by the company after it recommended earthmoving equipment manufacture in the late 1950s. Although not a popular machine, the SL-10 paved the way for bigger and better machines to come. *JKH collection*

The forerunner of today's LeTourneau loaders is this L-700, appearing in 1968. It was the first from the company to feature hydraulic power for its motions, doing away with the earlier rack-and-pinion design. The L-700 was in the 15-yard class. *JKH collection*

Northwest Engineering Company, having itself just been purchased by businessman Randolph Lenz, took over Terex Corporation from GM in 1986. In 1988, Terex Corporation succeeded Northwest Engineering as the parent company of the group. Recently, Terex decided to discontinue loaders and concentrate on its other equipment lines, most notably articulated trucks. The last loaders built were a batch of six Model 90Cs which left the Motherwell, Scotland, plant for Greece in 1994.

Volvo/Clark/Michigan Loaders

Clark Equipment Company began in 1903 and developed into a diversified industrial company. As part of its expansion program, Clark acquired the Michigan Power Shovel Company in 1953 and established its Construction Machinery Division at Benton Harbor, Michigan. At the same time, development was under way on a new line of rugged wheel loaders, the prototypes appearing later that same year. Although the Michigan power shovels only remained in production for a few years after the takeover, the Michigan name was retained to christen the new line of loaders. Three models were introduced at a public demonstration in 1954. These were the 75A, 125A, and 175A, providing stiff competition for all others in the field.

The Michigan range was expanded with the announcement of the Models 275A and 375A in 1957, together with wheel dozer versions designated Models 280 and 380. These machines had engines of 262 and 375 maximum horsepower and had operating weights up to 31 tons. The rapid increase in size continued with the giant 52-ton Model 480 dozer, announced a year later. This machine established the Michigan name in a league with the largest wheeled equipment yet built, and only five short years after the first Michigan prototype was developed.

Several more rigid-frame models were introduced; then in 1965, articulated Michigan loaders began to appear. By this time, the range had expanded to 11 models, from the small 1/2-yard 12B to the large 475A, a newly announced 12-yard articulated loader with 635 horsepower engine. The 475A and its upgrades, through B and C versions, lasted in the range until replaced by the similar-sized L480 in 1987.

It was big news in the industry when Michigan announced that its giant 675 loader was under development. Market research showed that earthmoving people were demanding rugged mobility in their loading tools, and larger wheel loaders would fit the bill. It was not only twice as big as Michigan's previ-

By 1981, the LeTourneau L-1200 was getting up there in size. The 1,200-horsepower loader, with a 21-cubic yard standard bucket, was the largest from the company at the time.

The Model LI, introduced in 1930, is an example of an early cable-operated loader, mounted on a Case tractor. This one is shown clearing surplus dirt from ditches along a Missouri highway in 1931. *Case Corp.*

ous largest 475 loader, it was the largest wheel loader ever built up to that time. The prototype was built in 1970 with two GM engines. Then from 1973 to 1976, a further 14 production models were built. These had twin Cummins engines totaling 1,270 horsepower and an operating weight of over 190 tons. The operator sat in a cab two stories above the ground and rode on four tires over 10 feet in diameter, the largest in the industry.

After the Clark-Michigan Company became a subsidiary of VME Group N.V. in 1985, the Michigan loaders were gradually merged into Volvo's Swedish-designed loader line, denoted by the L-series. By 1990, the L-series consisted of 10 machines from the L30 to the L480, covering bucket sizes from 1 to 12 1/2 cubic yards. The two Michigan-designed wheel dozers, 280C and W380, were still being offered.

By 1994, the Michigan name was dropped in favor of the Volvo name, and in 1995, VME Americas Inc. became Volvo Construction Equipment, as a wholly owned subsidiary of AB Volvo with headquarters in Belgium. Today the Volvo loader line consists of seven mod-els from the L50C to the L330C (bucket capacities from 1 1/2 to 9 cubic yards), plus smaller loaders from the Zettelmeyer, now also part of the Volvo group.

Wabco/Scoopmobile Loaders

A very important name in wheel loader history is Scoopmobile, a name invented in the 1930s by Mixer-mobile Manufacturers Incorporated of Portland, Oregon. Its famous line of three-wheel loaders under the name Scoopmobile started in 1939 with the 3/4-yard Model A. It had a single rear wheel that steered, and front-wheel drive on two large tires.

More Scoopmobiles came out in the 1940s. In 1949, the Model C was brought out and remained in production until 1966. These early models had a cable hoist for the bucket that ran up a vertical track. The bucket was dumped by gravity through a latch mechanism. The Model C was offered with a special high-lift arrangement in which the bucket was pulled up the vertical track to a height of 24 feet! This enabled the machine to load high bins and silos.

More three-wheel loaders were developed, including the fully hydraulic Models H and HP

The first four-wheel-drive integrated loader from Case was the Model W-9, in 1958. The W-9B illustrated is of 1966 vintage, and carrying a 1 3/4-cubic yard bucket.

which were introduced in 1952 and 1957. These models featured a single, centrally mounted bucket arm, probably the first loaders to do so.

Mixermobile is credited with building the first four-wheel-drive articulated wheel loader, the Scoopmobile LD-5, in 1953. Power to all four wheels was provided through an exclusive "Pow-R-Flex" coupling, permitting the two axles to oscillate independently, as well as providing articulation between the two frames.

By 1956, the Scoopmobile articulated line had been expanded to include the Models LD-8, LD-12, LD-15, and LD-20. The last model, at 4 cubic yards, held the world size record for a loader when it came out in 1954. Further new Scoopmobiles were introduced in the early 1960s.

The largest loader to date from Case in 1977 was the 4-yard W36. Until the recent "21-series" loaders, the operator's cab on Case loaders was attached to the front half of the articulated frame. *Case Corp.*

The current largest, and the largest loader ever offered by Case, is the 921B at 4 3/4 yards. It is an upgrade from the earlier Model 921, unveiled in 1992. *Case Corp.*

In 1965, Scoopmobile again came out with the world's largest wheel loader. This was the massive Model 1200 which offered buckets with capacity ranging from 10- to 20-yards (depending on material weight), and powered with a Cummins diesel developing 525 horsepower.

In 1968, the Scoopmobile line of wheel loaders was merged into the Construction Equipment Division of Westinghouse Air Brake Company, and the machines sold under the Wabco name. The line diminished soon after that date, and in 1974, the rights of manufacture were purchased by the Eagle Crusher Company, Inc. of Galion, Ohio. The machines continued to be built in dwindling numbers, until the final spark went out in 1989 when the last Scoopmobile left Eagle's works. As praise to the tenacity of the Scoopmobile design, the last machine built was a three-wheel Model HP, a machine needing only minor modifications from the machine launched some 32 years earlier.

The biggest loader for John Deere was the Model 844. Launched in 1977, it featured a newly developed 260-horsepower John Deere engine; its standard bucket held 5 cubic yards.

The John Deere G-series of loaders was introduced in 1993. A 644G demonstrates its loading height.

The 544H shown here is one from John Deere 's current line of H-series loaders. The 544H represents the latest in a long line of upgraded 544 loaders, going back to John Deere's first wheel loader, the original 94-horsepower 544, launched in 1967.

Chapter Four

SCRAPERS

crapers are the big digging and hauling machines seen on many types of construction jobs. The larger self-propelled types, running on giant rubber tires, are capable of moving vast quantities of earth at high speed. Also referred to by slang names such as buggies, pans, cans, or boxes, and by various trade names, scrapers evolved from a simple device drawn by horses to the high-speed earthmovers of today. Scrapers come in a wide range of types and sizes, and can be either self-propelled or pulled behind a wheeled or crawler tractor. This latter type, known as a towed or pull-type, is less frequently used today. It is almost superseded by small self-propelled types, or by other varieties of earthmoving equipment capable of performing similar tasks.

Early History

The history of the scraper goes back to the time when man first used animals to undertake earthmoving tasks. The original scrapers were pulled by horses and mules, and their earliest form consisted of a small scoop with handles controlled by a man walking behind.

By the 1870s, pull-type scrapers began to appear with wheels. An early type was invented by C.H. Smith & Company, a firm of railroad contractors in Iowa, who developed this "new" method for use on their own contracts. The idea was so successful that they were urged by others to build machines for sale. Thus, in 1879, a new company was born called the Western Wheeled Scraper Company at Mount Pleasant, Iowa. The company eventually moved to Aurora, Illinois. As described in Chapter 5, this company went on to build graders, and became a prominent force in the motor grader business. Another inventor was Abijah McCall, a blacksmith and earthmover of Fresno, California, who, with his partner, F. Dusy, came out with an improved pull-type scraper. With a pair of wheels at the front, this device eventually became known as the Fresno, after the area where it was invented. The name "Fresno" became widely used to refer to many types of drag, and wheeled, horse-drawn scrapers.

BASIC TYPES OF SELF-PROPELLED SCRAPERS

1. **Standard Self-Propelled**. The machines consist of a bowl, apron, and ejector, all capable of functioning independently through a hydraulic system. Some early types used cables. Variations include single or multiple engines, single or multiple bowls, two-wheel or four-wheel prime movers.

2. **Elevating.** In these machines, the apron is replaced by an elevator made up of two chains carrying a series of crossbars called flights. In loading, the elevator assists in lifting the material into the bowl. To dump, a sliding bowl floor is moved toward the rear. Reversing the elevator assists in dumping the load evenly. The elevator may be driven by hydraulic or electric motors. These scrapers do not require a push tractor to load.

3. **Auger.** This type of scraper is also a true self-loading type. Two vertically mounted augers are positioned inside the bowl so when rotated by hydraulic power, they assist in raising the material in the bowl. Its fewer moving parts give this type of scraper an advantage over the elevating type. In both elevating and auger scrapers, a full load is always ensured, since unlike standard scrapers, no more power is required to load the last yard of material than the first.

4. **Push-Pull.** This is a system rather than a type of machine. Two twin engine standard scrapers are equipped with a hook-up arrangement where two scrapers can be coupled together during the loading part of the cycle. Loading can be accomplished without assistance, as the power of the four engines is applied to loading each bowl in turn.

Large quantities of earth were moved using horses and mules with primitive scrapers, or "Fresnos," before the age of mechanized earthmoving. *JKH collection*

Early Pull-Type Scrapers

By the 1870s, steam tractors were first used to draw steel-wheeled scrapers. These were principally employed on the big railroad projects of the American Midwest. With the use of tractor power, scrapers of greater capacity were possible, but they had larger bowls that simply dragged their load rather than lifting it clear of the ground. Hence, they were known as the drag scraper.

As power of wheeled and crawler tractors increased in the early part of this century, several varieties of pull-type scrapers were developed by many manufacturers, very few of whom survive today. A popular type was known as the "rotary" scraper. This consisted of a cylindrical bowl, which was designed to rotate into the carry position after collecting its load. An operator-controlled release mechanism caused the bowl to dump its load by rotating a full 360 degrees, then returning to the carry position.

Early types included the "Atlas Power Controlled" scraper built by the Atlas Scraper Company, and rotary and carry types made by the Baker Manufacturing Company of Springfield, Illinois. The latter type, known as the Baker-Maney scraper, was designed to use singly or in a train of two to six units. The scraper consisted of a bowl suspended in a frame, controlled by power taken from the rear wheels. Often one scraper operator would control a train of scrapers. The operator had the busy job of hopping on and off every scraper to load each in turn. Then he rode the train to the dump, where the scrapers were emptied without stopping the tractor.

There was also the "Euclid Wheel Scraper" by the Euclid Crane & Hoist Company. Like the Baker-Maney, the bowl mechanism was driven by the scraper wheels. It

A slight improvement in efficiency resulted from mounting horse-drawn scrapers on wheels, the first of which appeared in the 1870s. Some early examples here have long since finished their working life. They are at the Reynolds Alberta Museum, Wetaskiwin, Alberta.

incorporated an automatic lift device to raise the cutting edge when the pull on the drawbar became heavy, thus minimizing the tendency to stall.

A review of the scrapers available in 1932 gives no indication of the phenomenal advances that were about to happen. Larger crawler tractors were just around the corner, and rubber-tired self-propelled scrapers were developed by the end of the decade. By 1940, heavy-duty pull-type scrapers of 30-cubic yard capacity were hauled by Caterpillar D8 tractors, and high-speed self-propelled Tournapulls of 42-cubic yard capacity were running on rubber tires. What a contrast from the small primitive steel-wheeled contraptions that were the "state-of-the-art" just eight short years earlier!

Dave Brainard brings to life the restored Baker-Maney scraper at a convention of the Historical Construction Equipment Association. Riding on the rear of the machine, the operator controls all scraper movements through hand levers. Power for the scraper motions is taken from the wheels via a chain drive.

R.G. LeTourneau pioneered mechanized earthmoving, and one of the first machines he made was this electrically powered scraper, known as the "Mountain Mover." Built in 1923, it was the third scraper designed by LeTourneau, and it held 12 cubic yards in two "buckets" that were filled separately. It was constructed using brazed metal instead of the usual riveted construction, typical of the day. The Mountain Mover is preserved at the LeTourneau University, Longview, Texas.

One of the first scrapers to operate from a cable control unit mounted on the tractor was this LeTourneau "Highboy." It got its name from its high-mounted tailgate, which swept out the load when dumping. The Highboy was built in 1929 and carried 6 cubic yards. *JKH collection*

LeTourneau "Carryall" Development

Invention of the scraper, as we know it today, is credited to Robert Gilmour LeTourneau, who had established his own earthmoving business in 1920. He took the primitive contraptions of the day and developed them into efficient earthmoving machines. Shortage of equipment in 1922 led R.G LeTourneau to start building scrapers for his own use. After experimenting with a drag scraper, he built a pull-type on wheels with 6-cubic yard capacity. Known as the "Gondola," it was significant for two important reasons:

1) It was built using brazed metal construction instead of rivets. After this machine, LeTourneau turned to electric welding, still in its infancy. Welding was at the "cutting edge" of technology in the mid-1920s.

2) The scraper motions were powered by electric motors, using rack-and-pinion drive. For LeTourneau, the rack-and-pinion drive was the chief method of transmitting power on mobile machines right up to his death in 1969.

The Gondola is preserved and is on display at LeTourneau University in Longview, Texas.

LeTourneau developed a scraper consisting of two or more buckets whereby each could be loaded in turn, with a consequent saving in power. He understood the principle that the last few yards of material loaded into a scraper take a much longer time to load than the first. The first scraper to demonstrate this concept was known as the "Mountain Mover" built in 1923. Incorporating electric motors, it featured two bowls, one telescoping inside the other. It carried a total of 12 cubic yards and was equipped with wide steel wheels to aid flotation. The Mountain Mover is now preserved and is displayed with the Gondola scraper at LeTourneau University.

The same year the Mountain Mover was successfully put to work, R.G. LeTourneau invented the world's first self-propelled scraper, although this turned out to be less successful. It was a long, cumbersome rig mounted on four large steel wheels. Electrically controlled from a DC generator driven by a gasoline engine, it had four telescoping buckets, and a fixed bucket at the front that incorporated the cutting edge. The fact that this scraper had a travel speed of only one mile per hour was most likely the reason a second machine was never built!

Abandoning self-propulsion for a time, R. G. designed some crawler-mounted pull-type scrapers beginning in 1925. One of these, built in 1926, is preserved at Micke Grove Park near Stockton, California. A succession of pull-type scrapers, all of different designs, were conceived and tested by the resourceful R.G. LeTourneau. The "Highboy" of 1929 was one of the first scrapers to operate from a cable control unit. It was named after the high frame above the bowl to which was

UPPER LEFT: This LeTourneau "Carryall" Model AU of 24-yard heaped capacity is in action in a deep cutting. It has two bowls, one running inside the other, so that less power is needed to fill them separately. Coming out in 1938, the AU was pulled by the largest crawler tractors of the time. *JKH collection*

TOP: Always thinking of doubling up in size, LeTourneau designed these Model J Carryalls to be pulled in pairs. Each carrying 12 cubic yards, they were operated from a four-drum winch on the rear of the tractor. *JKH collection*

The advent of large rubber tires prompted R.G. LeTourneau to build the giant Model A "Tournapull" in 1938. Its Caterpillar D17000 engine developed 160 horsepower at 950 rpm. Coupled to the super-sized Model NU Carryall scraper, it could carry 42 cubic yards. *JKH collection*

LEFT: The LeTourneau Super C Tournapull, coupled to the 15-yard LP scraper, was a popular machine in World War II, and well into the 1950s. The Super C shown here has been restored by owner Bill Graham, and is shown working on a county road job in Alberta, Canada, in 1988. The job was completed by Graham Brothers Contracting, using only antique equipment.

suspended a spring-loaded tailgate. The tailgate was pulled through an arc to sweep out the load.

In 1928, LeTourneau pioneered the cable control unit, in which the motions of the scraper were controlled from a double-drum winch mounted on the tractor. Although a relatively small, inexpensive unit, this was one of the most significant breakthroughs in earthmoving equipment.

R.G. LeTourneau, Inc., was incorporated in 1929 as a manufacturer and earthmoving contractor. However, the earthmoving business was discontinued soon after 1933 in order to concentrate on manufacturing.

The "Model A Carryall" of 9-cubic yard capacity was introduced in 1932 and was the first scraper to be known officially as a "Carryall." It was also the first to be equipped with pneumatic tires. The "Model B Carryall," introduced in 1933, was a significant milestone in scraper development, as it appears to be the first pull-type scraper to incorporate all the features that have since become standard, such as a bowl capable of being raised clear of the ground, an apron to drop down over the load, and a separate ejector to push out the load through the front.

The Model AU Carryall came out in 1938 and was a popular large pull-type scraper throughout the 1940s. The largest tractors of the day, such as the various models of the Caterpillar D8 and the Allis-Chalmers HD-19 when it came out in 1947, would pull a 23-yard (heaped) scraper.

LeTourneau "Tournapull" Development

With the advent of larger rubber tires, LeTourneau completed manufacture of the first high-speed earthmover, the Model A "Tournapull" in 1938. This machine featured many revolutionary concepts, some of which were adopted in all scraper designs to the present day. The two-wheel prime mover concept with the unique hitch, allowing the two-wheel tractor to swing more than 90 degrees in each direction, was the major innovation. In typical LeTourneau fashion, this first machine

This is an LTV-60 "Electric Digger" of 45-yard capacity built in 1963, one of the many variations of this configuration of scraper. Note that the operator could swivel his console and seat to face the direction of travel. The usual rack-and-pinion drives are present, providing power to all motions, including the telescopic bowl. *JKH collection*

The 1966 LT-360 Electric Digger was the biggest scraper ever built. One of the most powerful machines mounted on wheels, the behemoth boasted three bowls totaling 216 cubic yards in capacity, eight electric wheels, and eight GM 16V71 engines of 635 horsepower each. Its overall length was 200 feet, and its width was 19 feet 6 inches. No scraper has ever topped this one. *JKH collection*

A small 2.3-yard capacity Tournapull was this Model D4. It was made under special order from the U.S. Army Engineers, and could be air-lifted into enemy territory.

The 50-yard LeTourneau Model A-4 "Goliath" scraper had an electric motor in each wheel. This machine caused a stir when it was launched at the American Mining Congress in 1958. The scraper mechanism has distinctive rack-and-pinion drive, a feature that would become standard on all LeTourneau machines developed until the mid-1960s. *JKH collection*

LeTourneau-Westinghouse Company (Wabco) picked up the "Tournapull" line of scrapers when it purchased R.G. LeTourneau, Inc., in 1953. The scrapers were improved, and the line expanded. In 1962, the Model C-500 "Tournapull" appeared with twin 21-yard scrapers behind a 290-horsepower prime mover. In poor ground conditions, a second engine could be mounted on the rear scraper to power the rear wheels. *JKH collection*

Elevating scrapers were added by Wabco in the 1960s. The smallest was this Model 101, which has ancestry in the LeTourneau Model D Tournapull. The 101F was a handy 9-yard scraper with a 178-horsepower engine.

The giant Wabco 353FT was the largest elevating scraper ever built. Coming out in 1977, it could dig and carry 36 cubic yards, and could muster up a combined 1,025 horsepower from its front and rear engines. *Eric Orlemann collection*

Bucyrus-Erie Company started into the tractor equipment business in 1936 with this unique four-wheel pull-type scraper. All its movements (bowl, apron, and ejector) were worked from a single line from a winch on the tractor. Although not a success, the intricate linkages and cable reeving made for an interesting operation. Ahead of the action is an International T-40 TracTracTor. *Bucyrus International Inc.*

The largest scraper from Bucyrus-Erie was the B-250 at 27 1/2 heaped cubic yards. As seen here, the B-250 was usually found behind the International TD-24, the largest International tractor of the 1940s and 1950s. *Bucyrus International Inc.*

was designed in vast proportions. Fitted with the Caterpillar D17000 engine developing 160 horsepower at 950 rpm, the prototype achieved a speed of 20 miles per hour under tests. The Model A was hitched to a choice of Carryalls including the TU, RU, and NU of 24, 30, and 42-cubic yard heaped capacity.

There was no competition for these huge machines, and nothing like them had existed before. But although high-speed earthmoving by scraper had been born, like most innovations, the concept was initially slow to catch on. Coupled with some mechanical problems, the machines did not sell in large numbers. One creative contractor, Guy F. Atkinson Company, used a fleet of 13 Model A Tournapulls on its Hansen Dam Project at San Fernando, California, in 1938/39.

Undeterred by the slow sales, LeTourneau persevered with big scraper development, and up to six different versions of the A Tournapull were produced by the end of 1941. The A5 was powered by two 200-horsepower Cummins diesel engines mounted under separate front hoods. Each engine was connected to its own transmission and final drive by a hydraulic coupling, which synchronized the output of both engines. The transmission was actuated hydraulically and was one of the first true power-shift transmissions. The A5 was attached to the NU Carryall of 42-yard capacity, or to the huge 60-yard heaped capacity Model OU, a scraper size rarely exceeded since that time.

Thousands of crawler tractors and scrapers played a large part in winning World War II. R.G. LeTourneau,

Inc., supplied over 10,000 pull-type scrapers and over 2,000 self-propelled scrapers to the Allied armed forces. The most popular models supplied during the war were the Carryall Models FP, LP, and LS, many of which are still in use. Often, a U.S. Army nameplate can still be found on these scrapers under many layers of paint! The Model C Tournapull, introduced in 1940, was a great success. Fitted with the Model LP Carryall of 15-cubic yard heaped capacity, the Super C was one of the most popular scrapers through World War II and several years after. Other leading scraper manufacturers of the day, Caterpillar, LaPlant-Choate, Bucyrus-Erie, and Gar Wood, also reaped profits from their early pioneering efforts by supplying huge orders of scrapers and tractor equipment to the war effort.

A unique machine was the Model D4 Tournapull with Model Q Carryall of only 2.3-yard heaped capacity, made under special order for the U.S. Army Engineers. LeTourneau developed this very small self-propelled scraper, which could easily be airlifted into enemy territory to construct advance air strips. It was powered by a 45-horsepower Continental gasoline engine and the vehicle weighed only 3 1/4 tons.

After the war, new versions of the Tournapull A, B, and C models were launched by LeTourneau. Although the two-wheel tractor unit on these models had a mechanical drive to the wheels, all other functions operated electrically. Up to this time, all Tournapulls used the method of clutches and brakes for steering, similar to a crawler tractor. This feature was considered the

The Caterpillar No. 90 pull-type scraper was introduced in 1953 to match the power of the new D9 tractor, then under development. It was Caterpillar's largest to that time, at 27 heaped cubic yards.

A popular tractor-scraper team was the Caterpillar D9 coupled to the 28-yard (heaped) 463 scraper, which replaced the No. 90 in 1955. The team shown in the picture belongs to British contractor G. Wimpey & Company, which ran a large fleet of D9/463 outfits on its earthmoving jobs in the 1960s.

A mixture of Caterpillar D8 and D7 tractors with various equipment cut down the overburden on a British opencast coal contract in 1964. The D7 in the foreground is pulling a Bucyrus-Erie-designed Ruston-Bucyrus cable-operated ripper, which is also receiving down-pressure from the hydraulic blade of the D8 dozer in the rear.

main disadvantage of the Tournapull, as it made the machine prone to "jack-knifing." Accordingly, the new models were steered by an electric motor, pinion and gear assembly mounted between the tractor and scraper. All electric functions were controlled by small switches on the operator's control console. In 1948, the popular 9-yard Model D came out. With its successive generations, it remained in production for some 25 years.

To the surprise of many, R.G. LeTourneau sold his earthmoving equipment manufacturing business in 1953 to the Westinghouse Air Brake Company. Included in the sale were all the manufacturing rights and patents related to earthmoving equipment as well as the LeTourneau plants at Peoria, Illinois; Toccoa, Georgia; and Rydalmere, Australia. A condition of the sale was that LeTourneau would stay out of the earthmoving equipment business for a period of five years. The sale did not include the Longview, Texas, and Vicksburg, Mississippi, plants where LeTourneau continued manufacturing nonearthmoving equipment.

As a result of the Westinghouse purchase, LeTourneau-Westinghouse Company (L-W) was established as a subsidiary of Westinghouse Corporation. The original LeTourneau patents and designs were expanded and developed over the years by L-W, and its products became known by the name "Wabco."

Bucyrus-Erie Scrapers

Although R.G. LeTourneau performed much of the pioneering work in scraper development, other manufacturers were not slow to jump into the market with their own designs. Bucyrus-Erie Company, a firm most famous for its excavators, broke into the tractor equipment business in 1936. Bucyrus-Erie learned that International Harvester was expanding its range of crawler tractors and was looking for an exclusive supplier of tractor equipment to match to its tractors. In the early days of the industry, it was quite normal for tractor manufacturers to have other companies make equipment to use with their tractors. The tractor manufacturers could not afford valuable shop space to be taken up with metal fabrication. Instead, they allied themselves with a tractor attachment builder to build equipment exclusively for them. Bucyrus-Erie made a deal with International in late 1935 to supply tractor equipment for use with International's tractors.

Bucyrus-Erie's first scraper was a four-wheel machine operated by a cable from a single drum winch on the tractor. The single rope worked all three functions of bowl, apron, and load dumping through a complicated system of sheaves and linkages. The convenience of operation from a single drum winch was countered by high maintenance of the complicated mecha-

The 100-horsepower DW-10 was the first self-propelled scraper from Caterpillar when it was introduced in 1941. The scraper was built by LaPlant-Choate and had a capacity of 10 cubic yards. *Caterpillar Inc.*

Caterpillar's first two-axle motor scraper was the DW-21, which was released in 1951. It was born at the advent of Caterpillar's thrust to become the world's leading manufacturer of earthmoving equipment. The 18-yard struck capacity DW-21 was the forerunner of Caterpillar's broad line of scrapers introduced over the subsequent two decades. *JKH collection*

For those who preferred a four-wheel tractor, Caterpillar offered the DW-20 as an alternative to the DW-21. Both prime movers were powered by the same 255-horsepower Caterpillar D337 engine. On a good haul road, the three-axle scraper outfit could attain a higher speed than its two-axle counterpart.

nism. The machine obtained only limited success, and a new design soon followed.

The second series of pull-type scrapers from Bucyrus-Erie was still a radical design, but proved very durable, and remained in production for over 12 years. These were the S-series scrapers, built in sizes ranging from 5- to 12 1/2-cubic yard heaped capacity. They were operated from a two-drum winch, but the bowl was lifted from the rear instead of the more usual front lift arrangement. To dump, the movable scraper floor was hoisted from the rear, dumping the load forward.

In 1948, the S-series scrapers were upgraded with improved features. In the same year, the first of the B-series scrapers appeared, featuring the more conventional method of lifting the bowl from the front. The B-series consisted of the B-91, B-113, B-170, and B-250, ranging in heaped capacity from 10- to 27 1/2-cubic yards. The large B-250 scraper was designed to match the International TD-24 crawler tractor which had been introduced as the world's largest. These outfits were advertised in magazines and literature as the "Big Red Team," since both the tractor and scraper were painted in the bright International red.

65

Caterpillar 666 scraper (pictured) is receiving a boost from a DD9G (two tractors hooked together). First appearing in 1962, and upgraded to the 666B in 1969, it remains as Caterpillar's largest scraper. Carrying 54 cubic yards, this giant earthmover received 980 horsepower from its two engines. *Caterpillar Inc.*

The first Euclid scraper was this experimental Model 1SH with 4FDT tractor. It is shown being tested in 1938 and is receiving a boost from a Cletrac bulldozer. The Euclid displayed features that would become standard on Euclid's broad range of three-axle scrapers. The same tractor units were frequently seen pulling bottom-dump wagons. *Historical Construction Equipment Association archives*

Euclid was a pioneer of "twin power" in large earthmoving equipment. The first application on a Euclid scraper was this 16-yard (struck) twin outfit in 1949. The tractor unit was a 51FDT with a Detroit 6-71 diesel engine.

As an alternative to the elevating type, Caterpillar offers the auger scraper, another type of true self-loading scraper. This Caterpillar 657B is capable of picking up 44 cubic yards of dry soil using its twin augers to raise the load in its bowl.

This view shows the arrangement of the twin augers in the Caterpillar 675B scraper illustrated in the previous photograph. With the augers in motion, all the available tractive power of the scraper wheels can be applied to cutting the material and drawing it over the cutting edge. As the load fills into the bowl, the augers do their job of lifting the material up to overflow level.

The B-series scrapers saw Bucyrus-Erie through to the end of their association with tractor equipment in 1953. International Harvester followed Caterpillar's lead and decided to build its own tractor equipment. Thus, B-E responded by withdrawing from tractor equipment manufacture.

Caterpillar Pull-Type Scrapers

As already mentioned, it was common for specialty companies to supply attachments to crawler tractor builders, and Caterpillar was no exception. However, in 1946, Caterpillar commenced manufacture of its own pull-type scrapers. The first Caterpillar scrapers were the pull-type No. 70 and No. 80 models, designed to be hauled by the D7 and D8 tractors. Other models soon followed, until Caterpillar had a scraper designed specifically for each of its tractor sizes.

The No. 40, designed for the D4, was one of the first scrapers to be hydraulically operated from the tractor. It is interesting to note that throughout the 1970s and 1980s, many of the old cable-operated scrapers were converted to hydraulic operation like the Cat. No. 40.

In 1955, the first series of Caterpillar's pull-type scrapers began to be replaced by the 400-series. These were the models 435, 463, and 491, ranging in capacity from 17 to 35 cubic yards and designed to match the D7, D8, and D9 tractors. The No. 60, which first came out in 1947 to match the D6 tractor, found continued use in smaller applications and farm work and lasted in the Caterpillar line until 1972. By that time, Caterpillar had discontinued all its pull-type scrapers.

Other Pull-Type Scraper Manufacturers

By the end of the 1960s, the main crawler tractor manufacturers had gone full-circle. They had started the pull-type scraper manufacture in the 1940s or 1950s and stopped manufacture in the 1960s or early 1970s. Valuable shop floor space could be more profitably utilized in tractor fabrication. This once again left the market open to the specialized scraper manufacturers and there were many of them.

Some manufacturers like Rome Industries took over the designs of the tractor manufacturers. Others had a long history of lighter duty scraper manufacture and found a niche market in agricultural applications. Today, there are many successful scraper manufacturers like Reynolds, Miskin, and others that sell scrapers developed from the agricultural types to earthmoving contractors. This type is usually pulled by high-horsepower four-wheel-drive tractors.

Caterpillar Motor Scrapers

Built in 1941, the DW-10 was the first self-propelled or motor scraper from Caterpillar. It did not follow the two-wheel LeTourneau concept. Instead, Caterpillar opted for a four-wheel tractor outfitted with a Caterpillar 100-horsepower diesel engine, pulling a scraper of 10-cubic yard heaped capacity, manufactured by LaPlant-Choate. From 1947, Caterpillar offered its own No. 10 scraper to partner the DW10 tractor.

In 1951, the DW-21, forerunner of the present-day Caterpillar line of motor scrapers, made its debut. It was Caterpillar's first two-wheel tractor unit coupled to a cable-operated scraper of 18-cubic yard heaped capacity. It remained in production for nine years, receiving many design upgrades. Ninety-degree steering of the two-wheel tractor unit was accomplished by using two

The intermediate-sized twin-power Euclid TS-18 of 18-yard struck capacity was introduced in 1954. Launched at the same time as the S-7 and S-18, the three were the first "overhung" (single-axle tractor) scrapers from Euclid. *JKH collection*

A bird's-eye view of the famous Euclid TS-24 scraper. It has just picked up its 32-yard heaped load with the assistance of the D8 dozer in the background, and is about to head toward the fill at high speed. First appearing in 1957, the TS-24C is still available today under its Terex guise, representing a production life of 40 years, and still counting.

hydraulic rams between tractor and scraper. This arrangement afforded a safe, rigid connection at all times. Over the same time period the DW-21 was made, Caterpillar also offered a four-wheel tractor version of similar size, the DW-20. The intermediate-sized DW-15 four-wheel tractor and No. 15 scraper of 12 1/2-yard capacity followed in 1954.

The Caterpillar DW-series machines began to be displaced in 1960 with the unveiling of the first of the 600-series machines—the 619 featured 18-cubic yard heaped capacity. By 1962, a full line of 600-series scrapers was available with capacities ranging up to 54 heaped yards in the Model 666. The 666 twin-engined scraper with a four-wheel tractor had a combined power rating of 980 horsepower. The 666 was up-rated to the 666B in 1969 and lasted in Caterpillar's line until 1978. The 666 remains the largest scraper ever built by Caterpillar.

Caterpillar offered elevating scrapers starting in 1964 with the J619, based on an elevating scraper built by Johnson Manufacturing Company. Caterpillar expanded its elevating line to 11-, 16-, 22-, and 32-yard sizes through the 1970s. Caterpillar's largest, most powerful elevator was the 34-yard twin-powered 639D, which had a production run from 1979 to 1984.

Another type of scraper offered by Caterpillar is the auger type. This is a self-loading system offering an alternative to elevating scrapers. Hydraulically driven augers mounted vertically in the center of the bowl raise the material as it is loaded. Originally developed by Wotco in the mid-1970s, Caterpillar had adopted the principle by 1984 and offers auger versions of all their nonelevating scrapers today, including single- and twin-powered machines.

Euclid/Terex Scrapers

Euclid was one of the first companies to recognize the high-speed earthmoving capabilities of self-propelled scrapers. A prototype scraper known as the 1SH was in the field as early as 1938, the same year LeTourneau introduced his Model A Tournapull. Although only one model was built, the next few years saw Euclid experimenting with several self-propelled scrapers, including the overhung (two-wheel tractor) and four-wheel tractor types. However, during the remainder of the 1940s and the early 1950s, all Euclid scrapers were the four-wheel tractor design type.

In the late 1940s, Euclid started work on twin-power designs to meet the high production requirements of the great earthmoving projects following World War II. The commercial production of Allison's torque converter and semiautomatic transmission made this type of machine mechanically possible. The first twin was actually an 18-cubic yard bottom-dump hauler introduced in 1948 using the three-axle, four-wheel tractor configuration.

The latest from the long line of Terex scrapers (Euclid prior to 1968) is this TS-14D twin-engined model with struck capacity of 14 yards. Like its larger brother, the TS-14 is still counting the years of production since its launch in 1959. *Terex Corporation*

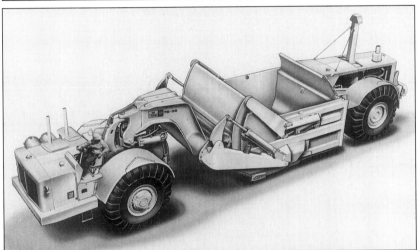

The most powerful overhung scraper offered by Euclid was the TS-32, introduced in 1966 with struck capacity of 32 yards. Its twin engines totaled 808 flywheel horsepower.

The twin-bowl, triple-engined TTS-14 was another combination unit from the extensive Euclid scraper line. The 444 horsepower from the three engines made this scraper a true self-loader. First coming out in 1963, several of these units operated in the 1960s.

BELOW: This is one of the outsized Euclid scrapers ordered by Western Contracting Corporation in 1964. The Tandem TSS-40 scrapers were powered by three Detroit Diesel 16V-71 engines, and the two bowls could hold 80 cubic yards (struck). These scraper outfits joined Western's massive fleet of earthmovers at the Castaic Dam job in California, where 71.4 million cubic yards of earth were moved in two years, one of the largest scraper jobs ever accomplished.

In 1957, Clark Equipment Company made its entry into the scraper business with three scrapers. One of those was the Michigan 210 scraper, which featured heaped capacity of 18 cubic yards. The 210 and its upgrades, including elevating versions, remained in production until Clark discontinued its scrapers in 1981. *John C. Sproule*

The giant Model 410 was Michigan's largest scraper. Introduced in 1964 to compete with the biggest scrapers on the market, its Cummins engine developed 635 horsepower, and it could heap a 44-yard load. However, only 20 of these giants were built. *Volvo Construction Equipment*

Typical of the many versions of elevating scrapers from Clark-Michigan was this Model 110-15 of mid-1970s vintage. This model was in the 15-yard class. *Volvo Construction Equipment*

The first twin scraper followed in 1949, using the same tractor unit, but with a hydraulic system added to operate the scraper. It was initially rated at 16-cubic yard struck capacity, but later was up-rated to 18 yards.

In 1954, three models of the overhung type of scraper (two-wheel tractor) were introduced by Euclid. These were the S-7 with 7 yard struck capacity, S-18 and TS-18 of 18-yard struck capacity. The small 7-yard scraper was a great success and remained in production until 1971. Larger overhung scrapers followed, including the famous TS-24 in 1957 and TS-14 in 1959. The 24-yard struck capacity TS-24 is still made today as the TS-24C by Terex Corporation, having undergone several modifications over its long production life of almost 40 years. The smaller 14-yard TS-14 has also been a huge seller and is still offered as the TS-14D by Terex, some 37 years after its introduction.

The huge 40-cubic yard TSS-40, with four-wheel tractor and powered by two GM engines developing 810 gross horsepower, came on the scene in 1963. Not content with the largest scrapers available at the time, famous earthmoving contractor Western Contracting Corporation ordered a fleet of Euclid TTSS-40 scraper units in 1964. On these, three 16V-71 engines provided the power, and the combination of the two bowls provided a struck capacity of over 80 cubic yards. These were the largest scrapers ever built by Euclid.

Another interesting Euclid model was the tandem TS-14, or TTS-14, which came out in 1963. Basically, it consisted of a fifth wheel mounted on the rear of a TS-14 scraper, and another TS-14 bowl with engine added on the rear. The three engines totaled 444 horsepower, making it a true self-loading scraper. As each bowl was loaded separately, the power of all three engines could be applied to each cutting edge in turn.

Euclid entered the elevating scraper market in 1964, by teaming up the S-7 tractor with 12-yard Model 12E-2 elevating scraper made by Hancock Manufacturing Company. The twin-powered unit, known as the S-12E, was the forerunner of larger elevating scrapers, including the company's largest, the 35-yard S-35E, introduced in 1968.

The most powerful overhung scraper offered by Euclid was the TS-32, of 32-yard struck, (43-yard heaped) capacity. It was launched in 1966, equipped with two GM engines for a total of 808 flywheel horsepower.

Euclid was a division of General Motors Corporation (GM) from 1953, but in 1968, GM's earthmoving products became known by the name Terex. The U.S. Justice Department ruled that GM must discontinue the manufacture of off-highway trucks in the United States for a period of four years and divest itself of the Euclid name. (See Chapter 6 for a history of Euclid and Terex.)

A 500-horsepower M-R-S Model 250 tractor is shown coupled to a 48-yard scraper in 1961. The M-R-S principle of traction was to use a four-wheel tractor to pull a four-wheel scraper. The unique weight-transfer system utilized a hydraulic ram between the tractor drawbar and the scraper gooseneck. When the going got tough and traction was lost, the operator activated the ram, transferring more weight to the driving wheels. *Taylor Machine Works*

This enormous Model 250-T was the largest scraper built by M-R-S. It could hold a whopping 90 cubic yards, and was boosted by a 430-horsepower engine in the rear! Note the hydraulic cylinder utilized to transfer weight to the tractor driving wheels. On this particular scraper, weight was not only transferred to the tractor for increased traction, but also to the rear-driving scraper wheels. *Taylor Machine Works*

Wabco Scrapers

As previously mentioned, the sale of R.G. LeTourneau's earthmoving equipment business to Westinghouse Air Brake Company spawned the LeTourneau-Westinghouse Company in 1953. At first, the new company continued to offer the machines designed by LeTourneau, but soon upgraded the old models in order to stay competitive. The original LeTourneau trade names "Carryall" and "Tournapull" were retained, but by the early 1960s, the name "Wabco" was used to identify the company's products.

By 1959, the Model B and Model C "Speedpull" scrapers began to appear. These were three-axle, four-wheel tractor scraper units capable of higher speed than the two-wheel Tournapulls, which continued to be offered in the B, C, and D sizes. The Model B Speedpull attained a top speed of 40 miles per hour with its rated load of 45 heaped cubic yards. It was equipped with a Cummins VT-12 diesel engine of 600 maximum brake horsepower.

Wabco also adopted the concept of adding a second scraper bowl for its scrapers. In 1960, the tandem Model B Speedpull hauled two 29-yard heaped scrapers. In 1962, the Model C-500 outfit ran two 21-yard heaped scrapers with a second engine on the rear unit, boosting the power to a total of 580 maximum brake horsepower.

Beginning in 1961, Wabco offered elevating versions for its scrapers. Initially, the scrapers were manufactured by Hancock Manufacturing Company, one of the pioneers of this type of scraper. Wabco aggressively promoted the elevating scraper throughout the 1960s and in 1966 introduced the Model 333F, which with 32 cubic yards of capacity, was the world's largest. This was soon followed by the twin-powered 333FT, boasting 34-yard capacity and 950 horsepower from its two engines.

By 1971, Wabco claimed that sales of elevating scrapers exceeded sales of its standard scrapers, and the company forged ahead with upgraded models in the 1970s, until the king of elevating scrapers came out in

The Wooldridge "Cobrette," on display at the 1957 Road Show. This smallest of the Wooldridge motor scraper line can carry a heaped 10 cubic yards, and is powered by a 171-horsepower engine. *JKH collection*

In 1959, Curtiss-Wright Corporation acquired the Wooldridge Manufacturing Company and continued the scrapers using the "CW" nomenclature. Shown here is a Model CW-226 with (heaped) capacity of 36 cubic yards and 360-horsepower engine. *Tom Berry*

1977. This was the Model 353FT, an upgraded version of the 333FT. The bowl heaped 36 cubic yards, and power from the two engines was increased to 1,025 horsepower, making it the most powerful production-model elevating scraper ever built. But ironically, this world record-beating 353FT signaled the end of the big elevating scrapers. Although a substantial number of large Wabco elevating scrapers were put to work, their size did not prove to be the most efficient way of moving earth. The elevating scraper proved expensive to operate, and contractors found that any job needing such large scrapers could be done more efficiently by using a fleet of standard scrapers assisted by a push tractor. With scraper sales generally declining, Wabco announced its exit from the scraper business in 1980, and the last was shipped the following year.

Clark-Michigan Scrapers

Michigan entered the scraper market in 1957, after a short development period. The scrapers were an outcome of the Construction Machinery Division set up by Clark Equipment Company in 1952. The Clark management decided the company would design its heavy equipment from first principles, rather than purchase an existing line. At first, three sizes were offered, the Models 110, 210, and 310, with 10-, 18-, and 27-yard heaped capacities. Although these three basic model designations were retained in the Michigan scraper line, many variations and upgraded models appeared throughout the 1960s and 1970s.

Michigan introduced its first elevating scraper in 1965. The scraper was designed and built by Hancock Manufacturing Company for attachment to the Michigan prime mover. Hancock, one of the pioneers of ele-

vating scrapers, built its first elevator type in 1956; the company was taken over by Clark in 1966. Naturally this led to the expansion of elevating options for the entire Michigan scraper line. In addition, Clark continued to market some of the Hancock models under the Hancock name until about 1972. The largest elevating scraper made by Clark-Michigan was the 310-H, which boasted 32-yard capacity and a 495-horsepower GM engine.

In early 1964, Clark-Michigan set its sights high, when it introduced the largest scraper ever to leave its shops. This was the Model 410, designed to compete with the Caterpillar 651, which had appeared a couple of years earlier. The massive 410 was slightly heavier than its competition and carried 44 cubic yards when heaped. The single-engine scraper was powered with a Cummins VT-1710-C diesel capable of 635 maximum horsepower. Unfortunately, sales of this machine proved disappointing, with only 20 units digging the dirt between 1964 and 1970, when it was discontinued.

Scraper production continued through the 1970s, with most models actually different versions of the Models 110 and 210 elevating types. In 1981, scrapers were discontinued from the Clark-Michigan line, and the plant at Lubbock, Texas, where they were built, was closed.

M-R-S Scrapers

A lesser known builder of scrapers is M-R-S Manufacturing Company, which made an indelible mark in the scraper business beginning in 1943. The letters stand for Mississippi Road Services, and the company started in Jackson, Mississippi, moving 20 miles north to Flora in 1946. Filling the need for high-speed earthmoving vehicles, M-R-S concentrated from the outset on four-wheel tractors with matching scrapers and wagons. The com-

This is a LaPlant-Choate C-114 pull-type scraper of 14-yard struck capacity. Allis-Chalmers acquired LaPlant-Choate in 1952, giving Allis-Chalmers its own line of scrapers.

Allis-Chalmers motor scrapers were developed from LaPlant-Choate designs. The midrange TS-260 came out in 1956, and was initially rated at 14 cubic yards in heaped capacity. Higher horsepower engines and design upgrades brought this model up to the 20-yard class by the mid-1960s.

pany's first efforts produced a 72-horsepower tractor and 8-yard bottom-dumping wagon known as the "Mississippi Wagon." (Read about haulers and wagons in Chapter 6.) From this first unit to the present day, every M-R-S tractor/scraper has utilized a four-wheel tractor. The company has stayed with the four-wheel tractor concept, believing it to provide better traction, higher speed, and lower maintenance than a two-wheel prime mover.

The typical configuration for M-R-S scraper units was a standard four-wheel scraper pulled by a four-wheel tractor. This arrangement allowed any brand of scraper to be pulled by the M-R-S tractor. However, most common were scrapers built by Wooldridge, whose pull-type scrapers were made specially for M-R-S tractors. The combined outfits were marketed by M-R-S.

A unique feature of the M-R-S design was the hydraulic weight-transfer system between the scraper and the tractor. A long hydraulic ram extended from the tractor drawbar to a high point on the scraper gooseneck. Operation of this ram adjusted the weight distribution between the scraper front wheels and the tractor rear wheels. Therefore, more weight could be transferred onto the tractor wheels to aid traction or during self-loading.

Some very large-capacity scrapers were developed by M-R-S in the 1950s and 1960s. The 500-horsepower M-R-S 250 tractor coupled with the Wooldridge OS-300B scraper (heaped capacity 41 yards) was billed as the world's largest rubber-tired earthmoving unit when it came out in 1955. On a good haul road, the outfit could reach 34 miles per hour in top gear. Coal scraper versions were also offered with huge capacities. One of the largest single scraper bowls ever made was the Model 250T, which could carry a heaped load of 90 cubic yards! This monstrous unit incorporated a 430-horsepower engine on the rear and was pulled by a 430-horsepower M-R-S tractor.

In the 1960s, M-R-S offered elevating scrapers designed by Hancock Manufacturing Company. M-R-S continued to offer standard and elevating 4x4 and 4x2 tractor and scraper combinations throughout the 1970s. In 1986, Taylor Machine Works, Inc., purchased M-R-S, and the full line is still available today on a manufacture-to-order basis.

Curtiss-Wright/Wooldridge Scrapers

Wooldridge was never a strong name in the earthmoving equipment field, although the company built machines over a long period. The Wooldridge Manufacturing Company of Sunnyvale, California, built scrapers in the 1930s, mainly for use in the western United States. In the early 1930s, the company had contracted with the Continental Roll & Steel Foundry to have the latter build Wooldridge scrapers under license for distribution in certain areas. In the mid-1940s, Wooldridge scrapers were made specially for M-R-S tractors, and the combined scraper units marketed by M-R-S.

Wooldridge also developed a range of self-propelled scrapers in the mid-1940s. They were known by various trade names such as the "Terra Cobra" which referred to a two-wheel tractor configuration, and the "Cobra Quad" which was a four-wheel tractor version. A smaller scraper, the "Cobrette," with a 7 1/2-yard struck capacity, was introduced in 1956. By 1959, the Cobra scraper line consisted of five models with struck capacities of up to 26 cubic yards. The Cobra scrapers featured a steering system known as the "Roto-Gear," which used no hydraulic rams. Instead, twin hydraulic motors applied torque through a gear reduction to a bull gear attached to the scraper yoke.

Wooldridge also continued its pull-type scraper line through the 1950s, using the trade names "Terra Clipper"

The largest of the original three Allis-Chalmers motor scrapers was the 20-cubic yard (heaped) TS-360 introduced in 1955 and built up to 1962. It was derived from LaPlant-Choate's first motor scraper, the TS-300, which was launched in 1947. The TS-360, unlike the other Allis-Chalmers motor scrapers, inherited the cable-operated scraper controls from the former model.

When the Fiat-Allis joint venture was formed in 1974, only the 100- and 200-series scrapers were continued from the former Allis-Chalmers range. The 261-B shown here was the single-engined elevating scraper offered by the company. It could self-load 23 cubic yards. The 200-series scrapers were phased out after 1988. *JKH collection*

and "Boiling-Bowl Scrapers." The line included six sizes of pull-type scrapers of up to 30-cubic yard struck capacity.

In 1958, the Curtiss-Wright Corporation of South Bend, Indiana, acquired the Wooldridge company. Curtiss-Wright continued to market the full scraper line as the CW-series. However, in the early 1960s Curtiss-Wright discontinued its involvement with earthmoving equipment, and the company focused in other directions.

Allis-Chalmers/LaPlant-Choate Scrapers

The LaPlant-Choate Manufacturing Company, Inc., was established in 1911 as a manufacturer of stump pulling and house moving equipment. It also built scrapers and other tractor attachments for Caterpillar in the early 1930s and provided Caterpillar with a scraper to pull behind its first wheel tractor, the DW-10 in 1940.

When the major tractor manufacturers began making their own tractor equipment in the 1940s, the independent scraper manufacturers looked to expand their lines, and LaPlant-Choate was no exception. It developed its own motor scraper line, beginning in 1947 with the 14-yard struck capacity TS-300, powered with a 225-horsepower Buda engine. As with other motor scrapers of that era, the TS-300 was operated by cables from winches on the tractor unit. The smaller TS-200 followed in 1950. These two motor scrapers, together with the full line of

The International Model 2T-55 was designed by the Heil Company, which International acquired in 1953. The 2T-55 was a single-engined conventional scraper of 13-cubic yard heaped capacity.

LaPlant-Choate pull-type scrapers, were made at the Cedar Rapids plant, where the company was based.

Allis-Chalmers Manufacturing Company acquired LaPlant-Choate in 1952, and for a short time, the original scraper models remained in the production line. From 1955 to 1957, Allis-Chalmers developed new models from the LaPlant-Choate designs, and introduced the TS-160, TS-260, and TS-360 with struck capacities of 7, 12 1/2, and 15 cubic yards.

In 1962, Allis-Chalmers expanded its motor scraper line in a big way. Caterpillar had just launched its big 600-series, and Allis-Chalmers responded with the biggest scrapers it ever made—Models TS-460 and 562 of 24- and 30-cubic yard struck capacity. The TS-460 was a single engine unit, which topped out the Allis-Chalmers single-engine motor scraper line. The Model 562 was a twin-engined giant featuring a modular concept in which the scraper could be operated with or without the rear engine. The engines involved were the Allis-Chalmers 25000, developing 435 maximum horsepower. The 562 was discontinued in 1966, but the TS-460 evolved into the "C" model in 1968 and remained until the advent of Fiat-Allis in 1974.

In 1974, Fiat S.p.A. of Italy purchased a majority interest in Allis-Chalmers to form the Fiat-Allis joint venture. Although the motor scraper line continued under the Fiat-Allis badge, scrapers were produced on a reduced scale, and the large scrapers were dropped. Only the popular-sized 200-series scrapers were continued. Evolving from the original Model 260, four 15-yard (struck) models were offered as single- or twin-powered and equipped with conventional or elevating scrapers. A new, smaller elevating scraper, the Model 161, was released in 1978.

The 200-series scrapers were phased out after 1988. Financial losses in the early 1980s prompted Fiat-Allis to discontinue manufacturing machines in the United States. Currently, Fiat-Allis in Italy produces only one scraper, the 15-yard Model 161.

Dresser/International Harvester/Heil Scrapers

An agreement was reached in 1953 in which International Harvester took over the scraper and bulldozer equipment lines formerly built by Bucyrus-Erie Company. The former B-E models were then sold under the International name.

In order to further bolster its earthmoving equipment segment, International also acquired the patents, designs, and manufacturing rights to two models of self-propelled scrapers from the Heil Company of Milwaukee, Wisconsin, in 1953. Earlier, Heil had introduced its two-wheeled tractor, self-propelled scrapers beginning in 1947 with the Model 2H700. When International took over the scrapers, they were known as the 2T-55 and 2T-75, with heaped capacities of 13 and 18 cubic yards.

To launch its newly acquired earthmoving lines, International staged the "International Industrial Power Roundup" in 1954 at their 4,200-acre proving grounds south of Phoenix, Arizona. Over 80 pieces of equipment were put through their paces in front of contractors, dealers, and bankers. The stars of the show were International's TD-24, the largest crawler tractor in the world, the motor scrapers, and the pull-type scrapers formerly made by Bucyrus-Erie. At that time, an I-H official said, "There's no foreseeable end to the present heavy construction boom, and we are determined to build the machinery to meet the demand necessary for the continual economic development of America and the free world."

In 1959 the first International-designed scrapers, the 295 and 495 Payscrapers with struck capacities of 24 cubic yards, replaced the 2T-55 and 2T-75. The 495 model utilized a four-wheel tractor unit, as the model number would suggest, and it was the largest scraper ever built by International. In 1963, a 14-yard (struck) Model 270 was released and beginning in 1965, International offered elevating versions of its scrapers.

In 1972, the International scraper line was completely revamped with the introduction of "System 400." The new same-size motor scrapers were available in different engine and elevating configurations, but all with the same basic scraper (14 yards struck). The four-model line consisted of single- or twin-powered, conventional or elevating scrapers. Soon after the introduction of the 400-series, larger scrapers were dropped from International's line. The small 11-yard elevating scraper, the E-211, was renamed the 412.

The International 295 Payscraper was the first of a new line of large scrapers designed by the company beginning in 1959. With a heaped capacity of 34 cubic yards, its engine was rated at 375 horsepower. A sister machine with a four-wheel tractor was also offered, known as the 495 Payscraper. The 295 shown here gets a powerful boost from a D500, International's largest wheel dozer. *The State Historical Society of Wisconsin*

The 400-series scrapers remained current until after Dresser Industries, Inc., purchased the Construction Machinery Division of International Harvester in 1982. However, all but the small Model 412 were discontinued in 1984. Today, the 412B is still offered as a Dresser machine under Komatsu America International Company.

John Deere Scrapers

John Deere's involvement in scrapers has concentrated only on the elevating types. As far back as 1957, John Deere 820 wheel tractors pulled four-wheel Hancock 8-yard elevating scrapers. In 1959, a prototype 840 close-coupled elevating scraper of 7 1/2-yard capacity was in the field, again using a four-wheel tractor. This model then evolved into the 8-yard Model 5010 scraper in 1962, and then the 9 1/2-yard Model 760 in 1965.

At Conexpo '69, John Deere announced a larger scraper, the 15-yard Model 860. It was the company's first to utilize a single-axle prime mover and proved to be a success. By the time Conexpo '75 came around, John Deere announced the replacement of the 760A scraper with the Model 762, also featuring a single-axle prime mover. In 1980, the 862 replaced the Model 860 as the

largest scraper in the John Deere line. Today, John Deere offers the 762B and 862B of 11- and 16-yard capacity.

R.G. LeTourneau Electric Diggers

No history of the scraper could be complete without mention of the monster scrapers known as "Electric Diggers" built by R.G. LeTourneau, Inc., in the 1960s. Although a large number of types and sizes were built, including the largest scraper ever built, the machines were never a real commercial success.

After R.G. LeTourneau sold the major portion of his equipment-building business to Westinghouse Air Brake Company in 1953, he designed a new line of earthmovers, which could not be marketed until 1958, according to the sales agreement with Westinghouse. Thus, all eyes of the heavy equipment industry were on the machine that launched LeTourneau's new earthmoving line, the 50-yard capacity four-wheel scraper model A-4. It was known as the "Goliath" and appeared at the American Mining Congress in 1958. It was the largest self-propelled scraper to date and the forerunner of things to come. It incorporated the familiar LeTourneau feature of rack and pinion with high-torque motors for the scraper motions.

In 1972, International again revamped its scraper line with the introduction of the "System 400" line. The 433 Payscraper shown here is a twin-engine conventional scraper with 21-cubic yard (heaped) capacity. The 400-series lasted in the line until 1984.

The 9 1/2-yard capacity JD-760 first started work in 1965. John Deere's entry into the motor scraper market dates back to 1957, when its wheel tractors were coupled to Hancock elevating scrapers. All John Deere's scrapers to date have been of the elevating type.

There is a right way and a wrong way to do most things. It is obvious as to which category this motor scraper belongs! This is the only machine featured in this book on which the author has no information. *Leigh Knudson collection*

All LeTourneau scrapers built after 1958 employed DC electric motors in the wheels, driven by diesel-electric power plants. Most of these machines were built in very limited numbers, or even on a "one-of-a-kind" test basis. There were coal scrapers with cabs at the rear or the front, as well as single-bowl scrapers with three wheels, four wheels, or six wheels. The creative minds of R.G. LeTourneau and his design team kept cranking the models out of the Longview plant. The most famous were the huge tandem- and triple-bowl outfits with multiple engines. The biggest scraper of all was the LT-360 Electric Digger with three bowls, having a combined capacity of 216 cubic yards. It moved on eight wheels measuring over 10 feet in diameter and was powered with eight engines of 635 horsepower each! It was the largest earthmover ever mounted on rubber tires.

Chapter Five

MOTOR GRADERS

The motor grader is probably the most familiar of all earthmoving machines. Seen on our highways clearing snow in winter or maintaining gravel roads in summer, the grader has coexisted with road traffic since the birth of the automobile. Before mechanized road transport, simple forms of graders consisted of nothing more than a board pulled by a horse. Today, the largest application for graders is still county and municipality road maintenance. A close second is their use by road contractors for general road construction and oiled surface preparation.

Way back in the horse-drawn era, a new type of grader appeared in 1885, an invention credited to J.D. Adams. What distinguished this grader was its adjustable leaning wheels. At the time, other graders consisted of a blade with a raising and lowering mechanism attached to the bed of a wagon. Adams observed that it was difficult to work on the sloping side of the road, and to solve the problem, he invented a crude grader with a blade set at a fixed angle and leaning wheels. His machine was called the "Little Wonder," and it found immediate success as the wheels could be cranked to lean against the sideways thrust of the angled blade. This leaning wheel principle has been a key feature of graders right up to the modern-day machines.

It wasn't long before animal power found itself competing with steam power to pull graders. Initially this was risky business, as some of the more flimsy types designed for horse power simply disintegrated when pitted against the super power of the giant traction engines of the day.

Prior to 1919, all graders were the towed type. The graders were pulled behind horse teams or behind tractors, and required its own separate operator. The operator stood on a platform at the rear of the grader, or if he was lucky, sat on a primitive board. Blade control was by hand—usually through cranks, gear reductions, or racks operated by wheels at the operator's station. In 1919, the Russell Grader Manufacturing Company brought out a self-propelled machine. Although primitive, it set the stage for Russell and other manufacturers to improve on this idea. Soon afterward, all grader makers included self-propelled models in their lines. Actually the word "grader" was not applied to these

In 1896, Adams produced the "Road King," a four-wheel, all-steel grader with an 8-foot blade and wheels that leaned either way. *JKH collection*

machines until the late 1930s. They were formerly known as road patrols, maintainers, or by various trade names.

Blade control by hand was tiresome and dangerous, especially with the higher-powered tractors coming into the field in the 1920s. Consequently, powered control was introduced, starting in the mid-1920s. Initially most were mechanical control, but some manufacturers like Galion and Huber pioneered hydraulic controls at this time. It took several decades for all grader manufacturers to graduate from mechanical to hydraulic controls. Some had semi-hydraulic systems operating mechanical clutches or linkages. Caterpillar did not change to hydraulic control until it introduced the G-series graders in 1973.

On the true grader, the blade, also called the moldboard, has a multitude of independently controlled operating positions. This allows the operator to accomplish many tasks that otherwise would require the use of hand labor. (See Sidebar.) In addition to the blade movements, graders are equipped with powered front-wheel lean and have capability to mount a dozer blade or snowplow on the front. Most graders can be equipped with a ripper or scarifier. This can be mounted ahead of the blade under the frame, or on the rear of the machine.

MOTOR GRADER BLADE MOVEMENTS

1. **Blade raise and lower.** Since the left and right sides of the blade can be independently raised, blade tilt can be performed. Thus, a side slope or cross-fall can be accomplished.

2. **Blade angle.** Mounted on a "circle" attached to a subframe, known as the drawbar, the blade can be angled to cast the material to the left or right sides as the grader moves forward. Or the blade can be completely rotated for reverse grading.

3. **Circle side shift.** In this motion the circle and its subframe or drawbar carrying the blade can be moved to the left or right. This allows the blade to reach out far beyond the wheels. In its extreme position, it allows the grader to position its blade in the bottom of a highway ditch while traveling on secure footing on the highway surface. In slope-trimming, the blade can be swung out to either side of the machine and positioned at any angle from horizontal to vertical.

4. **Blade side shift.** This allows the blade to slide within its mounting below the circle and permits the operator to negotiate the blade around obstacles such as road signs. It also allows windrows to be picked up from one side and distributed across the road surface.

5. **Blade pitch or cutting angle.** This is the rotation of the blade along its axis. Where the material has to be cut, such as peeling off topsoil, the blade can be sloped back producing a sharp cutting angle. For mixing, general blading, or carrying material to fill holes, the blade can be leaned forward for a blunt cutting angle.

Graders come in all sizes. Many companies have developed a niche market for small machines, designed for grading work inside industrial plants, housing developments, parks, municipal work, and other light-duty applications. With some exceptions, these small machines weighing five tons or less are built by manufacturers who don't compete with the big grader makers.

The grader becomes a production tool when used in surface mining operations where the largest graders are found. Beginning in the 1960s, some huge single-purpose graders were built for reclamation of spoil piles and road maintenance for the largest off-highway trucks. Because these large graders sell in very small numbers, manufacturers have tended to discontinue their production after a relatively short time. However, Caterpillar produced the successful 16-series and released the large 24-H model in 1996. These machines have allowed Caterpillar to dominate the large grader market.

An Adams Model 124 pull-type grader operating under the skilled hands of owner Bill Graham during a county road job in 1985. This restored machine, originally made from 1935 to 1945, is one of a fleet of antique construction machines used occasionally by Graham Brothers Contracting Ltd. to carry out present-day earthmoving contracts.

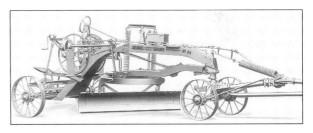

This Model 84 Leaning Wheel Grader from Adams shows the "steerable tongue" or tow bar, by which the grader could be steered independently from the tractor—a feature essential for ditch work, or for avoiding windrows. The steerable tongue was invented by Adams in 1912. *JKH collection*

In 1928, the No. 10 appeared as Adams' first self-propelled grader. Note that the grader movements are still controlled by wrist-wrenching wheels. *JKH collection*

WORLD'S LARGEST MOTOR GRADERS

Make	Model	Weight lbs	Power hp	Blade ft	Period Made
Galion	T-700	40,000	190	14	1955–1965
Huber	5D-190	30,000	195	14	1955–1957
Caterpillar	16	46,500	225	14	1963–1973
RayGo	Giant	106,000	636	20	1969–1978
CMI	Autoblade	65,000	450	18	1969–1970
Caterpillar	16G	60,150	275	16	1973–1995
Champion	100-T	202,000	700	24	1975–1989
ACCO	—	+/-400,000	1,700	33	1980
O&K	G-350	90,364	338	19	1980–1986
Komatsu	GD825A-2	58,250	280	16	1987–current
Caterpillar	16-H	60,150	275	16	1995–current
Caterpillar	24-H	131,000	500	24	1996–current

This is the Adams No. 102, a tandem-powered grader built from 1931 to 1934. *JKH collection*

The year after the Adams 660 grader came out in 1953, the J.D. Adams Company was purchased by LeTourneau-Westinghouse Co. The 660 was continued as a Wabco machine through "B" series upgrades, and was not discontinued until 1972. Over its life span, its engine power was increased from 140 to 190 horsepower.

Wabco/Adams Graders

The "Little Wonder" invented by J.D. Adams in 1885 was a small, two-wheel, horse-drawn grader with the blade set at a fixed angle, capably angling its wooden wheels to one side. This leaning wheel principle was eventually adopted by all other grader manufacturers, and it formed the foundation for a grader manufacturing company that would last almost a century.

In 1896, Adams introduced the Road King, a four-wheel, all-steel grader with an 8-foot blade, and wheels that leaned either way. The Road King, with upgrades, remained in the Adams line until 1922. The Adams Reclamation Ditcher was another popular model, which remained in production long after its introduction in 1905.

The grader business prospered, and by 1897 Adams was able to build his own factory in Indianapolis. Much later, in 1929, another plant was established at Paris, Ontario, Canada.

The J.D. Adams Company continued to develop new designs, which extended the scope of grader work. The first Adams self-propelled grader, the No. 10, appeared in 1928. In 1931, power-operated controls were installed on the larger graders. The mono-frame grader with an improved blade linkage appeared in 1935, and for the first time, the blade was able to extend to the side for trimming banks and shoulders.

In 1954, the J.D. Adams Company was purchased by LeTourneau-Westinghouse Company (L-W). The grader line was a good companion to the LeTourneau line of earthmoving equipment purchased by L-W a

The Wabco 555 grader, introduced in 1971, came equipped with a 175-horsepower engine and was in the 31,000-pound weight class. It was built for a short time in the 1970s by Northwest Industries in Edmonton, Alberta. *Henderson Photography, Edmonton, Alberta*

The biggest grader produced by Wabco was the Model 888. Unveiled in 1967, it was in the heavyweight class at 41,000 pounds. Pushing a 14-foot-wide blade, it was offered with a 230-horsepower engine. *Eric Orlemann collection*

The distinctive Allis-Chalmers tubular frame is exhibited by this pull-type grader of 1940s vintage. This restored example is being used on a county road job in 1988 by Graham Brothers Contracting Ltd. near Strome, Alberta.

The Allis-Chalmers Model W Speed Patrol was an extremely popular, reasonably priced grader. It was built around the Allis-Chalmers WC wheel tractor, and weighed only 3 tons. However, the specification says it could push a blade 10 feet wide!

The Allis-Chalmers BD-3 was one of four new graders announced by the company in 1948. It weighed just under 10 tons and came with a 78-horsepower engine.

In 1955, Allis-Chalmers' top-of-the-line motor grader was the Model 45 with operating weight of 25,600 pounds and a 120-horsepower engine.

The Fiat-Allis 100-C grader of the late 1970s started life as the Allis-Chalmers M-100 in 1962. Surviving through the formation of the Fiat-Allis joint venture in 1974, the 135-horsepower grader was not discontinued until the full Fiat-Allis grader line was replaced by the FG-series in the early 1980s. *JKH collection*

year earlier. Soon the two products stood side by side in distributor's yards and worked together on earth-moving jobs around the world. Both products, together with L-W's own trucks, were eventually marketed under the name Wabco.

The 1980s saw a decline in the grader market, and by 1983, graders were dropped from the Wabco line. The Indianapolis plant, which had been making graders since the turn of the century, was closed.

Fiat-Allis/Allis-Chalmers Graders

Allis-Chalmers purchased the rights to the grader line of the Ryan Manufacturing Corporation of Hegvisch, Illinois, bringing the company into the grader business in 1930. The graders became part of the Allis-Chalmers tractor division, which had already been bolstered by the acquisition of the Monarch crawler tractor line two years earlier. Established in 1925, the Ryan company had made its mark in the grader industry with a broad line of products. The Ryan acquisition meant that Allis-Chalmers was able to offer leaning-wheel graders with power control, a motor grader powered by the Allis-Chalmers Model U tractor, a leaning-wheel grader with hand control, and a line of small graders for maintenance work.

The Allis-Chalmers graders from the 1930s through the 1950s featured the distinctive tubular frame and drawbar, making the A-C graders instantly recognizable. Made from thick-walled steel pipe, this tubular design was even utilized on A-C pull-type graders.

The handy, light-duty Model W Speed Patrol was designed to give "relief for limited budgets," claimed the advertisements in the early 1940s. Built around the Allis-Chalmers Model WC farm tractor, it weighed only 6,000 pounds, but carried a 10-foot blade.

In 1944, grader production was moved to the Springfield, Illinois, works and by 1948 four new models were in production, the BD-2, BD-3, AD-3, and AD-4, ranging up to 21,600 pounds operating weight and 104 horsepower. The small Model "D" motor grader, introduced in 1949, incorporated many features from the larger graders. It was so popular that it remained in pro-

duction for over 20 years. In 1952, the AD-3 and AD-4 were supplanted by the AD-30 and AD-40 heavy-duty motor graders, and in 1955, the popular "45" grader was launched as Allis-Chalmers' top-of-the-line grader, with 120 horsepower.

The introduction of the 25,000-pound Model M-100 in 1962 heralded an entirely new line of graders. This line was expanded with additional models, as well as "B" and "C" upgrades. The prefix "M" was dropped in 1973, when the 100-C, 150-C, and 200-C rigid-frame graders came out, with engines of up to 160 horsepower.

In January 1974, Allis-Chalmers completed negotiations with Fiat S.p.A. of Italy to form the joint venture, Fiat-Allis. From that date, manufacture of construction equipment from the joint venture was shared between existing plants of both companies and bore the Fiat-Allis name. The M-series graders were continued until the early 1980s, when they were replaced by the Fiat-Allis FG-series. For the first time, Fiat-Allis offered articulated graders in its line.

In 1989, Fiat-Allis ceased manufacture of its earth-moving products in North America. Manufacture continues in Italy, where the grader line consists of six models from 80 to 196 horsepower. The top-of-the-line FG-105A, weighing just under 40,000 pounds, is the largest grader built by the company to date.

Clark/Austin-Western Graders

Although the Austin-Western Road Machinery Company manufactured many types of earthmoving equipment, its line of pull-type and motor graders made it famous. A company with a very long history, its two ancestors date back to the early days of mechanized earthmoving. In 1849, H.W. Austin and Co. was formed and eventually evolved into the Austin Manufacturing Company of Chicago. The Western Wheeled Scraper Company of Aurora, Illinois, was established in 1877, when it claimed to have built the first horse-drawn wheeled scraper.

Both companies prospered and expanded their product lines of road-building equipment. Included in their product lines were dump wagons, plows, rooters, drag scrapers, and wheeled scrapers known as Western Wheelers.

The early graders were surprisingly adaptable, with their blades incorporating most of the movements standard on motor graders today, including blade raise and lower, side shift, rotation, and tilt. Models included the "Little Steel Western," a light two-horse type, and the "New Western Reversible" grader. All operations were hand controlled through wheels coupled to gear reductions, cranks, or rack and pinions. Operators must have developed strong muscles to control these babies!

In one of the earliest corporate takeovers in equipment history, the Austin Manufacturing Company was

An early horse-drawn grader built by the Western Wheeled Scraper Company is represented here by the "New Western Reversible" grader. Note the rack-and-pinion axle extension arrangement so that the wheels could be positioned to avoid running over the previous windrow. A later method to achieve the same objective was the steerable tongue, featured first on Adams graders.

An early horse-drawn grader built by the Austin Manufacturing Company in 1917. This example is owned by the Sauder Museum, and is in fully restored condition.

A very advanced grader for its time, when launched in 1934, was the Austin "77" series of graders, in the 16,500-pound class. Offered in single- or tandem-drive versions and utilizing hydraulic controls, the "77" models boasted all the blade movements of today's modern grader.

Austin-Western was famous for its all-wheel-drive, all-wheel-steer graders, the first of which appeared in 1937. The 21,000-pound 99-H was one of the most popular, with its 13-foot blade machine and engines up to 80 horsepower. The 99-H shown here belongs to the Wyoming State Highway Department. *Berrien County Historical Association*

Austin-Western graders were made in England by Aveling-Barford Ltd. under license, beginning in 1950. The arrangement lasted until 1973, by which time Aveling-Barford had established its own line of graders. With an operating weight of 42,400 pounds, the 228-horsepower Super 700 was the largest Aveling-Barford grader in the early 1970s. *JKH collection*

purchased by the Western Wheeled Scraper Company in 1902. The Austin-Western Road Machinery Company was organized. All three companies operated as individual corporations, but under common ownership. The product lines were marketed as Austin or Western machines until 1934, when all three companies were merged into the Austin-Western Company.

About 1915, Austin pull-type graders were fitted with a steering tongue. Thus, the grader could be steered independently from the tractor pulling it. This device allowed the grader tracking to be offset relative to the axis of the towing tractor, so that the grader could straddle windrows or clean ditches.

Prior to the merger of Austin and Western in 1934, the grader line consisted of a wide range of machines. Horse-drawn blade graders were offered as well as 14 models of pull-type graders from both Austin and Western lines, ranging in weight from 1,330 pounds to 12,000 pounds. In sharp contrast to the seemingly outmoded pull-types, Austin also offered the "77" motor grader. This was an advanced self-propelled machine fitted with hydraulic controls, single or tandem drive, leaning front wheels, and all the blade movements of the modern grader.

In 1937, the Austin-Western Company introduced the first all-wheel drive, all-wheel steer grader. These features were great selling points as Austin-Western boasted no dead weight on an axle. The most famous all-wheel-drive grader was the 99-H introduced in 1947. This versatile machine, with operating weight of 21,000 pounds and 13-foot blade, was available with either International diesel or LeRoi gasoline engines in the 80-horsepower range.

The 99-H was also the first grader model adopted by Aveling-Barford Ltd. for manufacture in Britain, commencing in 1950. It was primarily sold in Commonwealth countries as the Aveling-Austin 99-H and was identical to the American model except for its British-built Leyland engine. The manufacturing arrangement between Austin-Western and Aveling-Barford lasted until 1973, when Aveling discontinued making the Austin line of graders. However, Aveling continued with its own line of motor graders developed during its association with Austin-Western. In 1997, the largest Aveling-Barford grader is the 47,000-pound Model ASG-021.

In 1959, the Austin-Western grader line graduated into the 100-series, consisting of the "Pacer" (four-wheel)

The top-of-the-line Austin-Western grader in the 1960s was the Super 500, with its 179-horsepower engine and 30,000-pound operating weight. The "Super" designation denoted a six-wheel, tandem-drive model. Graders in the "Pacer" line were four-wheel models. All models featured all-wheel-drive. *Berrien County Historical Association*

Showing its side-sloping capability, the Super 501 grader is one of the last graders to be produced by Clark Equipment Company. The 205-horsepower model weighed in at 37,000 pounds. Clark had taken over the former Austin-Western Company in 1971, and then came out with a consolidated line, consisting of the 301- and 501-series, in 1973. *Historical Construction Equipment Association archives*

The forerunner of today's Champion line of graders is this horse-drawn "American Champion" made by S. Pennock and Sons Co. of Kennett Square, Pennsylvania, in 1878. *William Barlow collection*

The Champion "Power Maintainer" was unveiled in 1928 as Champion's first self-propelled grader. Controls were still operated by hand. *William Barlow collection*

Power controls were featured for the first time on a Champion motor grader in 1936 when the "Hydraulic Maintainer" was launched. This was one of the last graders to feature the engine located ahead of the cab. The following year, Champion turned the prime mover around, giving its graders the present-day appearance of the rear-mounted engine. *William Barlow collection*

Showing its versatility, this Champion motor grader of 1948 vintage is fully equipped for snow removal. It sports a front-mounted "V-plow" and, as well as its regular moldboard, carries a "snow wing" on the right-hand side for stacking deep snow out of the way. *William Barlow collection*

Champion's updated 700-series graders came out in 1975, here represented by the midsized 740, powered by a 210-horsepower engine. *William Barlow collection*

and "Super" (six-wheel) versions, in sizes from the 100 to the 500. In typical Austin-Western tradition, every model featured all-wheel-drive. The top-of-the-line Super 500 was powered by a 179-horsepower GM 6V-71 diesel engine and had an operating weight of just under 30,000 pounds.

In 1971, Austin-Western, which had become part of the Baldwin-Lima-Hamilton Corporation in 1951, became a division of Clark Equipment Company. In 1973, the grader line was redesigned and consolidated into two basic ranges, the 301- and 501-series machines, covering the same size range as the earlier models. In 1978, grader production was transferred to Clark's Lubbock, Texas, plant, where the machines were marketed under Clark's Crane Division. Manufacture ended in 1981 when the plant closed.

Champion Graders

The Champion grader of today has a rich heritage, with roots reaching back well into the last century. In the early days, other road-building products were made. But since the early 1950s, the Champion Road Machinery Company based at Goderich, Ontario, Canada, has specialized in the manufacture of a single product—graders. Champion, however, has American origins in a firm owned by the Pennock family, based in Kennett Square, Pennsylvania. In 1875, S. Pennock and Sons Co. entered the road-building equipment business and the "good roads" movement, an organization that lobbied government for road funding. In 1889, the company was reorganized as the American Road Machinery Company, and the Good Roads Machinery Company was set up to market its products.

The company sold road-building equipment, including graders, across the United States and into Canada. In 1892, Copp Brothers Company Ltd. obtained the rights to manufacture products of the American Road Machinery Company in Hamilton, Ontario, Canada. They made the "Steel Champion" grader, after which the company would later be named. Following several name changes and reorganizations, the Canadian company became known as the American Road Machine Company of Canada Ltd. in 1909, and operated as a subsidiary of its American parent.

The American Road Machine Company of Canada was renamed the Dominion Road Machinery Company in 1915, and became more independent with a new charter. By 1929, the American Road Machinery Company was experiencing financial trouble and was sold, leaving the Goderich plant as the sole producer of Champion graders. The Dominion Road Machinery Company prospered over the years as an independent company, and gained a significant share of the grader market. In 1977, the name Champion became more than a trade-

This outsize giant was the world's largest grader when it was unveiled in 1975. The Champion 100-T was powered by a 700-horsepower Cummins engine, and weighed a massive 202,000 pounds. Only one grader has surpassed this machine for size. (See sidebar.) *JKH collection*

Showing off its mammoth size, Champion's 100-T is parked beside a couple of Caterpillar 14G motor graders. Designed to work with large surface mining equipment, the 100-T was offered by Champion until 1989. *JKH collection*

Champion announced its new Series V line of graders in 1996, one of which is shown here. The Series V machines range from 31,000 pounds to 40,600 pounds in operating weight. *William Barlow collection*

Various models of the Huber Maintainer have been in Huber's line since 1943. The 77-horsepower Model M-850-A is still made today. The Maintainer (pictured) is a 65-horsepower Model M-600 from 1970. *Huber Construction Equipment*

For a few years after Huber acquired the W.A. Riddell Corporation in 1957, the combined line of graders was marketed under the Huber-Warco name. The Model 4-DG (pictured) is from this era, and in the 23,000-pound class.

Huber claimed title to the world's most powerful grader when the 5D-190, at 195 horsepower, was unveiled. The 30,000-pound model was in production from 1955 to 1957.

The Huber D-1700 was the largest of a new line of graders launched by the company in 1966. It could be equipped with either GM or Cummins engines. *Huber Construction Equipment*

mark, when the firm changed its corporate name to the Champion Road Machinery Company Ltd.

The first Champion grader appeared in 1886. It was the first of the "Winner" series designed to be pulled behind two or four horses. The "Winner" was developed into the "Highway Patrol" of 1914, whose stronger design could withstand the strain of a tractor. Sometimes early graders were coupled to farm tractors to make a self-contained unit.

The "Power Maintainer" came out in 1928 as Champion's first self-propelled grader. The cab was positioned at the rear of the power unit, the machine featured solid rubber tires, and the blade controls were still operated by hand. In 1936, Champion introduced the "Hydraulic Maintainer," one of the earliest successful applications of hydraulic power controls on a grader.

The 1946 model had a 90-degree blade lift range with all movements controlled from the cab. In 1958, Champion's "power-plus" circle turning system was introduced. This replaced the conventional circle motor with twin hydraulic cylinders. By 1969, the range covered sizes from 100 to 190 horsepower.

In 1975, the first of Champion's 700-series appeared. Initially consisting of five models ranging up to the Model D-760 with an operating weight of 37,000 pounds, the line was later expanded to the larger 780 and the smaller 710.

Champion took a bold step in 1975 with the introduction of the world's largest production-model grader. The 80-T, which later became the 100-T, had a 700-horsepower Cummins engine, an operating weight of 202,000 pounds, and carried a 24-foot blade. It was designed to maintain roads in surface mines for large haulers or to reclaim vast areas of land. Champion sold the manufacturing rights of the 100-T to Dom-Ex Corporation of Hibbing, Minnesota, in 1989.

The Champion line still consists of the 700-series graders, but the line has progressed through several series upgrades. The Series V machines unveiled in 1996 range from 135 to 210 horsepower, with corresponding weights of 31,000 to 40,600 pounds. In 1997, Volvo Construction Equipment announced the purchase of Champion Road Machinery Company.

Huber/Warco Graders

The Huber Manufacturing Company was established in 1875 at Marion, Ohio. The company made a wide variety of industrial products, including steam tractors, threshing machines, and road rollers. In the Huber works during 1883, the company produced the very first Barnhart steam shovel, a noteworthy achievement. The following year, the Marion Steam Shovel Company was incorporated to build the Barnhart shovel. One of its first directors was Edward Huber, the founder of Huber Manufacturing Company.

With the Marion Steam Shovel Company safely on its way to prosperity, Huber left earthmoving equipment manufacture for several decades. In the 1920s, however, Huber built graders and introduced hydraulic control at the early date of 1926. By 1934, graders such as the Huber No. 3 were offered. This four-wheel grader featured hydraulic blade control with centrally mounted operator's station and engine at the rear.

The popular "Maintainer," introduced in 1943, was Huber's longest-lived machine. It looked like a farm tractor with a blade slung below its frame. The light-duty 66-horsepower Maintainer has survived through its various model upgrades to the present day, and is now sold by Huber as the Model M-850-A.

In 1957, Huber acquired the W.A. Riddell Corporation of Bucyrus, Ohio, another builder of motor graders, which was established in 1854. Riddell had the distinction of designing one of the very earliest motor graders back in 1921. It was a four-wheel, solid-tire rig with rear-mounted engine and virtually nonex-

Dating from the early 1900s, this is an early horse-drawn grader made by the Russell Grader Manufacturing Company. When Caterpillar purchased Russell in 1928, it established its motor grader line.

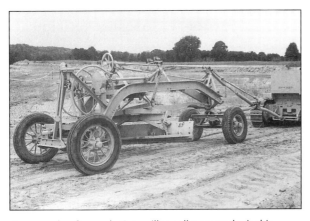

An example of an early Caterpillar pull-type grader is this hand-controlled No. 33 double-frame model. This example is owned by Bill Rudicill of Petersburg, Kentucky.

The Caterpillar "No. 9 Auto Patrol" was the first grader to have its engine mounted behind the operator. Coming out in 1931, the No. 9 was also Caterpillar's first rubber-tired motor grader, and was one of the first to feature power controls. It was powered by a 35-horsepower gasoline engine. *JKH collection*

istent operator accommodations. However, it was not the success the designers had hoped and was soon replaced by other models.

The Riddell graders became known by the trade name Warco, and for a while after the merger, were sold under the name Huber-Warco. In the mid-1950s, the line included some of the most powerful graders yet built. It consisted of the 4-D series of five standard transmission models in sizes from 75 to 123 horsepower, and the 6-D and 7-D series of four torque converter models ranging from 102 to 150 horsepower. The big 5D-190, made between 1955 and 1957, was billed as the world's most powerful motor grader, at 195 horsepower. Although not as heavy at 30,000 pounds, it competed with the biggest graders of the day, such as the Galion T-700.

In 1966, Huber introduced the D-1000 series graders with constant mesh transmissions and operating weights ranging from 23,000 pounds to 29,000 pounds. These graders had a distinctive rear-sloping engine hood. The largest, the D-1700, was equipped with Cummins or GM engines of up to 195 horsepower. The D models were soon followed by the F-1000 series, which boasted torque converter and power-shift transmissions.

In 1970, the Huber Manufacturing Company became a subsidiary company of A-T-O Inc., and relocated to Charleston, South Carolina, in 1977. The Huber grader line continued to be made in Charleston, although in diminishing numbers. In 1994, A-T-O (by then known as Figgie International) sold the Huber division to Enterprise Fabrications, Inc., which promptly returned the company to Ohio, this time to Galion. The first Huber machine, a Model M-850-A Maintainer, rolled out of the Galion plant in 1995. This small hydrostatically driven machine is the only grader being manufactured by Huber in 1997. However, it is a direct descendant of the first Huber Maintainer introduced in 1943, and has been in continuous production for some 54 years.

Caterpillar/Russell Graders

Caterpillar acquired the Russell Grader Manufacturing Company of Minneapolis, Minnesota, and garnered a new line of road maintenance products to add to its already popular crawler tractors in 1928. For many years Russell had produced pull-type graders, first for horse teams and then for early farm tractors. In 1919, the company began development of a self-propelled grader based on a 12-horsepower two-wheel Allis-Chalmers tractor. It was known as the Motor Hi-Way Patrol and it was the first of many Russell graders designed to fit around various brands of standard tractors.

Traction improved when Russell built a Motor Patrol around a Caterpillar 2-ton crawler tractor rated at 27 horsepower. Blade controls were hand operated and, surprisingly, blades up to 12 feet long were offered. When Caterpillar bought the company, Russell was experimenting with hydraulic controls but soon discarded them as unsatisfactory. The main disadvantages cited were leakage and unevenness of operation when more than one control was used at the same time. Caterpillar then developed reliable mechanical controls using screwed rods and worm drives operated through dog clutches. These were positive and not prone to creep like early hydraulic systems. The industry would have to wait until 1973 before Caterpillar introduced hydraulic controls on its G-series graders.

One of the most famous of the Caterpillar graders, the No. 12, was introduced in 1938. With its 12-foot blade, reliable mechanical controls, greater range of blade positions, and Caterpillar diesel engine, it replaced Caterpillar's line of pull-type and elevating graders. It progressed through several improvements and horsepower increases to the last series in 1959, when the No. 12 was replaced with the 12E. Over this period, engine power went from 70 horsepower to 115 horsepower.

A year after the No. 12 grader was released, Caterpillar introduced two smaller but similar graders, the 52-horsepower No. 112 and 35-horsepower No. 212. They were gasoline- or diesel-powered and available

Introduced in 1938, the Caterpillar No. 12 motor grader proved to be one of the company's most popular. With a 12-foot blade and mechanical power controls, it remained in the Caterpillar line until 1959, when it was replaced by the 12E.

The big No. 16 motor grader was the largest on the market when it was unveiled by Caterpillar in 1963. The 225-horsepower rigid-frame model with mechanical controls was made until 1973, when it was replaced by the articulated 16-G model. *Caterpillar Inc.*

An example of Caterpillar's articulated G-series graders, launched in 1973, is this 140G showing off its side-reach capability. The midrange 140G had a 150-horsepower engine. *JKH collection*

in single or tandem rear-wheel drive. Caterpillar started building large graders in the late 1950s. The first No. 14, rated at 150 horsepower with a 12-foot blade, appeared in 1959. In 1963, the first No. 16, with 225 horsepower and a 14-foot blade, hit the dirt. At 46,500 pounds, this machine was the largest grader on the market at the time.

In 1973, Caterpillar revamped its entire grader line with the introduction of the G-series. For the first time, Caterpillar had a line of articulated motor graders as well as hydraulic blade controls. The G-series graders proved to be even more popular than the earlier models and stayed in Caterpillar's line with little modification for over two decades.

In 1995, Caterpillar announced its H-series graders. Available in nine models, the line ranged from the 125-horsepower 120-H to the 275-horsepower 16-H. Included in the new lineup were two all-wheel-drive models—the 143-H and 163-H. New features included

an operator's cab with improved forward vision and electronically controlled transmissions.

The 24-H, a giant mining grader, was added to the line in 1996. At 131,000 pounds, it ranks as one of the largest graders ever built and comes with a Caterpillar 3412E engine rated at 500 horsepower. Prior to the 24-H, Caterpillar already boasted building the largest grader on the market, the 16-H, that replaced the 16-G a year earlier. (See Sidebar in this chapter.) Thus Caterpillar broke its own size record for graders and remains dominant in the big grader market.

Komatsu/Dresser/Galion Graders

The Galion Iron Works Company of Galion, Ohio, was founded by David Charles Boyd in 1907. In its early years, the Galion name appeared on a wide range of road-building and other construction equipment, such as drag scrapers, plows, wagons, stone unloaders, rock crushers, and a variety of "experimental machines." By

In 1995, Caterpillar announced its H-series graders, which ranged up to the 275-horsepower Model 16-H. At 60,150 pounds in operating weight, it was the largest grader in production at that time.

In 1996, Caterpillar's massive 24-H was unveiled. It was a grader over twice the weight of the existing largest grader on the market—Caterpillar's own 16-H. With a working weight of 131,000 pounds, and an engine developing 500 horsepower, this machine is targeted for the haul roads of the largest surface mines.

1911, Galion had begun production of a light-duty, horse-drawn road grader.

The company's success and product diversification brought about its reorganization in 1913, and a change of name to the Galion Iron Works and Manufacturing Company. The "Light Premier" was an early grader produced in 1915. It was billed as light enough for two horses, but strong enough for four. Its blade could be raised, lowered, angled, tilted, and shifted sideways, just like the blade movements on a modern grader.

Galion was famous for building some of the largest pull-type graders in the industry. Popular throughout the 1920s and 1930s, these huge machines were pulled by the largest traction engines and crawler tractors available. These graders outperformed other motor graders of the day. Galion continued selling its pull-type graders until 1945, long after other manufacturers discontinued pull-type graders.

In 1922, Galion was one of the first companies to develop a self-propelled motor grader. The tractor engine and transmission were located in the rear of the frame, and the operator cockpit was located near the center of the machine. Also in the 1920s, development work began on one of Galion's greatest achievements—the Galion hydraulic control. Used on both pull-type and self-propelled graders, this hydraulic system was one of the first to be applied to grader controls.

In 1929, Jeffrey Manufacturing Company of Columbus, Ohio, purchased the Galion organization, but the name of the company remained unchanged.

The motor grader line received the first power-shift transmission, which was a big leap forward, in 1955. Called the Galion Grade-O-Matic drive, it utilized a torque converter, output shaft governor, and power-shift transmission, providing simple two-lever control of speed and direction. The Galion T-700 garnered the world's largest grader title in 1955. Larger than anything else in the grader industry, it boasted 190 horsepower and an operating weight of over 40,000 pounds.

After exactly 60 years with the same name, the Galion Iron Works & Manufacturing Company was renamed the Galion Manufacturing Company in 1973. The following year a transaction was completed making Galion a division of Dresser Industries, Inc.

Galion introduced its modern-looking articulated grader line in 1979. It featured a distinctively sloped rear engine hood and was identified as the A-series for "Articulated." Initially three models were introduced, the A-500, A-550, and A-600, weighing up to 30,000 pounds. These models joined the rigid-frame models, which continued in the Galion line until the mid-1980s.

In 1986, the grader products took on the name of the parent company, Dresser, and the Galion name was temporarily dropped. In 1988, the grader line was consolidated into three articulated models named the 830, 850, and 870. That same year, Galion became part of the Komatsu Dresser Company (KDC) joint venture. The Galion name reemerged in 1992, when the Galion Division of KDC was established. (Galion back by popular demand!) From 1995, the three basic Galion graders were badged and renumbered to fit into Komatsu's GD series, and featured modified specifications. The Komatsu-designed GD825A-2 is its largest grader, weighing 58,250 pounds and producing 280 horsepower.

John Deere Graders

In 1967, John Deere entered the grader market with the advanced JD-570. This machine featured articulated

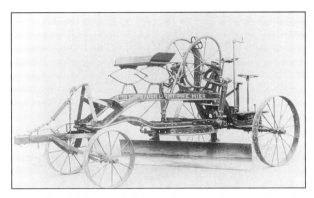

The Galion "Light Premier" horse-drawn grader came from the Galion Iron Works and Manufacturing Company in 1915. It was billed as "light enough for two horses, but strong enough for four." *Galion Historical Society*

Galion was famous for its huge pull-type graders, some of the largest ever built, and designed to pull behind the most powerful tractors available. The No. 14 shown here is equipped with scarifier, steerable tongue, 14-foot blade, and hand-operated controls. This heavy-duty piece of iron tipped the scales at 15,000 pounds. *Galion Historical Society*

A Galion pull-type grader cuts a steep bank and ditch. The advantage of the offset wheel arrangement is clearly demonstrated. This machine is equipped with hydraulic controls. *Galion Historical Society*

Galion developed one of the first hydraulic power grader systems in the 1920s. By the early 1930s, hydraulics were standard on all motor graders. An example of a 1932 "Galion Patrol" is shown here. *Galion Historical Society*

frame and front-wheel steering, which gave it excellent maneuverability. At that time, no other manufacturer offered articulation in graders. Currently, all grader manufacturers offer articulated-frame machines, with the exception of some of the small light-duty units.

John Deere unveiled the JD-770 grader at Conexpo 1975 in Chicago. This 33,000-pound machine was Deere's largest grader to date, and it featured innovative push-button hydraulic controls, instead of hand levers, on all motions except blade lift. Although this system was not the most reliable, it survived in the JD-770A from 1978 to 1986, when the new JD-770B reverted to lever control. The JD-770 was the only grader equipped with push-button controls.

The JD-672A and JD-772A, the first four-wheel-drive models, expanded Deere's 1978 line-up and weighed up to 35,000 pounds. The line has progressed through the B-series, introduced in 1986, and the C-series in 1997. The six-model lineup consists of tandem-drive models, as well as variable-horsepower, tandem-drive, and six-wheel-drive models from 140 to 205 horsepower. The variable horsepower model's engine output is automatically increased in the higher gears to maximize productivity when operating under heavy blade loads at higher speeds.

Other Large Motor Graders

Some of the very largest graders were not made by the most familiar grader manufacturers. CMI Corporation, famous for its automated profiling and paving equipment, came out with a giant grader in 1969. Named the "Autoblade," the 40-foot-long double-articulated unit had a power module at both ends, each consisting of a 225-horsepower diesel engine driving four wheels through hydrostatic drive. The eight-wheel-drive machine featured a centrally mounted cab that could swing 180 degrees to face in either direction. This, coupled with the ability to rotate the blade 360 degrees, eliminated the need to

The world size record was taken by Galion in 1955 when the T-700 was introduced, incorporating the new "Grade-O-Matic" control. This was Galion's name for its torque converter drive and power-shift transmission. Larger than any other grader yet built, the T-700 weighed 40,000 pounds and came with a 190-horsepower engine. *Galion Historical Society*

In 1979, Galion added the first three articulated graders to its line. The midsized A-550, with a 29,100-pound operating weight, is shown here. These graders were of a completely new design, with distinctive sloping engine hood. Other models of the same design were introduced until all Galion's rigid-frame machines were replaced by the mid-1980s.

Some bank grading performed by a Dresser 830 grader. The 27,800-pound grader was formerly the Galion A-450E, but was renumbered when parent company Dresser Industries temporarily dropped the Galion name in 1986. *JKH collection*

The Galion name returned when the Komatsu-Dresser joint venture was set up in 1992. Recently, the Galion graders were renumbered again, this time to fit in with the Komatsu nomenclature. This is the Komatsu GD670A, which is the same machine as the Galion 670 grader. They are in the 32,400-pound operating weight class.

The Komatsu GD825A is the flagship of the company's grader line. With its 16-foot blade, 280-horsepower engine, and 58,250-pound operating weight, it is definitely in the heavyweight class. From 1997, the GD825A has been marketed by Komatsu Mining Systems. *Komatsu America International*

The JD-770 represented a big jump in grader size for John Deere when it was unveiled at Conexpo 1975 in Chicago. It is demonstrating its 90-degree turning capability, helped by articulation. This 33,000-pound grader features the industry's first push-button controls for the blade movements. *JKH collection*

One of the John Deere graders from its current "C" series, introduced in 1997. The line consists of six models from 140 to 205 horsepower. *Deere & Co.*

back up over the grade to make another pass. In addition to heavy-duty grading, CMI promoted the Autoblade as a precision grader, suitable for fine grading in paving operations. The 65,000-pound machine could be guided in both alignment and grade from a fixed string line attached to pins on the ground.

CMI later produced more conventional-looking graders in their Autoblade series. The AG-55 and AG-65 graders had operating weights of up to 60,000 pounds and Caterpillar engines of up to 375 horsepower. All the CMI graders featured hydrostatic drive, and could perform precision grading from a reference line.

Graders produced by RayGo, Inc., could be categorized as either very small or very large. The minigrader, known as the Razor 350, was fitted with a 35-horsepower engine, and weighed only 5,250 pounds. By contrast, RayGo's other grader was known as the "Giant," and certainly lived up to its name. Like the CMI Autoblade, it was double-articulated and had a power unit at both ends, but the RayGo weighed 106,000 pounds compared to the Autoblade's 65,000. Both of the Giant's power units were GM 318-horsepower diesel engines, each driving a single axle. Although the RayGo Giant was suitable for heavy-duty leveling and reclamation of surface mines, its blade was fixed to the central frame instead of the usual circle mounting. The operator's cab was mounted on the rear frame, and suspended over the rear articulated joint, giving the operator a panoramic view of the blade and the front power unit. RayGo began manufacturing the Giant in 1969, after it had been developed and tested several years earlier by Ken Harris, a South Dakota contractor. RayGo, established in 1964, made its name in self-propelled compactors. It went out of existence in 1985 when CMI Corporation purchased the company. Rights to the RayGo products passed to Caterpillar Inc. in 1987.

CMI Corporation produced this giant grader, called the "Autoblade," in 1969. A power module with a 225-horsepower engine at each end propelled its eight hydrostatically driven wheels. The double-articulated grader carried a separate cab module, which could swivel so the operator could face the direction of travel. *CMI Corporation*

Orenstein & Koppel (O&K) make a full line of motor graders in Germany for worldwide distribution. From 1980, O&K made a huge mining grader known as the G-350. With an operating weight of over 90,000 pounds, this machine was the largest grader in production during the time. It was a true grader, with most of the blade movements of its smaller brothers, and found use in large mining applications where haul trucks were rapidly increasing in size. O&K sold 34 of the G-350 graders to many countries before it was dropped in 1986. The current O&K grader line consists of three sizes with operating weights from 23,800 to 35,000 pounds.

In 1980, Italian contractor Umberto ACCO created the world's largest grader ever. The one-of-a-kind monster was built for use on a major contract in Libya. With its 33-foot blade, front and rear engines totaling 1,700 horsepower, and 12 large tires, this beast dwarfed every other grader built to date.

The giant AG-65 was a more conventional-looking grader from CMI. With a Caterpillar engine of 375 horsepower, and a weight of 60,000 pounds, it featured hydrostatic drive. *CMI Corporation*

Another small company producing a big machine was RayGo, Inc. The "Giant" commenced manufacture in 1969, featuring double articulation and a 318-horsepower power unit at each end. At 106,000 pounds in operating weight, it was one of the largest graders ever built. *JKH collection*

O&K made its giant G-350 motor grader from 1980 until 1986. This 90,000-pound machine had all the blade movements of the smaller grader, but was designed to work with the largest haulers in surface mines.

The largest grader ever built was the behemoth ACCO made by contractor Umberto ACCO in Italy around 1980. This machine far exceeded in power and size anything resembling a grader before or since. It takes a 1,000-horsepower engine in the rear, and a 700-horsepower engine up front to push the 33-foot blade, utilizing traction from the ACCO's 12 tires. *Yvon LeCadre*

Chapter Six

OFF-HIGHWAY TRUCKS

Off-highway trucks range from the small site dumper used on construction jobs to the giant haulers found in surface mines, which are the largest trucks ever to roam the earth. Most have a rigid-frame with single- or tandem-drive axles, while others are of the tractor-trailer type, either with an articulated frame or consisting of a four-wheel tractor unit pulling a semitrailer. The latter type is usually found in surface coal mines, where the coal is hauled several miles on relatively flat roads. Off-highway trucks are more efficient at hauling material over longer distances than other types of earthmoving equipment, although they must be loaded by another machine, such as an excavator. Even conveyors, which are efficient at very long distances and have an advantage where the terrain is rugged, lose out to the flexibility of haul trucks when the loading or dumping points are constantly being changed.

As their name implies, off-highway trucks are unsuitable, and in most cases illegal, on public highways. Their width usually places them in the "wide load" category, and their wheel loading and axle configuration do not comply with highway weight regulations. Although the term "off-highway" implies that these trucks might be at home on rough, uneven roads, the opposite is in fact true; hard and stable roads are essential to run these large vehicles efficiently. Frames twist over uneven ground, resulting in premature cracking, so most open pit mines spend large amounts of money on road construction and maintenance to ensure their trucks run at lowest cost per mile.

Birth of the Off-Highway Truck

Before off-highway trucks were created, haulage vehicles were of the highway type. They were constructed of light-duty frames, flimsy bodies (often made of wood), and narrow wheels causing them to become stuck all too frequently. By the early 1930s, the excavators utilized to load these primitive trucks were comparatively well developed. As a result, the trucks were unsuitable to receive a cubic yard of dirt

Before the advent of the off-highway truck, railway transport was used, but contractors needed something less restrictive. They first turned to the only off-road vehicle available, the crawler tractor. Here, a Holt Caterpillar 10-ton tractor is hauling a train of dump wagons. *Ad Gevers collection*

Before Caterpillar entered the off-highway truck business, it offered rear-dump, side-dump, or bottom-dump trailers for its prime movers, whose normal duty was to haul scrapers. A fleet of Caterpillar PR-21 rear-dump units, with the trailers made by the Athey Corporation, are seen at a British surface coal mine.

Caterpillar's first entry into the off-highway truck market was in 1962, with the 35-ton Model 769. The one shown here is being loaded by a 110-B shovel on a British highway job.

After the company's first off-highway truck was launched in 1962, Caterpillar went straight into designing and testing a range of large electric-drive trucks. The 75-ton 779 prototype shown here was tested in 1964, and the production model hit the market in 1967. *JKH collection*

and rock dropped from a shovel dipper, and then carry a full load along an unmade road. Rail cars had been used successfully when the shovels were rail-mounted. Slow-moving wagons pulled by horses, steam traction engines, or crawler tractors were widely used, but a robust off-highway hauler was desperately needed when the shovels left their constricting rails and took to crawler tracks.

Although some earlier attempts had been made to beef up highway truck designs, it was the construction of the Boulder Dam (now the Hoover Dam) that bred true off-highway truck development. In the Mack section in this chapter, we will see how Mack redesigned some of its trucks for Boulder Dam use, and expanded into special off-road designs in the 1930s.

The first company to specialize in haulers designed and built for off-highway duty was Euclid Road Machinery Company of Euclid, Ohio, beginning in 1934. The off-highway truck filled a much-needed role in the earthmoving contractor's spread of equipment, and its success prompted many other manufacturers to enter the field. Some were established truck makers, such as Dart and Mack, while others were specialist off-road vehicle builders. Experience proved that a highway-type truck could not be beefed up enough for regular off-highway service. It wasn't enough just to strengthen the frame and axles. Every component of the unit, including wheel rims, springs, door hinges, even down to the last nut and bolt, had to be designed to withstand the most rugged conditions.

By the late 1930s, a number of off-highway truck types were available, including some very large capacity units. From 1938 to 1940, the Trojan Truck Manufacturing Company of Los Angeles, California, built the largest off-highway trucks. These monsters boasted a

The largest of the Caterpillar electric trucks was this 240-ton Model 786 coal hauler. With a cab and power module at each end for shuttle service, the unit ran on 16 tires. A total of five of these giant haulers went to work at the Captain Mine in Illinois in 1968. However, no more were built after this date. *Caterpillar Inc.*

Where grades are not too steep, a semitrailer can be attached to a standard truck to increase capacity. Here is a Caterpillar 776 tractor unit on test hauling a 110-ton rear-dump dump trailer built by Dart Truck Company. The 870-horsepower 776 is derived from Caterpillar's 777 rigid-frame truck, with a fifth-wheel trailer hitch installed instead of a dump box. *JKH collection*

capacity of 70 tons, two Caterpillar 190-horsepower D17000 engines, and triple tires on each of the four tandem rear wheels. Other off-highway specialist truck builders of the same era included the Hug Company of Highland, Illinois, in existence from 1922 to 1942, and the Six Wheels Inc. of Los Angeles.

The trailer-type haulers were pulled by a tractor unit, built from the earliest form of wagons pulled by horses, and later by steam traction engines. Caterpillar, LeTourneau, M-R-S, Dart, and Euclid manufactured these haulers at an early date. The modern wagon is pulled by a high-speed, wheeled tractor such as those made by Caterpillar, Euclid, and Komatsu. The wagons or trailers are built by specialist manufacturers, such as Maxter Industries Ltd. of Montreal, Quebec, who build rear- and bottom-dumping trailers up to 290-ton capacity.

Articulated Dump Trucks

Articulated dump trucks (ADTs), unitized tractor-trailer vehicles with an articulated frame, originated in Europe in the mid-1950s. Ranging in capacity up to 50 tons, these vehicles work mainly on construction sites

The 793C was Caterpillar's largest truck when launched at Minexpo 1996 in Las Vegas. An upgrade from the first 793 truck introduced in 1990, the 793C carries 240 tons and is equipped with a 2,166-flywheel horsepower engine.

An Isco IC-13R rear-dump hauler of 13-ton capacity, designed by Cline. The Isco name was used from 1972 to 1978, when Cline was a division of Isco Manufacturing Company, Inc. *JKH collection*

This is the Cline 50-ton rear-dump coal hauler that has been widely used in the Appalachian coal mining areas. It is still available from Cline Truck Manufacturing, Inc. *JKH collection*

One of a fleet of 10 Dart coal haulers delivered to Sunnyhill Coal Company, New Lexington, Ohio, in 1953. The tractor unit is a 300-horsepower Model 50S-BDT pulling a 60-ton trailer. At the same time, Sunnyhill purchased this Bucyrus-Erie 150-B electric shovel to load the trucks. *JKH collection*

This was the largest truck in the world when it left the Dart stable in 1951. Carrying a whopping 75 tons, the Model 75-TA was powered by two 300-horsepower Buda diesel engines. Only one of these was built, and it worked at the Bagdad Copper Mine in Arizona. *Kress Corporation*

This tractor-trailer combination is hauling 100 tons at a New Mexico coal mine. It is the Dart 95EDT, first appearing in 1960 as a 95-ton rear-dump hauler.

or small surface mines. Because of their four-wheel or six-wheel drive articulated design, ADTs have superb traction in adverse road conditions. The ADT is rapidly replacing scrapers in certain types of earthmoving application because an ADT carries as much and travels as fast as a similar-sized scraper, but it is more economical to operate. However, ADTs need an excavator or other equipment to load them.

Some early pioneers included Shawnee-Poole, Northfield, Whitlock, Camill, Morley, and Hudson from England; and Volvo (the originator) from Sweden. Of these, only Volvo survives today, but many others have sprung up along the way to offer much worldwide competition.

Among current producers of off-highway haulers who include ADTs in their line are Aveling-Barford, Caterpillar, Terex, O&K, and Volvo. As well, Bell (South Africa), Randon (Brazil), Moxey (Norway), Hydrema (Denmark), and DDT and Thwaites (England) specialize in manufacturing ADTs. Today, the largest ADT on the market is the 50-ton Fullback 650 built by Atlas Copco Wagner Inc. of Portland, Oregon.

Off-Highway Trucks Increase in Size

After World War II, sizes increased and many well-known highway truck manufacturers, including Autocar, Mack, Walter, International, Kenworth, and Oshkosh, continued off-highway vehicles in their production programs alongside the specialist manufacturers. However, the development of larger trucks was limited by the available size of engines, transmissions, and tires. This situation prompted Euclid to adopt twin power in the late 1940s, which involved doubling up on engines, drivetrains, and drive axles to allow heavier loads to be carried.

In the 1960s, truck design reverted to single-drive axle and single-engine designs as stronger, more powerful components became available. The cycle was repeated in the early 1970s, when increased demand for larger capacity once again exceeded technology. As a result, tandem-drive trucks reappeared in the largest sizes. Today, tires and engines have advanced to the point where the largest trucks in production are once again of the single-drive axle, single-engine design.

A major breakthrough came with the perfection of electric wheel drive, consisting of a diesel engine driving a generator. This provided DC electric current to a motor in each driving wheel. R.G. LeTourneau developed one of the first electric haulers in conjunction with Anaconda Company of Butte, Montana. This was the trolley-assisted TR-60, a 75-ton articulated hauler, which left the LeTourneau plant in 1959. That same year, Unit Rig brought out its prototype diesel-electric "Lectrahaul." Today, the debate rages between manufacturers as to whether mechanical or electric-drive trucks produce the lowest cost per ton hauled. Both types have their advantages.

Ralph Kress—Father of the American Off-Highway Truck

Since 1950, arguably, no single person has had a greater influence and impact on the off-highway truck industry than Ralph Kress. His family background was the Kress Carriage Company, builder of fire trucks from 1896. It supplied most of the fire trucks to the New York Fire Department in the first two decades of this century. Kress' background and talent allowed him to design many innovative vehicles. During his long career, he was a driving force behind the off-road hauler businesses of Dart, LeTourneau-Westinghouse (Wabco), Caterpillar, and Kress Corporation.

From 1950 to 1955, Kress was general manager of Dart Truck Company, which was founded in 1903. In 1951, he designed and built the Dart 75-TA, a 75-ton tandem drive, rear-dump truck powered by two 300-horsepower Buda diesel engines. It was the largest truck in the world, and was sold to the Bagdad Copper Mine in Arizona.

In 1955, Ralph Kress worked for LeTourneau-Westinghouse (Wabco) as a consultant. His task was to design a truck to put Wabco in the truck business. The outcome was a prototype 30-ton rear-dump truck of radical design. It featured a triangular box shape to lower the center of gravity, an offset cab, forward-sloping windshield, oleo-pneumatic suspension, short wheelbase, and high payload-to-weight ratio. These features set the standard for off-highway truck design for the next four decades.

In 1962, Ralph Kress joined Caterpillar. At this time, Caterpillar had already made seven preproduction models of the new 769 35-ton mechanical-drive rear-dump truck, but had not announced its entry into the truck market. Ralph started designing Caterpillar's electric-drive trucks, and developed the 779 75-ton and 783 100-ton haulers. Their prototypes were completed in 1964, and the 779 was put on the market in 1967. The side-dumping 783 featured three axles, front- and rear-wheel steer, and center-wheel drive. The culmination of Caterpillar's electric-drive truck program was the Model 786, a 240-ton coal hauler operating on the shuttle principle, with a drive module and cab at both ends. A total of five of these mammoth vehicles were built by 1968, and put into service at the Captain Mine of Southwestern Illinois Coal Corporation (now Arch Coal Inc.). The following year, Caterpillar announced the abandonment of its electric truck program, and purchased back those units already in the field.

When Caterpillar's electric trucks were abandoned, Ralph Kress moved to the Kress Corporation, a company

The first mechanical-drive, rigid-frame hauler to cross the 100-ton frontier was this Dart Model D-2771, in 1965. It was powered by an 800-horsepower engine. *JKH collection*

This Dart-designed Model 2085 is claimed to be the largest tandem-drive mechanical truck ever built. The 2085 measures over 40 feet long, is 15 feet 4 inches wide, and has a GVW of 293,000 pounds. Engines installed are in the 800-horsepower class. *Unit Rig, Div. Terex Corporation*

This is the original Euclid "Trac-Truk" of 1934, a rear-dump of 7-cubic yard capacity. The Euclid Road Machinery Company was the first company to specialize in off-road haul trucks. *Eric Orlemann collection*

The first application of Euclid's twin-power concept was in this bottom-dump coal hauler Model 50FDT from 1948. It features twin Detroit 6-71 engines, and an 18-cubic yard capacity.

The 1951 Euclid 1LLD was the real monster truck—the largest production truck of the day. With two engines under the hood putting out 600 horsepower, this giant rear-dump could carry 50 tons. By 1952, famous contractor Western Contracting Corporation was running a fleet of 30 of these units.

Not content with running a fleet of the largest trucks available, Western Contracting Corporation increased the capacity of the Euclid 1LLD to 150 tons by adding a rear-dump trailer and twin 375-horsepower engines. *Eric Orlemann collection*

The Euclid FD-series of 15-ton capacity rear-dump trucks was a welcome sight for many a quarry owner and surface mine operator. This very successful truck, small by today's standards, had a very long production run. As a 15-ton truck, it was in production from 1936 to 1963.

The giant Euclid R-X truck was offered with capacities of 85 to 105 tons. Introduced in 1965, the unusual R-X was designed with an articulated frame and four-wheel drive. With engines offered in the 700 to 1,000 horsepower class, the R-X soon became known as the R-105.

his son Ted had established a few years earlier. Ralph immediately went to work on a revolutionary new coal hauler, described under Kress in this chapter.

Current Off-Highway Hauler Situation

By the 1970s, the only companies making both highway and off-highway trucks were International and Mack. The other highway truck builders halted off-highway truck production at various times in the previous two decades. Truck builders had to specialize to survive. Those specializing in highway trucks found the market lucrative, and shied away from the relatively small market for off-highway haul trucks. It was too expensive to design larger and larger off-highway vehicles, often involving heavy steel castings, and different technology to that required for the familiar road vehicles.

Accordingly, Mack announced its exit from the off-highway hauler business in 1979. In 1982, International sold its off-highway Payhauler line to a new company, Payhauler Corporation. International's departure from the off-highway truck scene marked the end of an era. From that time on, highway and off-highway truck manufacture have proceeded as entirely separate industries, with no manufacturer producing both types.

The next sections of this chapter cover the histories and current situation of most prominent off-highway truck manufacturers.

Aveling-Barford

By 1939, Aveling-Barford, an English firm that had built road rollers since 1865, started building a site dumper based on a Fordson tractor. A larger 12-ton capacity site dumper was introduced in 1947. Then in 1958, the famous SN-series haulers of 30- and 35-ton capacity were introduced. The SN models were powered by Rolls Royce C8TFL or GM 12V71N engines, and attained speeds up to 33 miles per hour. In 1970, the entire line of Aveling-Barford trucks was replaced by the Centaur range, featuring offset cabs and capacities up to 50 tons.

The Centaurs gradually developed into the RD-series, and by 1980, this line consisted of six rigid-frame haulers from 17 to 50 tons. The haulers continued to grow and by the late 1980s, 55-ton and 65-ton models were added. The company was owned by British Leyland for several years from 1968, but is now independently owned. It continues the RD-series, as well as its RXD-series of articulated dump trucks of 24-ton and 28-ton capacity.

Caterpillar

Caterpillar's first haulers were semitrailer wagons pulled behind the company's DW-series wheel tractors. The first was the DW-10, which appeared in 1941, followed by the DW-20 in 1951 and DW-15 in 1954. These tractors, which normally pulled scrapers, could be attached to wagons of 11-, 22-, and 18-cubic yard capacities.

In 1962, Caterpillar entered the off-highway truck business with the 35-ton Model 769 that featured stylish curves around the cab area giving it a 1990s appearance. Caterpillar expanded its truck line in 1970 with the 50-ton 773, and the hugely successful 85-ton 777 in 1975.

Tractor-trailer bottom dump coal haulers are available from Caterpillar by equipping the truck chassis with

Making headlines around the world when it was introduced in 1971, the massive Euclid R-210 was driven by a gas turbine engine that developed 1,850 horsepower. The R-210 was double the size of its smaller companion, the R-105. Both models featured drive to all four wheels. *Eric Orlemann collection*

In the 1970s, Euclid offered this 120-ton tractor-trailer that utilized the twin-power concept with an extra engine mounted on the rear. Doubling up on the engines meant that, when the going was good, a second 120-ton trailer could be pulled behind the first. *JKH collection*

A popular coal hauler from Euclid in the 1980s was the CH-120 bottom-dumping unit of 120-ton capacity. The tractor unit is based on the Euclid R-85 rear-dump truck with a fifth wheel and trailer hitch provided. There are still many CH-120s running today, including this one giving good service at a western Canadian coal mine.

Euclid's current flagship hauler is the R-260, which was introduced at Minexpo 1996 in Las Vegas. Its capacity is 262 tons, the installed engine is 2,500 horsepower, and overall width is 25 feet 10 inches. *Wajax Industries*

a fifth-wheel arrangement instead of the dump body and hoist. Bottom-dump semitrailers can usually carry about 50 percent more than their rear-dump equivalent.

Since 1985, Caterpillar's line has included articulated dump trucks (ADTs) from 25- to 40-ton capacities in four-wheel and six-wheel configurations. The rights and designs for these trucks were acquired from the English truck maker, DJB Engineering Ltd., which was established in 1973. The ADTs are still built in the original DJB factory in England.

In 1985, Caterpillar boosted the top end of its truck line with the introduction of the 150-ton 785, followed the next year by the 195-ton 789. These were equipped with 1,290- and 1,705-horsepower Caterpillar diesel engines. Another boost came in 1990 with the launch of the 793 with a 240-ton capacity and 2,057-horsepower Cat D3516 diesel. These models have all since received upgrades, the 777D now running as a 100-ton truck. In 1998, Caterpillar announced the 797, its largest truck to date. With a gross vehicle weight of over 1.2 million pounds, it is 50 percent bigger than Caterpillar's 240-ton 793C, its previous largest. Except for its electric trucks designed by Ralph Kress in the 1960s, all Caterpillar's trucks have been equipped with mechanical drive and automatic power-shift transmissions.

Cline/Isco

Max Cline left Dart to form his own company in 1952. Cline Truck Manufacturing Company started cranking out a variety of heavy trucks, including crane carriers and underground trucks. A 35-ton 6x4 coal hauler became extremely popular in the Appalachians, and Cline's largest truck, introduced in 1970, was a 72-ton tandem-drive coal hauler with a 635-horsepower Cummins diesel.

Cline was a division of Isco Manufacturing Company, Inc., from 1972 to 1978. During that time, the off-highway trucks bore the name Isco. The lineup included rear-dump trucks from 13- to 50-ton capacities, and a tandem-drive

The first truck to leave the Peoria, Illinois, plant of LeTourneau-Westinghouse was this 80-ton "Haulpak" bottom-dump coal hauler. Traveling under its own power, it led the 1957 Thanksgiving Day Parade on its way to work at the Midland Coal Mine, 25 miles west of Peoria. *Komatsu America International*

A Wabco 85C "Haulpak" truck of 85-ton capacity is shown working at a Wyoming coal mine in 1975. Designed by Ralph Kress for LeTourneau-Westinghouse Company and introduced in 1957, the radical appearance of the Wabco Haulpak truck (rear-sloping box, offset cab, and forward-sloping windshield) was later adopted by most other off-highway truck manufacturers.

tractor unit capable of pulling 90-ton wagons. In 1979, the Cline name reemerged under new owner T & J Industries, Inc., which kept the company until 1985. From that date, Cline Truck Manufacturing, Inc., has operated as a division of C.B.T. Corporation, rebuilding older Cline trucks. It also offers its 50-ton tandem coal hauler, although none have actually been ordered since 1993.

Dart

Established in 1903 as a highway truck builder, the Dart Truck Company built its first heavy-duty off-highway truck in 1937. A diesel-electric tractor pulling two 40-ton trailers for coal hauling was built in 1939. In the early 1950s, Dart discontinued its highway truck line in favor of off-highway trucks, which it built in ever-increasing sizes. As already mentioned, Dart's tandem drive 75-ton Model 75-TA, designed by Ralph Kress in 1951, was a world record-beater for size. Then, in 1960, Dart came out with a 95-ton capacity, rear-dumping tractor-trailer unit known as the 95EDT. In 1966, the Model D2771 was the first mechanical-drive truck of regular two-axle configuration to beat the 100-ton barrier.

Dart offered both mechanical and diesel-electric drive in its truck line. By 1970, the line consisted of three sizes of two-axle mechanical-drive trucks in capacities up to 110-ton capacity, and 120-ton and 150-ton two-axle electric-drive trucks. The mechanical-drive models could also be equipped with trailers, giving capacities of up to 120 tons. Another interesting truck from Dart is the 85-ton Model 2080, claimed as the world's largest tandem axle mechanical-drive hauler. Introduced in 1980, it was popular for hauling coal in the Appalachians, and is still available today as the Model 2085.

After changing hands many times since its inception, Dart was acquired in 1984 by Unit Rig & Equipment Company of Tulsa, Oklahoma. In 1988, Unit Rig became

a division of Terex Corporation. Dart products have continued as a separate line, but are now built only to order.

Euclid

Euclid Road Machinery Company of Euclid, Ohio, was the first company to specialize in haulers for off-highway use. Starting as the Armington Electric Hoist Company in 1907, and continuing as the Euclid Crane & Hoist Company from 1909, the company's products included pull-type scrapers, rollers, wagons (crawler and wheeled), and tractor equipment such as dozer blades. Later, in 1931, the Euclid Road Machinery Company was incorporated to reflect the growing earthmoving business.

In 1933, the company experimented with a 5-yard bottom-dumping semitrailer intended for off-highway use, and pulled by a Chevrolet truck with shortened wheelbase. The next year, Euclid built its own off-road truck, a rear-dump type of 7-cubic yard capacity, christened the "Trac-Truk." The success of this truck established Euclid as the first company to specialize solely in off-highway haulers. In 1936, the initial version of the famous FD-series trucks hit the dirt with its 15-ton capacity. From then on, haulers grew ever larger to keep pace with larger shovels loading them.

To overcome the limitations of available engine and transmission power, Euclid pioneered the twin-drive concept in its rear-dump trucks in 1949, with the 34-ton Model FFD. This model contained two Detroit 6-71 engines, each driving one of its tandem axles through separate transmissions. The 1LLD 50-ton rear dump followed in 1951. Billed as the largest production truck in the world, the 1LLD was powered by two 300-horsepower Cummins NHRS engines. The demand for these large trucks came from famous earthmoving contractor Western Contracting Corporation. By 1952, they were running a fleet of 30 of these behemoths. In 1958, this contractor

With an oversize body to carry 170 tons of coal, this diesel-electric Wabco truck is working at a Wyoming coal mine. The engine installed has 1,600 horsepower. *JKH collection*

The behemoth tandem-drive Model 3200 truck was marketed by Wabco from 1971. It was equipped with a GM locomotive engine developing 2,000 horsepower, and was propelled by an electric motor in each rear axle. Initially rated at 200 tons, its capacity was later increased to 250 tons. It measured over 52 feet long and 24 feet wide. *Komatsu America International*

In 1978, Wabco launched an interesting coal hauler in the form of the "Coalpak." This rear-engined, bottom-dumping unit could carry 170 tons. It was powered by a 1,600-horsepower engine, and utilized electric wheel drive. This type of hauler is known as a "unitized" hauler because of its nonarticulated design. *Komatsu America International*

Designed by Ralph Kress when he joined the Kress Corporation, this 150-ton capacity unitized hauler has a rear engine and is mechanically driven through its rear wheels. A unique feature is the capability of turning its front wheels at right angles to the direction of travel for the tightest possible turns. The first fleet of Kress trucks was purchased in 1971 by the Captain Mine in Illinois. The one illustrated worked at Consol's Burning Star No. 4 Mine in Illinois. *JKH collection*

The CH-300, the largest truck ever built by Kress Corporation, went to work for the Coteau Properties coal mine in North Dakota in 1994. Carrying well over 300 tons, this huge vehicle is claimed to be the largest coal hauler currently in operation. *Kress Corporation*

had one of the 1LLDs rebuilt with twin 375-horsepower engines, and added a semitrailer that increased its capacity to 150 tons, resulting in a GVW of 590,000 pounds. More power was added in 1960, when twin 425-horsepower 12V71 General Motors engines were installed.

The R-X, a rear-dump hauler with a unique four-wheel-drive, articulated-frame concept, entered the market in 1965. A pair of tires on each of the four wheels carried an equal share of the loaded truck. It steered by use of hydraulic cylinders acting between the front and rear frames. Known as the R-105 from 1969, this truck came with engines ranging from 700 to 1,000 horsepower, and capacities from 85 to 105 tons.

Euclid experimented with a 210-ton capacity truck in 1971, having gas turbine power and electric wheel drive. Power came from an Avco-Lycoming 1,850-horsepower gas turbine. Although only one was built, the R-210 made headlines around the world. Like the R-105, the R-210 had equal weight distribution and electric drive to its four wheels.

Although the brand name has remained unchanged, Euclid has had several owners. In 1953, it became a division of General Motors. Then in 1968 it became a subsidiary of White Motor Corporation, following a Justice Department ruling. The ruling stated that GM had to discontinue the manufacture and sale of off-highway trucks in the United States for a period of four years, and divest itself of the Euclid name. The GM plant in Scotland was allowed to continue building trucks under another name. Thus the name Terex was given to the continuing GM

Starting at the top end of the scale, Wiseda's first truck was the 220-ton capacity Model 2450, introduced at the Las Vegas mining show in 1982. After tests, the truck was boosted to 240-ton capacity. The diesel-electric 2450 truck is powered by a 2,000-horsepower engine. In 1995, Liebherr acquired Wiseda, and the company became known as Liebherr Mining Truck, Inc. *Liebherr Mining Truck, Inc.*

The Mack Model AP "Bulldog" was an upgrade from the famous Model AC. This is one of two delivered to the Columbia Iron Mining Co. in 1934-35 for use at Desert Mound, Utah. It carries a steel "bathtub" body of 10-ton capacity. This style of body, as well as many other features on this AP truck, were developed at the Boulder Dam site beginning in 1931, where Mack ACs and APs played a major role in its construction. They were the first trucks on record to be built specially for off-highway use. *Eric Orlemann collection*

A Mack Model LR truck hauling two Easton side-dumping trailers. *JKH collection*

The L-series trucks represented Mack's off-highway truck line from 1940 to 1960. The popular 34-ton capacity Model LRVSW was equipped with a torque converter and a 400-horsepower engine.

The M-series Mack trucks, first appearing in 1960, were the mainstay of Mack's off-highway line until the company's withdrawal from that business. Shown is a Mack 75-ton M-series, bottom-dump coal hauler at work in a Texas coal mine in 1984.

products on a worldwide basis. Daimler-Benz acquired Euclid in 1977, and sold it to Clark-Michigan Company in 1984. The following year, Clark entered into a joint venture with Volvo AB of Sweden, and the VME (Volvo-Michigan-Euclid) name was established. In 1992, VME teamed up with Hitachi to form Euclid-Hitachi Heavy Equipment Inc., which makes the current line of haulers.

Currently, Euclid offers 12 rear-dump haul trucks from 32 to 262 tons in capacity. The largest, the R-260, was introduced at the Minexpo mining show in Las Vegas in 1996. The diesel-electric truck is

powered by a Detroit S-4000 diesel of 2,500 horsepower and has a GVW of 850,800 pounds. With the exception of the two smallest trucks in the line (R-32 and R-36), all Euclid trucks are now built in the Guelph, Ontario, Canada, plant, which the company acquired in 1972 from Bucyrus-Erie Company. The two smallest trucks are Volvo-designed, having a heritage from the former Swedish truck manufacturer, Kockums, and are built in Poland. A line of articulated dump trucks with capacity of up to 40 tons is also sold under the Volvo name.

The Liebherr Model 2420 truck was introduced into the 200-ton class at the Minexpo 1996. *Liebherr Mining Truck, Inc.*

Goodbary

Goodbary trucks were built from 1976 to 1980, taking their name from the company founder, E.R. Goodbary, formerly with the Unit Rig company. They were sold in capacities from 100 to 170 tons, and offered with engines in the 1,000- to 1,200-horsepower range. Goodbary trucks were diesel-electric drive, and were of the unitized bottom-dumping type. This meant that, unlike most bottom-dumping haulers, the unit had a rigid frame instead of an articulated design.

The rights to manufacture and market the Goodbary haulers were acquired by Dart Truck Company in 1980, but no further trucks were built.

Komatsu/Haulpak/Wabco

Wabco was formed in 1953, when R.G. LeTourneau's earthmoving business was purchased by the Westing-house Air Brake Company (WABCO). Although L-W senior management was committed to the earthmoving equipment business, it did not offer an off-highway hauler except for the Tournarocker (articulated rear dump) types inherited from R. G. LeTourneau. Accordingly, Ralph Kress was hired in 1955 to design a new line of off-highway trucks at the Peoria, Illinois, headquarters. The first two trucks were a 30-ton rear-dump and an 80-ton tractor-trailer, bottom-dump coal hauler with a 450-horsepower Cummins engine. The first Wabco truck left the Peoria, Illinois, plant and led the 1957 Thanksgiving Day Parade on its way to the Midland Mine, located 25 miles to the west.

By 1961, Wabco's truck line had expanded to include 22-, 27-, 32-, 42-, and 60-ton sizes. In 1965, the 120A rear-dump hauler was introduced, featuring electric wheel drive and a 930-horsepower V12 Fairbanks Morse diesel engine. The 120A was later upgraded to a 120-ton capac-

International first offered off-highway trucks in 1957. In 1963, the Payhauler 100 of 30-ton capacity was launched. It soon replaced the original 24-ton Model 95.

In 1973, Mack introduced its last off-highway truck—the "Mack-Pack." This unique vehicle was mechanically driven on all four wheels from a single 475-horsepower engine mounted on the rear frame. The bottom-dump outfit carried 35 tons and measured 46 feet 4 inches from front to rear. *Tom Berry*

The 180 Payhauler was the first of an entirely new line of trucks International brought out in 1963. The four-wheel-drive truck of rigid frame proved a great success in a niche market—locations where underfoot conditions are poor. The 180 first came out as a 45-ton truck, and capacity was later increased to 50 tons. *JKH collection*

Rimpull Corporation was established in 1971. Its mechanical-drive trucks became popular with some of the largest surface coal mining companies in the 1970s. Here a 150-ton Rimpull hauls coal in an Indiana coal mine in 1977.

As a direct descendent of the 180 Payhauler, shown in the previous picture, the Model 350 was adopted by Payhauler Corporation, a new company formed when International sold its construction equipment lines in 1982. After many upgrades, the current 50-ton Model 350C Payhauler is the truck now offered by the company. *Payhauler Corporation*

ity and GM 1,000-horsepower engine, and was also offered as a tractor-trailer rear-dump to carry 160 tons.

The 2,000-horsepower giant Model 3200 tandem-drive diesel-electric truck, equipped with a GM 645-E4 locomotive engine, was launched in 1971. Capacity was initially rated at 200 tons and later rose to 250 tons. It measured 24 feet wide and over 52 feet long. Wabco introduced a 120-ton mechanical-drive truck in 1978. That same year, the "Coalpak" unitized bottom-dump coal hauler came out. With a capacity of 170 tons, the Coalpak featured electric wheel drive and rear-mounted engine.

In 1984, Wabco became a division of Dresser Industries, Inc. Soon after, the entire truck line was revamped, and the Wabco name dropped. The new Dresser model designations now reflected the GVW of the vehicle, the line ranging from the 35-ton Model 140M with 140,000 pounds GVW to the 240-ton 830E at 830,000 pounds GVW.

In 1988, Japan's Komatsu Ltd. and Dresser Industries, Inc., began a joint venture for the manufacturing and marketing of construction and mining equipment in the Western Hemisphere—Komatsu Dresser Company (KDC). Since then, Komatsu has acquired 100 percent interest in KDC, and the trucks carry the name

Komatsu "Haulpak." Since 1997, they have been marketed under a new company, Komatsu Mining Systems. The "Haulpak" trade name continues, as it has since the inception of these trucks in the mid-1950s.

The latest top-of-the-line truck from Komatsu Mining Systems is the 930E with a payload rating up to 320 tons, and maximum GVW of 1,059,000 pounds. Apart from its size, the industry's first electric wheel drive utilizing AC motors was the real breakthrough. Launched at Minexpo Las Vegas in 1996, the 930E truck is 26 feet 7 inches wide, 24 feet high, and over 50 feet long.

Kress

The Kress Corporation of Brimfield, Illinois, makes the famous rigid-framed, bottom-dump coal carrier in capacities from 110 to 300 tons, including the largest coal hauler of any type currently offered. The Kress Corporation was formed in 1965 to design special purpose vehicles, such as slag pot carriers primarily for steel mills and smelters. This is the largest part of the company's business today, and Kress is now by far the world leader in this market.

In 1969, Ralph Kress joined his son's business and went to work designing a new off-highway coal hauler. Two years later, the first of five Kress haulers was put into service at the Captain Mine, in Illinois, replacing the 240-ton Caterpillar electric trucks as mentioned earlier. These were 150-ton unitized (rigid-frame), bottom-dump haulers with rear engine and 180-degree steering.

The Kress hauler is mechanical drive, and designed to haul its large load at up to 60 miles per hour on a smooth

The biggest Rimpull built to date is this CW-280 bottom-dump coal hauler. It is presently carrying 300-ton loads at a coal mine in Wyoming. *Rimpull Corporation*

Representing the line of Rimpull's rear-dump haulers is this RD-120, which can be powered by either Cummins or Detroit diesels in the 1,000-horsepower class. The unit shown is taking on a 120-ton load at a Wyoming coal mine.

A Terex R-65 rear-dump hauler in a deep open pit coal mine for British contractor Sir Lindsay Parkinson & Company. Built in Scotland and Canada, the R-65 was introduced in 1968. Its power comes from a GM 16V-71T engine developing 700 gross horsepower.

road. The four front wheels, straddle-mounted in pairs, are capable of turning 90 degrees to the truck frame, allowing extremely tight turns in a narrow coal cut.

The largest Kress trucks sold to date are three CH-300 units sold to Coteau Properties in North Dakota in 1994. Hauling more than 300 tons, they were the largest coal haulers operating in 1997.

Liebherr/Wiseda

Wiseda started at the top when it launched its first truck, a 220-ton monster, at the Las Vegas mining show in 1982. Established in Cardin, Oklahoma, the company concentrated on this one large model, which was tested

at several coal mining operations. The Model KL-2450 truck increased to a 240-ton capacity by 1985, and was the first in that size range on two axles. In the mid-1980s, fleets of Wisedas were sold to the Black Thunder Mine, Wyoming, the largest coal mine in the United States; to Australia's Mount Newman Mining Company; and other locations.

The KL-2450 is an electric-drive truck with General Electric DC motors in the rear wheel hubs. Power is offered from a Detroit, Cummins, or MTU diesel engine in the 2,000-horsepower class.

In 1995, Liebherr-America, Inc., acquired Wiseda, and the new company, Liebherr Mining Truck, Inc.,

The largest Terex mechanical-drive truck was this 33-14, unveiled at the American Mining Congress Show in Las Vegas in 1978. It is in the 120-ton class and is powered by a 1,200-horsepower (gross) Detroit 12V-149T1 diesel. *Eric Orlemann collection*

First built as a prototype in 1971 at the Canadian plant of General Motors Diesel Division, the Terex 33-15 electric-drive truck of 150-ton capacity was the first of GM's new line of trucks to be marketed after the imposed four-year hiatus. The 33-15B shown here has been up-rated to 170 tons, and carries a Detroit 16V-149T1 engine with 1,600 gross horsepower. GM retained its electric truck line when it sold its mechanical-drive, off-highway trucks and other earthmoving lines to IBH in 1981. *Jack Grimes photography*

was established. The Model KL-2450 was continued, and a year later, a new smaller model was added, the KL-2420 in the 190- to 210-ton size rating. The 340-ton KL-2680, launched in 1998, featured an AC wheel motor drive system. The new truck, with engine choices of MTU and Cummins up to 3,200 horsepower, was jointly developed by Siemens and Liebherr, and today competes with the largest trucks on the market.

The latest truck development from Liebherr is the IL-2600. Resulting from a Technology Licensing Agreement between Liebherr and BHP Coal Pty. Ltd. (Australia), a truck of radical new design has reached the prototype stage. The IL-2600, in the 240- to 300-ton class, is designed from a "clean slate," with the objective of decreasing structural weight, thereby increasing the payload-to-weight ratio. The design features four inline rear wheels, straddle-mounted in pairs. The rear frame has no lateral support, so necessary strength is provided by a beefed-up truck box.

On January 1998, Liebherr established a new division, Liebherr Mining Equipment Company, to market its haul trucks and largest of its hydraulic excavators. New model numbers were issued—the KL-2420 became the T252, the KL-2450 became the T262, and the KL-2680 became the T282.

In 1985, General Motors finally sold its Titan truck line to Marathon-LeTourneau Company (now LeTourneau Inc.) of Longview, Texas. The line was subsequently expanded and upgraded. Since 1987, LeTourneau has offered its "T" series electric-drive trucks, ranging up to 240-ton capacity. The 200-ton T-2000 shown here is offered with either Cummins or Detroit power in the 2,000-horsepower class. *LeTourneau Inc.*

The biggest truck in the world! At the time of writing, the heaviest and most powerful truck ever built is the famous Terex Titan 33-19, first shown at the American Mining Congress show, Las Vegas, in 1974. Designed to carry 350 tons, the behemoth measures over 67 feet long, 26 feet wide, and boasts a GVW of 1,209,500 pounds. Each of its 10 11-foot tires weighs 3 1/2 tons. The Titan 33-19's reign as the world's largest truck is about to be eclipsed after nearly a quarter-century, as larger trucks are being developed by the world's truck manufacturers. *JKH collection*

Currently the largest of the new 33-series trucks from the Terex plant in Scotland is the Model 33100 at 100-ton capacity. Its engine is a Cummins KTA38-C of 1,050 gross horsepower. *Terex Corporation*

Mack

Mack Trucks Inc. of Allentown, Pennsylvania, is one of America's most famous highway truck builders with its history dating back to 1902. From the outset, Mack established a reputation for building heavy-duty reliable trucks used in all kinds of industries. In 1915, the famous Model AC was released. When a major order of 150 units was placed by the British Army in 1917 during World War I, Army officers dubbed the rugged vehicles "Bulldog," after their likeness to the British canine. The heavy-duty chain-driven Bulldog found its way onto many earthmoving projects and under steam shovels of the 1920s and 1930s. The AC remained in the Mack line until 1938, by which time, over 40,000 had been built. In contrast to the size of today's "heavy" trucks of over 300 ton capacity, Mack classified the AC models from 7 1/2- to 10-ton capacity as its "Heavy-Duty" series. They were at the leading edge of truck size and technology. It is amazing how far we have come in the last 60 years!

The success and reliability of the Mack Bulldog, and the need for a robust off-highway vehicle, intensified Mack's interest in the off-highway hauler market. Beginning in 1931, Mack played a major role in hauling rock for the famous Boulder Dam project (now Hoover Dam). In fact, Mack designed heavy-duty trucks specifically for the job. Mack AC, and the larger Model AP from the same family of trucks, were used in large numbers on this project. The APs were specially modified for rugged off-highway use. Still chain-driven, they had heavy steel bodies of rounded design to withstand rock loading and dumping. The larger trucks were tandem drive, and in 1932, some were fitted with aluminum bodies that enabled them to carry 25-ton loads. The APs at Boulder were regarded as the first trucks in the industry to be expressly designed

Unit Rig rapidly expanded its electric truck line-up to this 200-ton model by 1968. Equipped with a 1,650-horsepower engine, the M-200 was not only the largest truck on the market, it attained that capacity on only four wheels. The M-200 shown here is being loaded at a coal mine in southern British Columbia, Canada, by a new O&K RH-120C hydraulic excavator. *Steen Ahlberg, O&K*

Unit Rig & Equipment Company burst on the scene in 1963 with its 85-ton M-85 "Lectrahaul" electric-drive truck. The electric-drive principle found immediate acceptance with the world's surface mines. *JKH collection*

for off-road use. The ruggedness of these Macks led to the expression "Built like a Mack truck."

Mack increased its off-highway presence in the 1930s and 1940s with the F-series, introduced in 1937 with GVW up to 100,000 pounds. From 1940 to 1960, Mack catered for the off-highway industry with the L-series of four-wheel and six-wheel tandem trucks. The largest was the LYSW of 40-ton capacity, which was fitted with a 450-horsepower Cummins NVH12V1 engine. But more popular was the LRVSW of 34-ton capacity, powered with the same engine as its larger brother.

In 1960, a new line of trucks, the M-series, with modern styling, started to replace the L-series. The line consisted of both single- and tandem-drive axle types, denoted by the suffix AX and SX model designations. The largest were tandem-drive units reaching to 100-ton capacity in the M-100SX by 1966. Only three of the largest were made, but the smaller 70-ton M-70SX, unveiled in 1965, and its successor, the M-75SX in 1970, were much more popular. These were fitted with 700-horsepower Cummins engines.

In 1973, the Mack-Pack, a unique articulated bottom-dumping hauler of 35-ton capacity, was released. All four wheels were driven from a rear-mounted Detroit 12V71N 475-horsepower engine. The front wheels were driven via a prop shaft over 20 feet long, running through a trough in the body. The Mack-Pack was Mack's last fling at the off-highway market. In 1979, the company withdrew from the off-highway truck market, and the last truck left the factory in 1981.

Michigan

Well known for its wheel loaders and scrapers, Clark Equipment Company added an off-road rear-dump haul truck to its line in 1965. It was the modern-looking T-65 of 65-ton capacity, equipped with air-over-oil suspension, and offered with Cummins or GM diesels of 700 horsepower. Intended to be the first of a line of haulers, the T-65 had only a short life, with about eight being built. These all operated in the United Kingdom in various open pit coal mines. Michigan was not involved in off-highway haulers again until it purchased Euclid in 1984.

M-R-S

M-R-S Manufacturing Company (Mississippi Road Services) originated the "Mississippi Wagon" in 1943. This was a bottom-dumping four-wheel trailer pulled behind a heavy-duty four-wheel tractor. This hauler's distinctive feature was its load transfer capability. A hydraulic cylinder mounted between the tractor drawbar and the yoke of the trailer could lift the front trailer axle, transferring weight to the rear tractor wheels. So when the going was good, all the load was carried by the trailer. In soft ground conditions, the weight could be transferred back to the driving wheels for maximum traction.

M-R-S developed a line of haulers from 13- to 20-ton capacity based on International prime movers. By the 1950s, M-R-S was producing a range of its own tractors in sizes up to the Model 250, with 500-horsepower Cummins diesel power. These pulled wagons up to 50-ton capacity. The M-R-S tractors were often found pulling M-R-S and other brands of scrapers (Chapter 4). M-R-S products are still available today from Taylor Machine Works, which purchased M-R-S in 1986.

This is the Unit Rig BD-180, one of the largest coal haulers available in the 1970s. With a choice of engines up to 1,600 horsepower, the BD-180 was designed to carry 180 tons of coal. *JKH collection*

At the time of writing, the largest truck from Unit Rig is this MT-4400 Lectrahaul, announced in 1995. Rated at 260-ton capacity, this electric rear-dump hauler is powered with an MTU 396 diesel of 2,467 horsepower. *Eric Orlemann*

Payhauler/International

In 1957, International burst onto the off-highway truck scene with the Models 65 and 95 Payhaulers of 18- and 24-ton capacity, powered by 250- and 335-horsepower International engines. Through upgrades, the 65 lasted in the line until 1973, by which time the 65C was rated at 22 tons. The 95 remained until 1965 when it was supplanted by the Payhauler 100, released a couple of years earlier as a 30-ton truck. The 100, in its final B-series version, was in production from 1967 to 1971.

In 1963, the Payhauler 180 made International's big breakthrough in the off-highway truck market. The truck was designed from a totally new approach, with convention cast aside. The result was a four-wheel-drive, rigid-frame, 45-ton rear-dump hauler with dual tires all around, and the front the same size as the rear. This configuration, with equal weight distribution on each wheel, was a resounding success. It found a niche market on construction sites and surface mines, especially where soft ground was encountered. Competition from other manufacturers was nonexistent. In 1968, the line was expanded with the Payhauler 140 (36- and 40-ton sizes) and Payhauler 180 (45- and 50-ton sizes). So successful were these models, International had discontinued all its other off-highway models by 1973. That year, the Payhauler models were revamped and renumbered as the 330, 340, and 350, covering the same size range.

When International sold its construction equipment lines in 1982, the off-highway Payhaulers were sold to a new company, named appropriately, Payhauler Corporation, established at Batavia, Illinois. However, only the 50-ton Model 350B was marketed. It featured dozens of improvements and eventually evolved into the 350C. Terex Corporation purchased Payhauler in 1998, and the niche market for this unique truck continues.

Rimpull

Rimpull was established in 1971, and began developing a line of mechanical-drive haul trucks. The company's slogan was "Back to Basics." At the time, most manufacturers were promoting electric trucks with elaborate drive and suspension systems. The first two 100-ton Rimpulls were delivered in 1973, and by 1975, fleets of 150-ton bottom-dump coal haulers had been sold to several coal mining companies. From 1975 to 1980, Rimpull produced over 50 vehicles for the 1,000-plus horsepower class, more than any other manufacturer of mechanical-drive trucks. During this same period, Rimpull delivered over 75 vehicles in the 100-plus-ton payload class.

By 1979, Rimpull offered a line consisting of five rear-dump models ranging from 65- to 120-ton capacity and five tractor-trailer bottom-dump haulers from 100- to 170-ton capacity. In 1980, a 200-ton capacity bottom-dump unit with a 1,200-horsepower Detroit engine was introduced.

Today, mechanically driven Rimpull trucks offer rear-dump designs from 85- to 120-ton capacity. The bottom-dump line has been expanded even further to include the 180-ton CW-180, as well as the 300-ton CW-280, which is presently working in a western coal mine. It is powered by Detroit or Cummins engines of 1,600 horsepower.

This is the original Mississippi Wagon, which put M-R-S Manufacturing Company in the hauler business. This early version is built around an International tractor. Note the hydraulic cylinder mounted on the towing hitch, the distinctive M-R-S feature that can transfer weight from the trailer to the tractor driving wheels to increase traction. *Taylor Machine Works*

Long before the present-day LeTourneau company offered its electric-drive trucks, the former R.G. LeTourneau Inc. experimented with a great variety of electrically driven trucks. The picture shows the one and only TR-60, delivered to the Anaconda Company at Butte, Montana, in 1960. Its electric wheels could either be powered from its own diesel engine, or from a trolley system utilizing an overhead line pickup, saving diesel fuel. The 75-ton hauler is now preserved in the Butte Mining Museum. *JKH collection*

Terex

A U.S. Justice Department ruling was the impetus behind the birth of Terex in 1968. General Motors (GM) had to discontinue the manufacture and sale of off-highway trucks in the United States for a period of four years, and divest itself of the Euclid name. (See under Euclid.) Terex was the name assigned to all GM products, which included trucks and other earthmoving equipment lines, made in the plant in Scotland.

Thus in 1972, GM reentered the off-highway truck market with a new line of models known as the 33-series. The first was the 33-15, a 150-ton diesel-electric rear-dump hauler, which had appeared as a prototype a year earlier. The 33-series trucks were rapidly introduced from 1971 to 1974, filling out a seven-model lineup from the 22-ton 33-03 to the giant diesel-electric 33-19. The 33-19 was known as the "Titan," the world's largest truck, at 350 tons in capacity. The Titan and the 33-15, both electric trucks, were built by the GM Diesel Division in London, Ontario. The other 33-series eventually replaced

WHY ONLY ONE TEREX TITAN?

After the Terex Titan went to work, the world coal markets softened, and most mines had to cut back on production. Many new mine developments could have utilized the Titan. Instead, most mining companies rebuilt aging equipment rather than purchase new machines at ever-increasing prices. Those companies that did purchase new trucks wanted proven units with a large worldwide population. Thus, 33-19s weren't in demand and no more were built.

Large capacity trucks are not a thing of the past. Several current truck designs exceed 300-ton capacity. Tires and engines have increased in size, but technology to make the trucks more user-friendly has improved drastically since the Titan was designed over 25 years ago. The new trucks are able to be carried on just four wheels rather than the six-wheel configuration of the Titan. Modern large trucks have a higher payload-to-weight ratio, resulting in less fuel per pound needed to carry the load. They also have higher road speeds, making them altogether more efficient for today's demanding user.

Several highway truck manufacturers ventured into off-highway vehicles at different times in the past. Here a Kenworth LW-848 is attached to a 70-ton coal trailer for work in a western Canadian coal mine. It is powered by a 370-horsepower Cummins engine.

Autocar was another famous highway truck builder who ventured into off-highway models. Shown is a Model AP-40 of 40-ton capacity, powered by a Cummins VT-12 engine developing 600 horsepower. *American Truck Historical Society archives*

the R-series, which had been in continuous production at GM's Scottish plant since its establishment by Euclid in 1950. The largest Terex mechanical-drive truck was the 120-ton 33-14, introduced in 1978.

Accolades for the largest and heaviest truck ever built go to the 33-19 Titan. It was unveiled at the American Mining Congress Exhibition in Las Vegas in October 1974. The behemoth measured almost 67 feet long by 26 feet wide, weighed 509,500 pounds empty, and boasted a GVW of 1,209,500 pounds. Using the same diesel-electric drive technology as GM's railroad locomotives, the Titan was powered by a 16-cylinder GM 16-645E4 engine, was rated at 3,300 horsepower, ran at a low 900 rpm flat out, and had a 315-rpm idle speed. The Titan ran on ten

40.00x57 tires, which are over 11 feet in diameter, and weighed in excess of 3 1/2 tons each. A unique feature was its rear bogie, which was made to steer automatically with the front wheels, to reduce tire scuffing.

The 33-19 was more than double the size of Terex's next largest truck—the 150-ton 33-15. It spent most of its working life at the Balmer Mine of Westar Mining Ltd. in British Columbia. Today the Titan is restored, and is a tourist attraction at Sparwood, British Columbia.

From 1981 to 1983, Terex was owned by the German conglomeration IBH, although the Terex electric trucks were retained by GM. When IBH failed, GM purchased Terex back, then sold it to Northwest Engineering Company in 1986. The following year, Terex Corporation succeeded Northwest as the parent company name. In 1988, Terex purchased truck builder Unit Rig of Tulsa, Oklahoma, giving the company a broader range that included electric-drive trucks.

Meanwhile, the Scottish plant unabatedly continued to roll out the 33-series mechanical-drive haulers, introducing new models and updating others throughout the 1980s and 1990s. In 1992, Terex made an agreement with German O&K to build Terex trucks badged with the O&K name. In 1997, five sizes from 35 to 100 tons were offered as O&K Models K-35, K-40, K-45, K-60, and K-100. These same trucks are sold as the Terex 3335, 3340, 3345, 3360, and 33100. Terex also offers a line of four articulated dump trucks up to 40-ton capacity. In late 1997, it was announced that Terex had purchased O&K's mining division which includes the haul trucks.

LeTourneau/Titan

When the Terex Division of General Motors was sold to IBH of Germany in 1981, GM retained the diesel-electric product line, which included the 33-15B and 33-19 Titan. Both models were made at GM Diesel Division at London, Ontario. The 33-15B was up-rated to 170 tons. Since the Titan name was well known, it was adopted for the GM Division. Only the 33-15B model was marketed, and inside a year, it changed into the 33-15C, with a long list of improvements.

In 1985, the Titan Division was sold to Marathon-LeTourneau Company of Longview, Texas (now LeTourneau, Inc.), putting that company back in the hauler business after an absence of almost two decades. Since the 1920s, R.G. LeTourneau, Inc., has made many different types of haulers. Most haulers were trailer types with a rear- or bottom-dumping design towed behind Tournapulls. (Chapter 4) In 1960, the first of LeTourneau's TR-series electric-drive trucks went to work for Anaconda Company's Berkeley Pit in Montana. This was a trolley-assisted rear dump carrying 75 tons. After a productive life, this truck is now preserved at the

Butte Mining Museum, Montana. Other TR models followed, including the 30-ton Model TR-30 in 1963, and the TR-100, a side-dumping electric 100-ton hauler.

Today's LeTourneau trucks incorporate several design improvements on the 33-15C acquired from GM. In 1987, LeTourneau came out with the T-2000 series of trucks. Initially ranging from 170- to 200-ton capacity, the line was boosted in 1990 with the 240-ton Model T-2240.

Unit Rig

Established in 1935 to build oil well servicing equipment, Unit Rig & Equipment Company first entered the off-highway truck field in 1963 with the M-85 diesel-electric truck. However, a prototype electric truck made an appearance in 1960. Using the trade name Lectrahaul, the line soon expanded to include nine models of trucks, with General Electric wheels, and payloads from 85- to 200-ton capacity. In 1968, Unit Rig introduced the world's largest truck—the M-200. This remarkable vehicle was the first to attain 200-ton capacity on only four wheels.

The Lectrahauls enjoyed immediate success and paved the way for general acceptance of the electric wheel drive truck in the world's surface mines. By 1979, the 2,500th Lectrahaul had been delivered, and the company boasts it has produced more diesel-electric trucks than all other makes combined.

Unit Rig produced the BD-145, a rigid-frame, bottom-dump hauler of 145-ton capacity, which ran at the Captain Mine, in Illinois, in 1977. It had a 1,200-horsepower rear-mounted engine, and of course, the drive was through electric wheels. Only one BD-145 was built before it was updated to the similarly designed 145-ton capacity BD-30. Unit Rig also developed large bottom-dump, tractor-trailer coal haulers, such as the 180-ton capacity BD-180 that was first delivered in 1972. When the BD-240 went to work at the Caballo Mine of Carter Mining in Wyoming in 1986, it claimed the title of the world's largest bottom-dump truck. Carrying 240 tons, the BD-240 tractor unit is based on the 170-ton Mark 36 rear-dump hauler. Bottom-dump hauler size continued to grow, and in 1997, the largest offered by Unit Rig was the BD-270, a 270-ton model with engine choices of up to 2,000 horsepower.

Unit Rig today also offers six sizes of rear-dump trucks from 120- to 320-ton capacity. The 260-ton MT-4400 was the largest available when it was introduced in 1995. The prototype MT-4800 features AC electric drive made by General Atomics. At 320 tons, this will be the largest Lectrahaul to date.

Unit Rig became a division of Terex Corporation in 1988. The line remained unchanged, as the electric-drive trucks complemented the mechanical-drive trucks in the existing Terex line.

Famous for its range of wheeled loaders, Clark-Michigan started in the haul truck business in 1965. The T-65 model of 65-ton capacity could be powered with Cummins or GM engines of 700 horsepower. Although Clark had sights on further truck sizes, the truck line plans never materialized, and the short-lived T-65 was the only model built. *Volvo Construction Equipment*

Another make of truck with a short life was the V-Con, made by the Peerless Manufacturing Company in 1971. This giant was rated at 260-ton capacity. Running on four pairs of straddle-mounted wheels, it was fitted with an Alco 3,000-horsepower locomotive engine. Marion Power Shovel acquired the rights to the V-Con trucks in 1973. *Eric Orlemann collection*

V-Con

The Vehicle Constructors Division (V-Con) of Peerless Manufacturing Company, Dallas, Texas, was formed in 1969, with a vision of building the world's largest mining truck. It did. In 1971, V-Con started testing the Model 3006. Rated at 260 tons, and fitted with an Alco 3,000-horsepower locomotive engine, the diesel-electric truck moved on eight wheels, straddle-mounted in pairs. It was first tested at the Pima Mine in Arizona.

The 3006 truck, and the V-Con large-wheel dozers described in Chapter 2, attracted the attention of Marion Power Shovel Company, which acquired the V-Con Division in its entirety in 1973. Several truck sizes were offered and heavily promoted, but nothing more was achieved in sales.

Goodbary trucks were built only from 1976 to 1980. They were of the bottom-dump unitized type with electric drive to the rear wheels only. The unitized-frame design was said to combine the advantages of the rear-dump rigid-frame type with the tractor-trailer bottom-dump hauler. The Model CP-2400 shown is equipped with a Cummins KT2300 engine of 1,050 horsepower. It is carrying a 110-ton load of coal for a western Canadian mine in 1986.

The Holland Loader Company offers the Model 180 bottom-dump hauler, capable of carrying loads of up to 200 tons. The tractor unit is fitted with a Cummins KTA1150C diesel of 600 horsepower. The trailer is of a unique clamshell design which splits down the center when dumping. The doors form a 16-foot-wide opening when fully open, as shown in the picture. *Holland Loader Company*

The "Cradle-Dump" trailer coupled to the "Hug Lugger" tractor was one of the first methods of hauling large volumes of earth offered by the LeTourneau company in the 1930s. Developed jointly by LeTourneau and the Hug Company, the trailer could carry 45 tons of material, while the tractor was the Caterpillar diesel-powered Hug Model 100 with four-wheel drive.

The Trojan Truck Manufacturing Company built the world's largest trucks from 1938 to 1940. With an enormous payload of 70 tons, these outsize vehicles were equipped with a pair of Caterpillar D17000 diesel engines. Note the triple tires on each of the rear wheels. A 1938 Fageol truck heads the trailer outfit hauling the Trojan to the job site. *Leigh Knudson collection*

Other Off-Highway Trucks

Internationally, several manufacturers have built large trucks over the years. Examples include the French-built Berliet 100-ton tandem truck of 1958, and the Secmafer line of trucks, of up to 150 tons, built in the mid-1970s. Currently, Perlini in Italy makes a full line of mechanical-drive trucks of up to 100-ton capacity.

Belaz, located at Minsk in the former Soviet Union, claims to be the world's largest maker of off-highway trucks, building 4,000–4,500 units per year. Belaz introduced a 200-ton truck in 1981 and currently supplies trucks in capacities from 33 to 310 tons. The largest, the Model 7550, is an articulated-frame design, powered by a Russian-made, low-speed locomotive engine and propelled by DC electric motors in all four wheels. The Model 7550 is the largest Belaz makes, but it remains in prototype stage. In 1997, the prototype had achieved five years of operation.

Chapter Seven

LARGE CABLE EXCAVATORS

The cable-operated excavator is the earliest documented self-powered machine ever used to move earth. Its earliest form, the steam shovel, has roots going back to the very first mechanical excavator, the Otis Steam Shovel of 1835. (Chapter 1) Today, cable excavators have been all but eclipsed by other types of equipment, such as hydraulic excavators, wheel loaders, and tractor-mounted attachments. The cable excavators that do survive are the large shovels and draglines, usually electrically powered, and found in surface mining and quarrying operations. Chapter 8 describes the very largest shovels, the stripping shovels, while Chapter 9 covers walking draglines. This chapter traces the development of the intermediate-sized two-crawler excavators, featuring the primary manufacturers.

Hundreds of manufacturers have designed and built cable-operated crawler excavators, but relatively few have ventured into sizes much above the 6-cubic yard size which are classified as quarry and mine machines. These have included Weserhutte and Menck & Hambrock from Germany; Ruston & Hornsby from England; and Clark/Lima, Manitowoc, P&H, Bucyrus-Erie (now Bucyrus International), Marion, and American Hoist from the United States; as well as some makers in the former Soviet Union.

In the category of cable-operated machines greater than 12 cubic yards, the list shrinks to just four manufacturers in North America (Bucyrus-Erie, Marion, Manitowoc, and P&H) and some from the former Soviet Union. From the beginning, these manufacturers have supplied the entire world with this category of excavators.

The boom in surface mining in the 1970s brought larger two-crawler shovels to load the larger trucks. Into the 1990s, the truck size increased to well over 300 tons. Since customers demand three-pass loading of these large trucks, shovel manufacturers have responded. Consequently, unlike the giant stripping shovels and walking draglines, which reached their peak size nearly three decades ago, the two-crawler electric shovel has continued its upward trend in size.

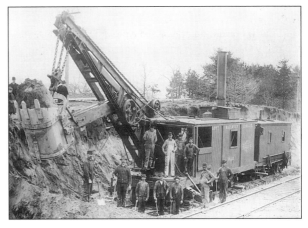

The Bucyrus Foundry and Manufacturing Company was established in 1880. It commenced building shovels when it took over manufacture of the Thompson railroad shovel in 1882. The machine shown here was built in 1890, and like most shovels sold in the 1800s, was employed in railroad construction. The modern-day Bucyrus giant mining shovels can trace their ancestry back to this machine. *Bucyrus International*

This is how the first crawler steam shovels looked in the early years of this century. It is an Erie Model A built by the Ball Engine Company from 1916. The shovel is loading a Packard truck in a Lowell, Massachusetts, stone quarry. *JKH collection*

The Bucyrus 50-B steam shovel made a big impact in heavy-duty loading applications when the Bucyrus Company launched it in 1922. The 2-yard shovel was eventually made available with gasoline, diesel, or electric power. It survived until 1934, after the Bucyrus and Erie companies had merged in 1927. *JKH collection*

The 120-B was the first heavy-duty revolving shovel specifically designed for quarry and surface mining work. It combined the ruggedness of the railroad shovels of the previous era with the revolving capability of the long-boom stripping shovels. First built as a 4-yard machine, it revolutionized the shovel industry. Later it became a 5-yard shovel, and remained in production until 1951, after over 400 had been built. *Bucyrus International*

The Bucyrus-Erie 210-B, introduced in 1961, was a large two-crawler diesel-electric dragline. It could swing an 8-cubic yard bucket on a 120-foot boom, and it weighed about 260 tons in operation. *Bucyrus International*

Electric mine and quarry shovels feature separate electric motors for each motion (i.e. hoist, crowd, and swing) and receive power via a trailing cable on the ground.

With the takeover of Marion by Bucyrus in 1997, and with Manitowoc discontinuing its single large dragline model, the expanding world market for large cable-operated electric mining shovels is today supplied by just two manufacturers, Bucyrus and P&H.

Bucyrus Large Crawler Excavators

The Bucyrus Foundry and Manufacturing Company was established in 1880, and the present-day Bucyrus International Inc. can boast a rich heritage of specialization in the crane and excavator industry. From the smallest yard crane to some of the largest machines ever to roam the earth, no other company has built such a wide variety of types and sizes of excavating machines. From its floating dredges, tractor equipment, hydraulic excavators, drills, cranes, walking draglines, wheel excavators, and other special equipment, the name Bucyrus has been synonymous with moving the earth.

Several famous names in excavator manufacturing have been acquired by Bucyrus over the years. Bucyrus-Erie Company was formed in 1927 when the Bucyrus Company took over the Erie Steam Shovel Company. Other excavator acquisitions include the Vulcan Steam Shovel Company (1910), Atlantic Equipment Company (1912), Monighan Machine Company (1932), Milwaukee Hydraulics Corporation (1948), Ransomes & Rapier Ltd. (1988), and Marion Power Shovel Company (1997). The company changed its name from Bucyrus-Erie Company to Bucyrus International Inc. in 1996.

Bucyrus-Erie's large two-crawler excavators were a natural progression from its smaller excavators, and filled the gap between these and its giant stripping shovels. From the 1920s, Bucyrus pioneered the "quarry and mine" electric shovels, described later in the chronology

An example of a long-boom stripping shovel mounted on two crawlers is this Bucyrus-Erie 280-B. Normally a 15-yard shovel in standard form, the 90-foot boom on this long-range version permits only an 8-yard dipper. Operating weight is 572 tons. *Bucyrus International*

A midrange electric shovel is this Ruston-Bucyrus 150-RB, made in Lincoln, England. The machine shown carries a dipper of 7 cubic yards. It is loading a Terex R-45 truck at a South Wales coal mine for contractor Sir Lindsay Parkinson & Company.

The largest two-crawler shovel from Bucyrus currently is the 495-B. Introduced in 1990, its dipper range is from 40 to 80 cubic yards, and the standard shovel version has an operating weight of 1,228 tons. *Bucyrus International*

The first excavator built by Harnischfeger Corporation was this P&H Model 210 in 1914. It carried a 1 1/4-cubic yard bucket, and remained in production until 1925. *Harnischfeger Corporation*

The first P&H electric shovel was this Model 1200WL in 1933. With a 2-yard dipper, it was the forerunner of the present-day range of giant mining shovels from Harnischfeger, now the world leader in this type of excavator. *Harnischfeger Corporation*

The world's largest shovel on two crawlers was this P&H 5700LR when it went to work in 1978 at the Captain Mine of Arch Coal Inc. in Illinois. This was the long-boom version of the 5700, which carried a 25-yard dipper on a 90-foot boom. In this configuration, the 5700LR weighed just under 1,800 tons. *Harnischfeger Corporation*

section in this chapter. In the early 1950s, the entire Bucyrus line of electric shovels was replaced by the 110-B, 150-B, and 190-B redesigned models, covering sizes up to 9 cubic yards. These models moved away from the twin-stick, rack-and-pinion type of crowd drive in the earlier design, to the single tubular-stick, rope crowd type. From here the trend was upward in size, keeping pace with growing truck capacity.

The magnificent diesel-electric 210-B came out in 1961 as an 8-yard dragline on two crawlers. In 1972, Bucyrus introduced the 295-B 21-yard shovel, popular for over a decade. The 34-yard 395-B followed in 1979, the first to utilize AC motors and B-E's patent computerized "Acutrol" control, a solid-state computer-driven system. The present two-crawler shovel range spans from the 195-B to the 495-B. In 1990, Bucyrus introduced the 495-B, the largest Bucyrus mining shovel, with a dipper range from 40 to 80 cubic yards and an operating weight of 1,228 tons.

P&H Large Crawler Excavators

Harnischfeger Corporation (P&H) large crawler shovels and draglines have a long pedigree, going back to the company's founders, Alonzo Pawling and Henry

Harnischfeger, in 1884. The company built its first excavator, the gasoline-powered Model 210 in 1914. It carried a 1 1/4-yard dragline bucket and remained in production until 1925. From this model, an extensive range was developed up to the early 1930s. In 1935, an entire new excavator line was launched, incorporating welded construction.

The first electric shovel was the P&H 1200WL, which was built in 1933. With 2-yard capacity, it was the forerunner of the present-day P&H mining shovel line. The basics of the modern P&H shovel, such as crowd motor mounted on the boom and twin handles to support the dipper, were incorporated into the early machine.

P&H was one of the few excavator manufacturers to intensively promote its line of electric shovels in the 1930s and 1940s. This gave P&H the capability to build excavators in sizes larger than the economic limit imposed by the fuel cost of diesel machines. When the going was good in the small "construction-size" market in the four decades from the 1920s, and hundreds of excavators were being sold each month, most makers were content to compete only in this size range. Although P&H did very well in the small machine market, its electric shovel expertise allowed it to continue to prosper after the small machine market dwindled in the 1960s. This mining machine success (spurred on by the popular 15-yard 2100-series electric shovels) allowed P&H to become the dominant force in the cable shovel industry. Today, the P&H 5700XPA version ranks as the world's largest excavator on two crawlers.

P&H also developed some large two-crawler draglines from basic shovel models. In 1954, the 8-yard diesel-electric dragline model 1855 hit the market and was P&H's largest excavator at the time. The 1855 was superseded by the 10-yard diesel-electric 2155 dragline in 1962. Only two of

The P&H 1900AL electric mining shovel is typical of the machines produced by Harnischfeger in the 1970s and 1980s. In its standard form, the 1900AL carried a dipper of 12 cubic yards, and weighed just over 400 tons. The machine shown is owned by contractor Taylor Woodrow and is removing overburden at a British opencast coal mine. *JKH collection*

The first of the P&H excavators designed specifically as a dragline was this Model 1855. Available as a diesel-electric or straight electric machine, the 1855 was introduced in 1954, and could carry an 8-yard bucket on a 160-foot boom. The machine shown is working in a Pennsylvania coal mine. *Harnischfeger Corporation*

A P&H Model 2155 diesel-electric dragline with a 140-foot boom and a 10-cubic yard bucket, stripping coal near Steubenville, Ohio, for the Ohio Edison Coal Company. First going to work in 1962, the Model 2155 replaced the earlier Model 1855 as the largest two-crawler dragline in the P&H line. *Harnischfeger Corporation*

Harnischfeger launched its largest two-crawler dragline, the Model 2355, in 1981. Much larger than the earlier machines of this type, the 2355 can swing an 18-yard bucket on a 160-foot boom. Its operating weight is 765 tons, and it uses the power of two big diesel engines of 2,000 horsepower to drive its motor-generator sets.

Another view of the P&H 2355 diesel-electric dragline, showing the independent electric motor drive to the two crawlers. The machine shown is stripping coal at a western Pennsylvania surface coal mine.

these were ever built. Then, after a hiatus of some 18 years, P&H launched the much larger 2355 in 1981. This state-of-the-art, two-crawler dragline in the 18-yard class is supplied with either diesel or electric power. The diesel version comes with a choice of two big Cummins, Caterpillar, or GM engines, totaling approximately 2,000 horsepower. Its operating weight is 765 tons with 160-foot boom.

Marion Large Crawler Excavators

As one of the pioneering steam shovel manufacturers, Marion Power Shovel Company was established in 1884 as the Marion Steam Shovel Company at Marion, Ohio. Marion evolved into a leading manufacturer of excavating machines. The company went head to head with Bucyrus and manufactured similar products such as railroad shovels, dredges, cranes, walking draglines, and drills. Marion's excavator range extended from the smallest 1/2-yard shovel to the largest shovel ever put to work—the Marion 6360. This behemoth excavator worked at the Captain Mine, Illinois, with a 180-cubic yard dipper!

Marion achieved many notable "firsts" over the years. In 1911, the first long-boom stripping shovel hit the dirt in North America. The company followed it with a succession of record-breaking giant machines. (See Chapter 8 for the story of the stripping shovels.) In 1939, Marion entered the walking dragline business and produced some of the largest models in the world. (Chapter 9)

In the 1960s, Marion gradually withdrew from the small machine market, concentrating instead on large two-crawler excavators above the 10-yard class, walking draglines, and blast hole drills. However, the long-running 3-yard 101-M and 4 1/2-yard 111-M machines were produced at Marion until 1975, and in India under license for several years after that date.

Marion made some famous record-breaking two-crawler excavators, which are described in the Chronology section in this chapter. Over the years, Marion has also designed and built several large two-crawler draglines. A large machine of this type, the 183-M was a diesel-electric 9-yard shovel or dragline introduced in 1956. It remained in the Marion line until 1974 when it was upgraded to a 10-yard dragline, the diesel-electric 184-M. In 1970, the 17-yard 195-M was released as a full electric dragline. Certain customers preferred crawler draglines over walking draglines for applications requiring extensive mobility, or work in confined spaces such as at the bottom of a pit. The largest Marion two-crawler dragline, and currently the largest in the world, was sold to a customer in Australia in 1990. This is the 305-M, which carries buckets of up to 24 cubic yards and weighs 1,225 tons. Only one 305-M has so far been built.

In an effort to increase the dipper capacity of a given shovel size, Marion designed the unusual "Superfront" shovel. An extensive testing program had been carried out starting in 1967 to enlarge dipper size. A Marion 101-M was retrofitted with the first Superfront featuring a 5-cubic yard capacity and representing an increase of 66 percent over its standard dipper size. Further testing with two existing 15-yard Marion 191-Ms proved the concept.

The Superfront's increased capacity comes from its geometry, and the weight saved by the replacement of the

The Marion Steam Shovel Company was established in 1884 to manufacture "Barnhart's Steam Shovel and Wrecking Car." Like all railroad shovels, the Barnhart was mounted on standard railroad trucks, and its boom swung just over 90 degrees to each side. This machine was the forerunner of the giant super shovels built by the Marion company many decades later. *JKH collection*

Coming out in 1948, the popular Marion 111-M was a convertible excavator, available as a shovel or dragline. In standard format, the 111-M was a 4 1/2-yard excavator, although the machine in the picture has a long boom for stripping shovel duties, and a correspondingly smaller dipper of 4 cubic yards. It is uncovering coal for the Ohio River Collieries Co. Marion retained the 111-M in its line until 1975. *JKH collection*

A Marion diesel-electric, two-crawler dragline of 9-cubic yard capacity. The Model is the 183-M, which was in production from 1956 until it was replaced with the 10-yard 184-M in 1974.

The magnificent Marion 195-M came out in 1970 as an 17-yard all-electric dragline. Its operating weight was 527 tons, and it could carry booms up to 160 feet in length. The machine illustrated is working for British contractor G. Wimpey & Company on a coal stripping job in Wales. *JKH collection*

The largest two-crawler dragline ever built is this Marion 305-M, which is working in Australia. It can be equipped with buckets up to 24 cubic yards, and booms up to 255 feet long. This super dragline has crawlers 10 feet wide and, in operation, weighs 1,225 tons. A large crawler dragline is preferred in some applications because of its mobility, although it will exert a higher ground pressure than a similar-sized walking dragline. *Marion Power Shovel Co.*

boom by a stiff leg. The digging action causes the hoist and crowd motions to work together as the dipper moves up the bank. A movable mast causes the whole front end to rotate about the stiff leg foot pins, exerting large crowd forces. Under the control of the operator, the Superfront allows the dipper to rotate relative to the dipper handle.

The 204-M was the production model Superfront, offered with a standard dipper of 30 cubic yards. Marion's first order for the Superfront came from the former Soviet Union—a large order consisting of 10 Model 204-Ms, which were shipped over a five-year period beginning in 1976. Additional 204-Ms were shipped to Australia, New Guinea, and to coal mining companies operating in the western United States.

Keeping pace with the increasing size of off-highway trucks, Marion designed the 57-yard capacity 301-M to load 240-ton trucks in three passes. The first of these 1,150-ton shovels was sold in 1985. In 1995, the 301-M was upgraded to the 351-M, which made it Marion's largest two-crawler shovel. It has a similar dipper range to its predecessor, and weighs 1,300 tons.

In 1997, two giants in the earthmoving business merged. Bucyrus International, Inc. (formerly Bucyrus-Erie Company) purchased Marion Power Shovel Company. The sale marked the end of a 113-year era of intense competition between two major players.

Clark-Lima Large Crawler Excavators

Having established a popular line of crawler excavators since its origins in the Ohio Power Shovel Company in 1928, the Lima Locomotive Works of Lima, Ohio, built two large Model 1600 crawler cranes in 1943. In 1948, the 1600 graduated to the Model 2400, a diesel-powered machine of heavy proportions. It featured air-controlled clutches and brakes. The machine was initially offered as a 6-yard shovel or dragline, or 110-ton crane. The 2400, and the 2400B upgrade, eventually became the mainstays of Lima's excavators and crawler cranes. The clean lines, curved-house design, and distinctive appearance attracted many shovel enthusiasts to the 2400.

The durable and reliable 2400 proved to be a particular favorite with coal stripping contractors in the eastern United States and overseas. A Lima advertisement in 1960 proclaimed that over 60 Lima 2400s were working in Great Britain.

Lima Locomotive Works underwent a number of transformations over the years, including buy-outs and mergers. Lima Locomotive Works became the Lima-Hamilton Company in 1947, Baldwin-Lima-Hamilton Corporation (BLH) in 1950, and then Clark Equipment Company purchased BLH in 1971. Finally, the excavators became known as Clark-Lima.

In a radical departure from conventional shovel design, Marion announced the "Superfront" shovel in 1974, some seven years after the prototype was tested on a 101-M base machine. Permitting a bucket size increase of up to 66 percent over the standard machine, the "Superfront" has the capability to rotate its dipper under the control of the operator.

The production model of Marion's "Superfront," known as the Model 204-M, is shown here loading a Rimpull 120-ton truck in a Wyoming coal mine. The dipper size is 27 cubic yards. The Superfront's increase in dipper capacity comes from its geometry, and the weight saved by the elimination of the boom.

The largest two-crawler shovel built by Marion Power Shovel Company is the 351-M, the first going to work in 1995 as an upgrade from the former 301-M, which it replaced. It was also Marion's last model to be introduced before the company was taken over by Bucyrus International in 1997. The 351-M shown here is working for Suncor in the Alberta tar sands in Canada. It is loading 240-ton trucks in three passes with its 57-cubic yard dipper. *Marion Power Shovel Co.*

Dating back to 1948, the Lima 2400 was a favorite among surface coal mining companies for three decades. Its 6- to 8-yard shovel capacity was very suitable for small- and medium-size sites, and its diesel power offered mobility impossible for its electric counterparts. The machine shown here is working for contractor G. Wimpey & Company at a coal mine in Wales.

Another popular cable excavator was the Manitowoc 4500, which first appeared in 1947 as a 5 1/2-yard excavator, convertible to dragline. The 4500 shovel pictured is loading a Euclid 63-ton bottom-dump wagon.

The largest Manitowoc excavator was the 6400, introduced in 1977 as a 15-yard dragline. In usual Manitowoc tradition, the 578-ton machine was diesel-powered, with a second engine in the lower works to power the crawlers. The prototype 6400 is shown under test without its house. *JKH collection*

The 8-cubic yard Manitowoc 4600 competed for popularity with the same-sized Lima 2400, and both achieved sales in large numbers. The diesel-powered 4600 came out in 1963, replacing the previous 4500. The standard machine is powered with a 430-horsepower engine for the main draw works, and a second 215-horsepower engine for swing and propel. The 4600 is still included in Manitowoc's production line. *Manitowoc Engineering Co.*

In 1969, the 2400 evolved into the 2400B, an 8-yard shovel/dragline or 150-ton crawler crane. Although it continued to sell well, sales dropped off by the late 1970s. In a last effort to prolong its manufacturing life, a redesigned 2400-BLS brandishing a 12-yard shovel dipper was offered, but only two of the BLS versions were sold. A larger Lima crawler machine entered the market in 1974—the Lima 7707. However, this machine was only available as a 300-ton crawler crane with no dragline or shovel options.

In 1981, manufacturing of all Clark-Lima products was discontinued, and the plant was closed. Some of the patents were acquired by Grove Manufacturing Company, although no more machines were made. Today, MinnPar Inc. of Minneapolis, Minnesota, controls the manufacturing and distribution of parts for Clark-Lima machines.

Manitowoc Large Crawler Excavators

The Manitowoc Company Inc. has been known by several different names, and has operated a number of divisions since its inception in 1902 at Manitowoc, Wisconsin. The company began building excavators in 1928, when it contracted to build the small 3/4-yard crane known as a "Speedcrane," designed by Roy and Charles Moore. Manitowoc developed larger crawler cranes in the 1930s, then large government orders for cranes during World War II helped to strengthen the company's product line.

Manitowoc's famous reputation for large crawler cranes allowed it to gain a substantial share of the large crawler shovel and dragline market. The 5 1/2-yard diesel-powered Model 4500 was introduced in 1947 and became the mainstay of many surface coal mining operations in the Midwest and in Pennsylvania. Its successor, the 8-yard 4600, followed in the same tradition, and solidified Manitowoc's position in the intermediate-size excavator field.

The largest Manitowoc excavator was the big diesel 6400, introduced in 1977 as a 15-yard dragline. This machine had a separate diesel engine mounted in the lower works to provide propelling power. Its operating weight was 578 tons, and it could swing booms up to 200 feet long. The last 6400 left the factory in 1984.

Today, Manitowoc offers a wide range of cranes with lifting capacities up to 1,400 tons, and crawler draglines from 4 to 8 cubic yards.

American Large Crawler Excavators

The American Hoist & Derrick Company of St. Paul, Minnesota, was established in 1882. Famous for its large lift cranes of all types, including giant pedestal-mounted derrick cranes, locomotive cranes, and crawler cranes, the company's move into the large crawler dragline market was a natural avenue of expansion. Since 1961, when the 900-series models (which could be rigged as 4-yard excavators) were introduced, size has spiraled upward. The 1100-series cranes were introduced in 1971, followed by the 1200-series in 1977, carrying 7-yard and 11-yard dragline buckets. The 1200-series (consisting of the Model 12210 and its updated Model 12220) are the largest draglines produced by American. The company offered the 1800-series walking dragline at the tail end of the 1970s—but there were no takers.

Today the company is known as the American Crane Company, having moved its manufacturing operations to Wilmington, North Carolina, in 1987. The company offers a wide range of cranes with lifting capacities up to 800 tons.

Two-Crawler Stripping Shovels

Many of the two-crawler cable-operated shovels could be fitted with a boom of extended length. Thus, the two-crawler shovel could then do the work of a stripping shovel, although on a smaller scale than the giant multicrawler machines described in Chapter 8. The long boom and correspondingly long stick or handle allowed the shovel to dump the material far enough away so that it didn't have to be hauled away in trucks. These types of stripping shovels were most popular in the 1940s and 1950s in the shallow-overburden coal regions of Ohio, West Virginia, and western Pennsylvania.

Many excavator manufacturers that didn't typically supply excavators to the surface mining industry offered the long boom option. Thus, many makes of smaller stripping shovels, such as Osgood, Lorain, and Northwest, were seen at work in the coal fields. Of course, the dipper capacity was considerably less than a conventional shovel fitted with its regular boom. However, the extra reach and the elimination of haulage vehicles offset the smaller dipper capacity, and these machines proved profitable for their owners.

Chronology of Large Two-Crawler Cable Excavators

The German firm, Menck & Hambrock, came out with a 5 1/4-yard shovel in 1924, ranking as the world's largest on two crawlers at that time. The Model J weighed 290 tons, and was offered with either steam or electric power. The massive Model KRA, a giant long-boom stripping shovel with a 6 1/2-yard dipper, followed in 1927. This model was furnished with a four-crawler undercarriage and weighed 540 tons.

During the 1920s, excavation with shovels that loaded trucks or rail cars became prevalent and organized. There were still many railroad shovels that provided heavy and robust power for digging hard rock. But these could not rotate 360 degrees, so loading vehicles was

The 1200-series excavators introduced in 1977 by American Hoist & Derrick Company were the largest produced by the company. The diesel-powered Model 12210 could swing a 9-yard bucket on a 140-foot boom. The machine shown here is stripping coal in western Pennsylvania for Grampian Coal Company.

This Koehring 1205 is an example of a stripping shovel from a manufacturer not normally associated with surface mining equipment. Long booms could easily be attached to base machines, but correspondingly smaller dippers resulted. The machine in the picture carries a 3-yard dipper on a 40-foot boom. The 1205 could also be fitted with a 50-foot boom and 2 1/2-yard dipper. *JKH collection*

The Osgood 1006 is another fine example of a long-boom stripping shovel derived from a base machine. It could carry a 2-yard bucket on a 35-foot handle with a 45-foot boom. Working weight was 87 tons. *JKH collection*

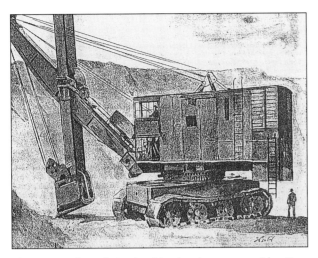

The German firm of Menck & Hambrock came out with a 5 1/4-yard shovel in 1924, taking the world size title for a two-crawler excavator. It weighed 290 tons and was offered with steam or electric power. *JKH collection*

awkward. The shovels of the day that could swing 360 degrees were long-boomed gangly outfits, not robust enough for hard digging. This market demand led the Bucyrus Company to design a shovel that combined the robustness of the railroad shovel with the 360-degree rotational capability of the stripping shovel.

Enter the 120-B—the world's first mine and quarry shovel designed for loading rail cars or trucks. First built in 1925 as a 4-yard machine, and later up-rated to 5-yard capacity, it revolutionized the shovel industry. Over 300 had been built by the time it was finally discontinued in 1951. Most were electric, but a few were steam-powered. The 120-B was the forerunner of other Bucyrus quarry and mine shovels, larger and smaller, designed on the same lines, such as the 85-B, 100-B, and 170-B.

Marion took the title for the world's largest shovel on two crawlers in 1951 with the sale of the first 191-M to Western Contracting Corporation. This 10-yard shovel was diesel-powered and had three engines total-

The title for the world's largest excavator on two crawlers was taken by Marion in 1951 with the sale of the first 10-cubic yard Model 191-M to Western Contracting Corporation. The 191-M, with its upgrades over the years, turned out to be a very successful machine for Marion, as 157 were shipped, with the last one in 1989. Although normally an electric machine, five of the total were made with diesel-electric power, including the first one, shown here. It is powered with three diesel engines totaling 1,700 horsepower. *JKH collection*

ing 1,700 horsepower. This machine was used on dam construction in South Dakota, along with several more 191-Ms, and on many other jobs by Western Contracting. After being disassembled and reassembled about 12 times during its long life, it was cut up for scrap in 1993. The 191-M turned out to be a very successful machine for Marion, as repeat orders were received from mines and contractors around the world up to 1989. Out of a total of 156 units built, only five were diesel-powered; the rest were electrically powered.

The 191-M held its title as the world's largest on two crawlers until Marion broke its own record in 1962 with the 291-M, a 15-yard shovel with a 90-foot boom. Only two were ever built. They have been owned and operated by Peabody Coal Company since new, and were still operating in 1997 at the Rochelle Mine in Wyoming, as 36- and 40-yard coal shovels.

In 1978, the P&H 5700LR shovel took the title for the world's largest shovel on two crawlers. The first unit went to work at Arch of Illinois' Captain Mine, carrying a 25-yard dipper on a 90-foot boom, and weighing just under 1,800 tons. This machine has since moved to one of Arch's properties in West Virginia, and is now operating as a 44-yard loading shovel with a correspondingly shorter boom. The XPA version of the 5700 offered now has dippers of up to 80 yards and an operating weight of 2,100 tons, which has reinforced its position as the world's largest shovel on two crawlers.

Marion broke its own size record for a two-crawler excavator when it came out with the 291-M in 1962, a 15-yard shovel with a 90-foot boom. Only two of this model were built, but they were successful machines for their owner, Peabody Coal Company, which was still operating them in 1997.

The giant of the two-crawler excavators today is the P&H 5700XPA. With a dipper range of up to 80 cubic yards, its operating weight is 2,100 tons. The Dresser Haulpak 240-ton truck in the picture is dwarfed by this 5700XPA electric shovel working in Australia. *Harnischfeger Corporation*

Chapter Eight

STRIPPING SHOVELS

Stripping shovels are the true giants of the machine world. The size and scale of them is awe-inspiring. The 15,000-ton *Captain* shovel is included in this exclusive group and is the heaviest piece of equipment ever to move under its own power on land. Only ocean ships have a greater movable mass than these monster machines.

The largest stripping shovels are found in surface coal mines, while smaller sizes have typically worked in limestone quarries. Stripping shovels work the same way as the cable shovels described in Chapter 7, however, they are larger, and don't load another vehicle. Regular shovels depend on haulage trucks to carry the material away, but the stripping shovel's gigantic proportions allow it to dig from a high face, swing around, and pile the material clear of the working area. These colossal machines operate in surface coal mines and dig long strips or cuts, casting the material into the adjacent strip, where the coal has already been removed. It's similar to large-scale field plowing where the furrow being cut is turned over into the adjacent furrow.

Stripping Shovel Description

Large stripping shovels are mounted on eight crawler tracks arranged in pairs at each corner of the lower frame. Each two-crawler assembly is attached to a large vertical hydraulic cylinder for leveling the machine, which allows it to travel over undulating ground. The leveling is usually done automatically by means of a pendulum system, which directs the hydraulic fluid to and from the four cylinders to keep the machine on an even keel. Each crawler assembly is steered by horizontal hydraulic rams which move the front pair, or the rear pair, in unison.

Stripping shovel fronts, or long boom shovels, can also be mounted on certain models of two-crawler excavators as covered in Chapter 7.

Up until the mid-1920s, steam or electricity powered these mighty shovels. Since the 1920s, the big stripping shovels have been exclusively electric-powered. Interestingly, power jumped from steam to electric, without the

The earliest known revolving stripping shovel was this rail-mounted machine built by John H. Wilson & Company in 1900. Used in England to uncover iron ore by Lloyds Ironstone Company, it had a 1 1/2-cubic yard dipper on a boom 70 feet long. It weighed 78 tons. This first machine had a working life of 54 years.

typical diesel phase seen in other types of excavators. Electric motors or steam engines could be fitted to the machine exactly where power was needed, as opposed to transmitting power by means of long shafts, gears, or chains, when a single power source is used. Imagine having a chain or a drive shaft to power a shipper shaft halfway up a boom measuring over 200 feet long!

Operation

Operating a large stripping shovel is a very precise science that takes careful planning. Because of the high ground pressure under its crawlers, the stripping shovel must always operate on a very stable footing, such as uncovered coal. If it runs off the solid material onto soft ground, disaster can strike. It can quickly sink and become stuck. When the biggest machine on the site is stuck, there is nothing to pull it out! So this

A long boom was fitted to this Vulcan Model K railroad-type shovel in 1908, making it into a stripping shovel. With only a part-swing boom, its limitations in this type of work are apparent. Note the chute for dumping coal onto the shovel to power its steam boiler. This machine is fitted with traction wheels rather than the usual rail-mounting. The action is taking place near Lily, Kentucky, for Laurel Engineering Company. *Bucyrus International*

Another English stripping shovel was this Grossmith in 1908. It carried a 3-yard dipper on a boom 80 feet long. In 1926 the machine shown here was converted from steam to electric power. However, the owners must not have felt too confident with the new-fangled electric power, as the conversion retained the original boiler and steam engines, so that in case of failure to the electrical equipment, the machine could still be operated using steam.

is avoided at all costs. It may take other equipment several days to excavate around the large shovel and haul in dry material, before the huge machine can be driven out under its own power.

Pit wall failure is another hazard to avoid. Sometimes the pit wall where the shovel is working becomes unstable, and large chunks of rock crash down to the floor of the strip mine. This can partly bury the machine. A wall failure can occur without warning, and the stripping shovel cannot always escape because of its slow propelling speed.

When work is completed, these large machines can't be lashed down to a flatbed semitrailer and hauled away. They must be dismantled. The shovels are broken down into small enough pieces to be moved from one site to another. In some cases, shovels have been dismantled and reerected several times during their lives. Moving a machine of this size takes a crew with special skill and a lot of experience. A new machine may need more than 250 truck or rail car loads of parts to complete delivery.

Early Development

Stripping shovels were invented around the turn of this century, and gradually increased in size over the years. In the 1960s, their size skyrocketed and the machines became colossal wonders. During the 1960s, the decade of the giants, both stripping shovels and walking draglines (Chapter 9) reached sizes that have never been surpassed.

In 1885, Wright & Wallace, a coal mining contractor, used a land dredge to strip coal near Danville, Illinois. This is the earliest documented application of a stripping-type machine. The contractor bought an old dredge made of wood, removed the hull, and mounted the machine on rollers. He installed a wooden boom 50 feet long and a dipper of 1 1/4-cubic yard capacity. Several similar land dredges were made before the turn of the century, but these wooden machines had very short working lives.

The first long boom (stripping) shovel, as we know it today, was a fully revolving machine built in 1900 by John H. Wilson & Co. in England. Operated by Lloyds Ironstone Company to uncover iron ore, it carried a dipper of 1 1/2-cubic yard capacity on a 70 foot boom that provided a 60-foot dumping radius. The 78-ton unit was mounted on rail tracks, and was regarded as a marvel for its day when most excavation work was done by hand. This stripper was so successful that it had a working life of 54 years.

Another long boom shovel was used at a coal mine near Lily, Kentucky, in 1907. The surface mining coal company installed a long boom on a Vulcan Model K railroad-type shovel, and used it to strip overburden.

With the restriction of only 180 degrees of swing, the machine had limited success, and subsequent development of stripping shovels involved only the full-swing (360-degree) type.

In 1908, the Grossmith was built, another early example of a full-circle stripping shovel. Used in England for mining brick clay, this giant machine carried a 3-yard dipper on a boom 80 feet long, and it rotated on a swing circle 18 feet in diameter. A dipper tilting device, operated by a steam turbine motor, was a novel feature. The angle of the dipper could be adjusted relative to the arm, which gave the shovel a greater floor-cleaning radius. However, this system did not survive the jolting of the dipper and was soon discarded. In the 1960s, much larger shovels with tilting dipper devices made a return, after a gap of some 60 years.

In 1911, the Marion 250, built by Marion Steam Shovel Company, was the first U.S. full-circle long boom stripping shovel. It was put in service at Mission Field near Danville, Illinois. It set the stage for large-scale, mechanized stripping of minerals by surface mining methods. This steam-powered, rail-mounted machine had a working weight of 150 tons, and a 65-foot boom carrying a 3 1/2-yard dipper. Even at this early date, Marion had pioneered the concept of leveling the machine by utilizing a hydraulic cylinder under each corner of the lower frame. This concept has been incorporated into every Marion stripping shovel built since.

When a coal stripping customer ordered one new Marion 250 in preference to two Bucyrus machines (a railroad shovel and a dragline) to strip the same amount of coal in tandem, the response from Marion's main rival was immediate. The Bucyrus engineering department came out with competitive machines a few months later: the 2 1/2-yard 150-B and the 3 1/2-yard 175-B stripping shovels. These were also rail-mounted steam machines, but instead of using hydraulic jacks, Bucyrus opted for a three-point suspension system with screw jacks to level the machine.

Electric Control

In 1919, both Marion and Bucyrus applied an improved control system to their electric machines called Ward Leonard control. It produced precise variable speed similar to steam power, and proved well suited to excavators. Ward Leonard uses AC-powered motor generator

A Bucyrus 225-B stripping shovel owned by Clemens Coal Company stripping overburden at Minden, Missouri. The 225-B carried a 6-yard dipper and was available with steam or electric power. This view shows an initial or "box" cut being made, and demonstrates the usual lack of dirt room in such operations. *Bucyrus International*

The first revolving stripping shovel in the United States was the Marion 250 of 3 1/2-cubic yard capacity. Purchased by Mission Mining Company in 1911, it was operated near Danville, Illinois. Another early user was T.J. Forschner Coal Company. Their machine, shown here, was one of 19 ordered by coal companies between 1911 and 1913. *JKH collection*

The Bucyrus Company worked fast to come out with a stripping shovel to compete with Marion's 250. The first was the Model 150-B, which came out in 1912, shown here operating for C.F. Markham Coal Company at Fuller, Kansas. The shovel was leveled by a screw jack system, and carried a 2 1/2-cubic yard dipper. *Bucyrus International*

The Marion 350 is the machine that took title to the world's largest mobile land machine when it came out in 1923. A 560-ton roving monster was certainly an eye-opener in the days of the Model T Ford and silent movies. A total of 47 of these giants were built until 1929. *JKH collection*

The last remaining Marion 360 machine has been preserved at the Diplomat Mine Museum site near Forestburg, Alberta, Canada. Built as a dragline in 1927, the machine was moved to Canada and converted to a shovel in 1950. It worked at the Diplomat Mine until 1980. Now restored, it is on display to the public during daylight hours throughout the year.

One of the few stripping shovel competitors to Marion and Bucyrus was the British firm of Ransomes & Rapier Ltd., who built them for only seven years from 1934. The machine shown here is a rail-mounted Model 5360 at work in 1974 for the British Steel Corporation in one of its ironstone strip mines. The 710-ton machine carried a 10-cubic yard dipper on a 104-foot long boom.

The introduction of the Bucyrus-Erie 950-B stripping shovel in 1935 heralded both a world record holder and a new design of stripping shovels. The 30-yard machine incorporated many new features that are still found in modern-designed machines of today, like the tubular dipper handle. This 950-B is shown dropping 30 yards of overburden onto the spoil piles at the Buckheart Mine of United Electric Coal Mining Companies. *Bucyrus International*

sets to power DC motors for the machine's motions. With Ward Leonard control, maximum pull is available at motor stall speed, and a motor will not burn out when overloaded. The first models to receive the control system were the Bucyrus 225-B stripping shovel and the Marion Model 300-E. Since then, Ward Leonard control became standard on all large stripping shovels.

Crawler Tracks

In 1925, the Bucyrus 320-B was the first stripping shovel to be equipped with crawler tracks. The 320-B was introduced a year earlier as a 7 1/2-yard rail-mounted machine. The four rail trucks were replaced with eight crawler tracks mounted in pairs at each corner.

Later the same year, Marion quickly responded by placing crawler tracks on their world record size Model 350, which had an 8-yard dipper.

While crawlers had proved themselves on smaller machines, they were slow to appear on stripping shovels, due mainly to high cost, and to the fact that rail mountings were manageable and economical. However, by 1927, most new stripping shovels were ordered with crawlers, even though they added about 40 percent to the cost of the machine.

The Race for Larger Machines

In 1923, Marion broke the world size record with the Model 350, a mobile machine weighing no less than 560 tons. This giant had an 8-yard dipper and 90-foot boom and was the world's largest mobile land machine of any type ever constructed up to that time. Initially rail-mounted, the 350s were equipped with crawler tracks from 1925. The tracks were driven by the main hoist motor upstairs in the revolving frame, via the center pintle. Then power was routed through a long train of bevel gears, shafts, and spur gears, to each of the four crawler assemblies through a series of jaw clutches. A further set of jaw clutches split the drive to power the steering of each crawler assembly through screwed rods.

To propel the 350, the operator in the cab had control of the main hoist motor, but no control over steering. A person on the ground had to run around under the machine, heaving heavy jaw clutches and sliding gears in or out to effect steering. He carried a heavy iron tube, which he placed over the levers to obtain greater pull. Another duty of the ground operator was to level the machine. Marion used its patented hydraulic leveling device, but leveling the four large jacks was not automatic. Guided by two pendulums attached to the frame, the ground operator used valves to divert hydraulic oil to or from each cylinder until the machine was level. Such large-scale use of hydraulics on a machine this size in the 1920s is truly amazing.

Imagine the sight of this monster machine eating up the countryside, taking 8 cubic yards at each bite and dumping it half a football field away. The massive proportions of this machine sharply contrasted with the automobiles of the era, which had spindly wheels and light chassis. All this was at a time before sound movies were in the theaters—even before the era of welding!

The 350-series machines were a great success with 47 units sold before production ceased in 1929. The last one to operate finally shut down in 1980 at the Diplomat Mine near Forestburg, Alberta, Canada. It is now preserved in the Diplomat Mine Museum, on the site where it once operated.

Size continued to spiral upward. Both Marion and Bucyrus introduced stripping shovels of 12-cubic yard capacity in 1927. Marion debuted its 5480 that weighed almost 1,000 tons and incorporated most of the 350's proven features. The Bucyrus 750-B became the first in a

A new world record holder was launched in 1929 by Marion with its Model 5600. Purchased by the United Electric Coal Companies initially with a 15-yard dipper, it was later converted to a dragline, and then back to a shovel with a dipper of 26 yards. Although only one of this model was built, it had an interesting career, with its final years spent as a cross-pit bucket wheel excavator. *JKH collection*

A big breakthrough in stripping shovel design occurred in 1940, when Marion introduced the knee-action crowd on the new 35-yard Model 5561. The machine pictured is working at Middle Grove, Illinois. The "ruler" on the side of the machine enables the foreman to measure the depth of cut for his daily volume records without having to throw a tape over the high wall! *JKH collection*

The most famous of them all, the *Mountaineer*, carves its way through the rich coal fields of eastern Ohio. The Marion 5760 was purchased by the Hanna Coal Company (now Consolidation Coal Company). The giant machine carried a 60-yard dipper and featured a passenger elevator running up its center pin. *JKH collection*

ADVANTAGES OF THE KNEE-ACTION CROWD ON STRIPPING SHOVELS

1. The crowd machinery is moved to the gantry, near the machine's center of rotation, minimizing swing inertia.
2. The dipper handle is connected to a movable stiff leg instead of the boom. This removes all torsional and bending stresses from the boom, so that the boom can be made considerably lighter.
3. The action of the movable stiff leg allows the dipper to move in a long horizontal sweep at ground level. This results in a long cleanup radius, and positions the dipper teeth so that they will not gouge into the coal being uncovered.
4. The crowd motion is capable of producing a tremendous downward force at the toe of the bank, just where it's needed in hard digging.

long, distinguished line of giant stripping shovels produced by that company.

In 1929, Marion claimed title to the world's largest land machine again, when the 1,500-ton Model 5600 was sold to the United Electric Coal Companies for work in southern Illinois. Only one example of the gigantic 5600 was ever built. This 15-yard machine spent periods of its life in various configurations. In 1933, it was converted to a 20-yard dragline, the largest dragline ever put to work at that time. Then in 1957, the 5600 was converted into a bucket wheel excavator. (Chapter 10)

Now it was Bucyrus-Erie's turn to make a move on the world's largest machine title, and this they did handsomely in 1935 with the cutting edge 950-B. This massive stripping shovel with its 30-yard dipper contained a host of innovations The front-end arrange-

Bucyrus-Erie's biggest shovel in the 1950s was the 1650-B. The first one went to Peabody Coal Company in 1956, and was named *The River Queen*, after the mine in Kentucky where it worked. After some 13 years at River Queen, the 1650-B saw action at two more mines in Kentucky for Peabody, before being sold to Green Coal Company to work at their Henderson County Mine, also in Kentucky. *Bucyrus International*

ment with single tubular dipper handle operated by wire ropes was the most notable. The two-part boom was pinned at its center and tied back to the gantry with two heavy beams. The handle's tubular design allowed it to rotate, thus minimizing stresses on the handle and boom caused by unbalanced loads on the dipper. The 950-B also featured a counterbalanced hoist, with a moving counterweight at the rear of the revolving frame, connected to the dipper hoist drum through its own set of cables. The counterweight balanced the weight of the empty dipper allowing more hoisting power to be applied to filling it.

The lower works of the 950-B did not escape radical improvements either. A propelling motor was mounted in each of the four crawler assemblies, eliminating the previous complicated system of multiple gear trains and shafts or chains. And for the first time on a Bucyrus-Erie machine, a hydraulic leveling system was introduced, dispensing with the earlier screw types.

Marion's 1940 knee-action crowd was the next major design breakthrough because it featured a totally new design for the front-end geometry of stripping shovels. The Model 5561 was the first to receive the new front end, which, with its 35-cubic yard capacity, claimed a dipper size record yet again. The long handle and stiff leg design appeared to fold like an insect's leg, thus it was nicknamed the "grasshopper." The effective and efficient knee-action crowd became standard for all subsequent Marion stripping shovels, and much later some Bucyrus machines. By 1945, the 5561 had grown to 40-cubic yard capacity.

Era of the Super Strippers

In 1955, news stories reported that a shovel of unbelievable proportions was being built in eastern Ohio. The stories were true, and the machine that created the whirlwind of attention was the "Mountaineer."

Dismantling a Marion 5760 known as *Big Paul* at the River King Mine of Peabody Coal Company in 1964. It had worked at the Illinois mine from the time it was new in 1957, and was destined to move to Peabody's Hawthorne Mine in Indiana. The large stiff-leg derrick is shown lifting off the gantry of the super stripper. *JKH collection*

This Marion-built monster was the lead machine of a new era of super strippers. The 60-yard dipper took its first bite for the Hanna Coal Company (now Consolidation Coal Company) on the cold winter day of January 19, 1956. With the worldwide publicity this machine received, the *Mountaineer* was one of the most famous big strippers. However, this was only the beginning. It was hard to fathom that a shovel exactly three times its size would be built by the same manufacturer only a decade later!

The *Mountaineer*, designated the Marion 5760, had an operating weight of 2,750 tons, and the top of its boom rose 160 feet into the air, as high as a 16-story building. It even had an elevator inside its center pintle to carry the crew from ground to cab level. The size and scale of the machine and what it could accomplish were astounding. The shovel's range allowed a dipper load of 90 tons to be dug from the face, deposited the length of a football field away, and stacked over 10 stories high. It could move 7,500 tons of material each hour, which was almost three times its own weight.

The size of stripping shovels that followed the *Mountaineer* grew astronomically. Almost immediately, Bucyrus-Erie responded with the similarly sized 55-yard 1650-B "River Queen," ordered by Peabody Coal Company for its River Queen Mine in Kentucky. Then, Marion upgraded the 5760 to the 5761 in 1959 and increased dipper size by 10 more yards.

In 1960, Bucyrus-Erie took the next huge jump forward in shovel size with an order for the world's largest shovel, the 3850-B, with a dipper capacity of 115 cubic yards. Amazingly, it was almost double the size of the largest shovel then in operation!

The following is taken from the press release:

"Bucyrus-Erie to Build Record Shovel. A contract to build a mammoth stripping shovel, the largest mobile land machine ever built, has been awarded to Bucyrus-Erie Company, according to an announcement today by President Robert G. Allen. The shovel will be built for Peabody Coal Company, St. Louis, Missouri, for a new mine in western Kentucky (Sinclair Mine). It will be more than twice the size of any shovel now in operation.

"Merle C. Kelce, Peabody president, stated the purchase of this shovel is a continuing part of Peabody's

Before the first Bucyrus-Erie giant 3850-B shovel was put in operation, Peabody Coal Company ordered a second one of the same model with a dipper holding a whopping 140 cubic yards. The picture shows the second 3850-B in operation at the River King Mine, Illinois. The hydraulic leveling cylinders can be seen extended to level the machine on this uneven pit floor. The protruding cab gives the operator a good view beyond the boom. *Bucyrus International*

Erection of the Bucyrus-Erie 3850-B in a pit created for the purpose. The "low-level" erection avoids the need to ramp the machine down to the coal level to commence work. It also minimizes the lift height for components brought in at ground level. The stiff leg derrick, seen in the background, would do most of the heavy lifting. In this progress picture, the lower works are almost completed and assembly of the revolving frame has just started. *Bucyrus International*

The immense size of the 140-yard dipper of this 3850-B shovel is dramatically captured in this photograph. The dipper was designed to move 44 million cubic yards of overburden annually. Power requirements to run this machine are equal to those required for a city of 12,000 people. *Bucyrus International*

modernization program. It is expected to lower the cost of mining deeply buried coal, which otherwise could not be recovered by the strip mining method.

"Power requirements for this electrically operated machine are equal to that required for a city of 12,000 people. Fifty-two electric motors, ranging from 1/4 to 3,000 horsepower, will operate and propel this giant stripping shovel. The machine will be controlled by a single operator located in his air-conditioned cab five stories up. A passenger elevator will provide access to the cab."

The Bucyrus-Erie engineering team assigned to the 115-yard shovel offered the following statistics to underscore the great size of the machine:

"In 50 seconds, the shovel will pick up 173 tons of material, dump it 464 feet away, and swing back for the next bite. Overburden moved in one month could fill all the cars in a train stretching from Pittsburgh to Chicago. The shovel boom will tower 210 feet—as high as the deck

of the Golden Gate Bridge, 56 feet higher that the Statue of Liberty, 45 feet higher than Niagara Falls."

A little over a year after the first 3850-B was announced, and before the machine went into operation, Bucyrus-Erie received an order for a second 3850-B from the same customer. This time Peabody wanted a new shovel for its River King Mine in Illinois, but needed a productivity even greater than that expected from the first 3850-B. With a boom some 10 feet shorter, the dipper capacity was increased to 140 cubic yards. In 1964, the second 3850-B went into service. Both 3850-Bs had operating weights between 9,000 and 10,000 tons, and were the largest ever built by the Bucyrus-Erie Company.

The Bucyrus-Erie 1850-B was another super stripper. Wielding a 90-yard dipper on a 150-foot boom, it was named *Big Brutus*. This 5,500-ton shovel went to work for Pittsburg & Midway Coal Mining Company at West Mineral, Kansas in 1963. After only 11 years of work, this modern machine

One of the few stripping shovels saved from the scrapper's torch is the Bucyrus-Erie 1850-B *Big Brutus*. The 90-yard shovel now stands as a landmark in the Kansas prairie scenery near West Mineral. It is maintained by its preservation group, Big Brutus, Inc.

This view shows the intricate erection process of a large stripping shovel. The Bucyrus-Erie 1850-B takes shape near West Mineral, Kansas. As usual, a stiff leg derrick is the main lifter. Note the extensive cribbing used to support the boom while it is being welded. At the time this picture was taken, the boom was being raised. *Bucyrus International*

was idled, but not scrapped. It now stands high and proud on public display near West Mineral, having been restored by Big Brutus, Inc., a nonprofit organization dedicated to the restoration and preservation of the shovel.

The race for the largest stripping shovel effectively ended in 1965 when Marion broke the shovel size record for the final time. The incredible Marion 6360 was named the *Captain*, and truly was the captain of all shov-els. This behemoth is still the largest machine of any type to have moved under its own power on land.

The following is an extract from an article that appeared in the November 13, 1965, issue of *Business Week*:

"It stands 21 stories high, it weighs around 15,000 tons and it rolls over the ground under its own power. It is manned by one engineer and one oiler. No, it's not a tall railroad train—it's the most powerful excavating machine ever built, and it just happens to be also the largest self-propelled 'mobile' land vehicle.

"Marion Power Shovel Company built the super scoop for Southwestern Illinois Coal Corporation's Captain strip mine near Percy, Illinois. (Now Arch Coal, Inc.) Its bucket takes 180 cubic yards of overburden at each bite; that's 300 tons of earth and rock. And it takes a mouthful every 1 minute and 12 seconds.

"The electric-powered shovel dug its first dirt in mid-October close to its assembly site. Mine officials expect it will be active 85 percent of the time, 24 hours a day, seven days a week, uncovering enough coal each day to fill 155 to 165 railroad cars."

The 6360 shovel looked liked most other Marion stripping shovels, with its eight crawler tracks, hydraulically leveled lower works, and its knee-action crowd. However, what set this shovel apart were its gigantic proportions. It featured twinned dipper doors, and each separately hinged half weighed 15 tons! This was the only shovel to have two dipper doors.

Four pairs of crawlers using two electric motors in each pair propelled the 6360 to a top speed of 1/4 mile per hour. Each crawler was 45 feet long and 16 feet high, and each crawler shoe measured 10 feet across and tipped the scales at 3 1/2 tons. Inside the house, eight motors powered the two hoist drums, four motors powered the crowd motion, and a further eight motors rotated the machine. All these motors operated on DC current provided by four AC motor-generator sets with a total of 21,000 horsepower.

The active life of the *Captain* shovel came to an abrupt end on September 9, 1991, when a disastrous fire burned for several hours in its lower works. It was suspected to have started when a hydraulic line burst, spraying fluid over live electrical panels. The fire was fueled by a build-up of grease and oil in the swing circle area, and was difficult to extinguish. After assessing the damage, mine officials considered the cost of repairs too great, so the machine was scrapped in late 1992. During its lifetime, the 6360 shovel moved about 810 million cubic yards of overburden. That was well over three times the quantity of material excavated for the Panama Canal! After the fire, mine officials moved in a 105-yard Marion 5900 shovel from another part of the mine to carry on the duties of the stricken *Captain*.

The heaviest self-propelled machine ever to move on land was the greatest stripping shovel of them all, the Marion 6360, named the *Captain*. Weighing 15,000 tons, this engineering marvel was erected at the Captain Mine of Southwestern Illinois Coal Corporation in 1965. This view shows how the shovel could uncover two seams of coal simultaneously with its 180-cubic yard dipper. Digging to the side uncovered the upper seam; digging straight ahead uncovered the lower seam on which the shovel is standing.

The 15,000-ton weight of the Marion 6360 can be appreciated from this rear view showing the man on the ground. Note the maintenance crane on top of the gantry traveling on its own rail track. Each of the eight crawler assemblies is 45 feet long and 15 feet high. The driving motors inside the house total 21,000 horsepower!

The last two stripping shovels produced by Bucyrus-Erie were the *Silver Spade* (105 yards) and the *Gem of Egypt* (130 yards), both purchased by Consolidation Coal Company for work in Ohio. They were 1950-Bs, which featured the knee-action crowd under special arrangement from Marion. The *Silver Spade* is shown here. Plans are afoot to preserve this giant, once its working days are over. *Bucyrus International*

Stripping Shovel Epilogue

Although the race for larger and larger shovels had ended, the manufacturers didn't realize it. They designed even larger machines, but there were no takers. Among others, Bucyrus-Erie designed the 4850-B at 220 yards and the 4950-B at 250 yards. This latter shovel would have had a weight of 18,000 tons supported on 16 crawlers, four per corner. There was even talk of a 1,000-yard shovel! But these designs never left the drawing board.

Although there were no more record-breakers, several other stripping shovels were manufactured until the last one was built—a 105-yard Marion 5900, which started work in 1971. This actually was the same machine that replaced the 6360 at the Captain Mine. Bucyrus-Erie's last stripping shovel, a 130-yard 1950-B named the *Gem of Egypt*, was put to work in early 1967 by the Hanna Coal Company (now Consolidation Coal Company) in southeastern Ohio. This joined an earlier 1950-B (the *Silver Spade*) which was put to work by Hanna at the same location. The 1950-B was the only Bucyrus-Erie equipped with a knee-action front end. A special arrangement had to be made with Marion, whose patents had previously covered this design to produce this type of front end.

Although immense in size, the stripping shovel is limited to the depth of overburden it can remove. Unlike a dragline, which can sit on the surface and move into advantageous positions to gain dumping reach, the shovel sits on the coal in the bottom of the cut where its range is limited. As "shallow" coal reserves are exhausted, stripping shovels are being retired. Today, only a handful of stripping shovels still operate.

Throughout the history of shovels and draglines, the intense competition between Marion and Bucyrus was readily apparent. The competition was never more intense than in the area of stripping shovels. The rivalry between these two companies goes back to their founding in the 1880s. Over the decades, engineering innovations and machine size records switched from one company to the other many times. Then in 1997, Bucyrus International, Inc., purchased the Marion Power Shovel Company, ending a rivalry that had lasted 113 years.

With very few exceptions, Marion and Bucyrus have supplied the entire world market for large stripping shovels. A few manufacturers attempted to make this type of machine in the early part of the century. In addition, stripping shovels were built in England by Ransomes & Rapier Ltd. over a seven-year period beginning in 1933. The German firm Menck built some in the 1920s, and a few have been built in the former Soviet Union for use in that country. But there was never any serious competition to Marion and Bucyrus, whose names will forever be synonymous with stripping shovels.

The last stripping shovel to be built was this Marion 5900 in 1971. Originally sold to Amax Coal Company for work at the Leahy Mine in Illinois, it is now working at the Captain Mine of Arch Coal Inc. The 5900 carries a 105-cubic yard dipper and, in operation, weighs approximately 7,000 tons. *Eric Orlemann collection*

Even the largest mobile machine is vulnerable to fire. After a disastrous fire on September 9, 1991, the Marion 6360 super shovel was damaged beyond repair. In this picture, taken after the fire, the severity of the damage is not apparent, but the fire centered around the swing circle in the guts of the machine, and the cost of repairs proved prohibitive. The *Captain* was scrapped in late 1992. *Eric Orlemann*

Chapter Nine

WALKING DRAGLINES

Looking like a large crane to the untrained eye, the walking dragline is a digging machine. It is mostly found in surface mining operations, large sand and gravel pits, or limestone quarries. Occasionally, large construction projects, such as canals and dams, have made good use of the walking dragline's appetite for large volumes of earth.

A crane carries a lifting hook, but a dragline belongs to the family of excavators, and carries a digging bucket suspended from its boom by hoist ropes. Another set of ropes drags the bucket up the working face toward the machine as it collects its load. When full, the bucket is hoisted, and the machine swings to dump its contents in a pile off to the side.

Ever since its inception in the late 1800s, the surface mining industry has demanded excavators that move immense amounts of material efficiently, and the walking dragline fits that bill handsomely. As draglines developed in the 1930s, a well-organized dragline operation was found to be the most efficient method in all but the hardest of materials.

Unlike the stripping shovels (chapter 8), which are limited in the depth of overburden they can handle, a walking dragline is very flexible in operation. It has the capability to dig deeper, rehandle material, and work on a bench below ground level. Because of the wide-open spaces of a strip mine, walking draglines are not restricted in size. Consequently, walking draglines constitute some of the largest machines ever to move on the earth. The high cost of dismantling and erecting these giant machines is insignificant when averaged over their lifetime, which can be 30 years or more.

The first dragline machine was built in 1904. It was a homemade affair built by contractors Page & Schnable to fill a specific need on the Chicago Drainage Canal. It was a simple derrick fitted with a swinging boom controlled by winches, and carried a 1-yard bucket.

Following the success of this first machine, Page built more draglines for use on its own contracts, and also started building them for sale. The Monighan

This flimsy wooden contrivance was the first dragline devised by John Page of Page & Schnable, contractors. The part-swing boom could carry a 1-yard bucket operated by a steam derrick. The machine was assembled to fill a specific need on the Chicago Drainage Canal, on which the contractors were working. *JKH collection*

An early method of moving draglines was by use of skids and rollers. The Bucyrus Class 24 dragline, the world's largest when it was built in 1911, was one such machine. It carried a standard 3 1/2-yard bucket on a 100-foot boom. The last remaining Class 24, shipped in 1917, is currently being preserved in Alberta, Canada.

Machine Company, a local Chicago firm owned by John Monighan, built the draw works while Page built the rest of the machine. Eventually, building draglines proved more profitable than contracting, and Page Engineering Company was incorporated in 1912.

Even though several other manufacturers entered the dragline business up to 1912, no one had developed any means of propelling the machines. They were mounted on rails, or on skids and rollers, and pulled themselves along by means of the dragline bucket. This was a cumbersome, tortuous, and time-consuming motion. One typical skid-and-roller dragline was the Bucyrus Class 24 steam machine, many of which were made from 1911 to 1930. When it was first built, the Class 24, with its 3 1/2-yard bucket on a 100-foot boom, ranked as the world's largest dragline. The last known remaining Class 24, and probably the oldest dragline still existing today, is at the Coal Valley Mine near Edson, Alberta, Canada. This steam-powered example was built in 1917, and at the time of writing, the Canadian Institute of Mining & Metallurgy (CIM) is spearheading a project to move this machine, and preserve it at the world-class Reynolds Alberta Museum, Wetaskiwin, Alberta, in recognition of CIM's Centennial Year in 1998.

Monighan engineer Oscar Martinson revolutionized the dragline industry by placing two shoes, one on each side of the dragline's revolving frame. In 1913, the Monighan 1-T became the first "walking" dragline, and the first walking device was known as the Martinson Tractor.

The walking system on a dragline is very simple in operation. To take a step, the shoes are rotated in a circular motion by means of an eccentric drive, so that they touch the ground simultaneously. Further rotation lifts the leading edge of the dragline's circular tub off the ground, pulls it ahead the distance of one step, and gently lowers the machine back on its base. The shoes continue to rotate, and the process is repeated for the next step. Changing direction (steering) is just a matter of swinging

The first walking dragline was this Model 1-T designed by the Monighan Machine Company in 1913. The 1-yard machine was propelled by shoes on each side of the machine, a device known as the "Martinson Tractor." *JKH collection*

This 7-cubic yard capacity Bucyrus-Monighan 7-W is shown taking a step. As the eccentric cams rotate, the shoes are pressed to the ground, raising the leading edge of the tub off the ground. In high position, about 80 percent of the dragline's weight is transferred to the shoes. *Bucyrus International*

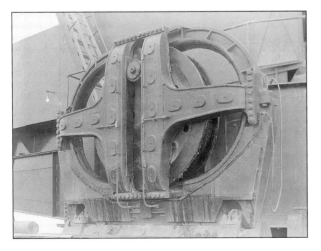

In 1925, Monighan improved its walking system to the type shown, still in use on many machines today. The eccentrically mounted cam turns in its oval track to move the shoes in a circular motion. *Bucyrus International*

It is no surprise that this first walking system from Page was not a resounding success, due to its complicated setup of gears, racks, and chains. In this system, the entire base of the machine was lifted clear of the ground. *JKH collection*

Soon after Bucyrus-Erie acquired the rights to the Monighan draglines in 1932, the company designed the largest yet built. A 12-yard bucket swinging on a 250-foot boom, the world's longest, meant that this dragline was twice the size of the previous largest. The machine, known as the 950-B, was shipped to Brazil in 1935. *Bucyrus International*

the machine to point in the desired direction when the shoes are off the ground. The shoes on the Martinson Tractor were suspended by chains as shown in the illustration. An important advantage of the walking dragline is the very low ground pressure exerted by the large-diameter base on which the machine sits while digging. When walking, only about 80 percent of the machine's weight is transferred to the shoes, which can also be made with large dimensions to reduce ground pressure. Walking draglines always walk backwards, as they must walk away from the hole or pit being excavated.

Page and Monighan had dissolved their relationship and each was producing his own draglines by the time Page Engineering was incorporated. Thus the Martinson invention gave the Monighan machines a superior advantage. Martinson improved his walking system in 1925 by eliminating the suspension chains, and sub-

stituting a cam wheel running in an oval track in a frame pivoted to the shoes. As credit to Martinson, this design has remained current on machines up to the present day. Bucyrus-Erie Company (now Bucyrus International, Inc.) took a controlling interest in the Monighan company in 1932, and renamed it the Bucyrus-Monighan Company. However, it was operated separately out of the Chicago works until the mid-1950s.

Meanwhile, Page began designing a walking system for its machines. In contrast to the Monighan system, Page came out with the most complicated system imaginable. To walk, the entire revolving frame and house ran on rollers inside another heavy frame, while the machine was lifted completely off the ground by three legs, two in front, one in the rear. All movements were powered by large numbers of chains, racks, and gears. In 1926, Page revised this propelling mechanism and perfected a vastly

The Bucyrus-Monighan 5-W first appeared in 1935, and was offered with diesel or electric power. The 5-yard dragline was very successful, and a total of 141 were built in Monighan's Chicago plant and the Ruston-Bucyrus plant in Lincoln, England. *Bucyrus International*

Chicago plant, and a further 62 were built in the Ruston-Bucyrus plant, Lincoln, England, over a production life that lasted until 1971.

In the late 1930s, two other walking dragline names emerged—Rapier and Marion. The British firm of Ransomes & Rapier Ltd. unveiled its first dragline in 1938, the Rapier W170. It carried a 4-yard bucket on a 135-foot boom, and featured the patented Cameron & Heath walking system, in which the shoes were attached to an eccentric cam running in a roller bearing. Ransomes & Rapier was established in 1869, and built an array of heavy equipment, including locomotive cranes and large dockside cranes. In 1914, it built the company's first excavator, a rail-mounted steam shovel.

The Marion Steam Shovel Company entered the walking dragline market in 1939 with the diesel- or electric-powered Model 7200, swinging a 5-yard bucket on a 120-foot boom. Later, 7200s carried 7-yard buckets. The following year, Marion came out with a 10- to 11-yard walker named the Model 7400. And then the big one! In 1942, Marion introduced the 7800, the world's largest dragline, capable of 30 cubic yards on a 185-foot boom. Launching the 7800 was an impressive achievement for Marion, which had only been in the dragline business for three years. The 7200, 7400, and 7800 were three extremely successful draglines that remained in Marion's product line for over 20 years. In the case of the 7400, more than 90 were sold from 1940 to 1974, for an incredible manufacturing life of some 34 years. The first Marion 7200 was still working some 55 years after it was built, and there are also several Marion 7800s in service at the time of writing.

Then in 1951, a Rapier machine claimed the world's largest dragline title. Although its 20-yard bucket had been exceeded earlier, the Rapier W1400's 282-foot long boom, and its operating weight of 1,880 tons, was much larger than any machine built at that time. The W-1400 was the first dragline to use tubular boom construction with compressed gas in the members to detect cracking. The cantilever-type, triangular-shaped boom can be instantly recognized as a unique Rapier feature.

In 1961 Rapier returned with an even larger machine, the W1800, reestablishing the company as the builder of the world's largest dragline. Weighing over 2,000 tons, and carrying a bucket of 40 cubic yards, the first W1800 went to a large open pit coal mine in South Wales, operated by George Wimpey & Company. Other W1800s worked on British ironstone stripping. One is still operating at Estevan Coal Company's Boundary Dam Mine, Saskatchewan, Canada.

Two years after the W1800 went to work, Marion startled the dragline world with the introduction of its Model 8800 in 1963. This world record-beater repre-

improved system, which was so good, it lasted on Page draglines for the next 60 years. A little more complicated than the Monighan system, it used eccentric drive to the shoes, which were attached to the machine by walking spuds or legs.

Soon after Bucyrus-Erie took over the Monighan company, the 950-B, the largest dragline built up to that time, was launched. The 950-B swung a 12-yard bucket on a 250-foot boom, which was the longest in the world. Shipped to Brazil in 1935, it was double the size of the previous largest walking dragline. Although only one was built, it laid the foundation for much larger draglines, which would appear over the next three decades.

At the small end of the scale, the Bucyrus-Monighan 5-W was unveiled in 1935. It was a diesel- or electric-powered machine with a 5-yard bucket on a 120-foot boom. A total of 79 of these popular draglines were built in the

The British firm of Ransomes & Rapier Ltd. first entered the walking dragline business with this W170 in 1938. It carried a 4-yard bucket on a 135-foot boom. The W170 shown here is uncovering ironstone in central England, where it worked until it was scrapped in 1971.

This is the first walking dragline built by Marion. It is a Model 7200 shipped in 1939, and it was known to be working some 55 years later! The picture was taken at the American Aggregates' gravel pits near Indianapolis, Indiana. The 7200 normally carries a 7-yard bucket.

The most popular Marion walking dragline was the 7400, first coming out in 1940. Over 90 were shipped until the last one left the plant in 1974. In the 11-yard class, the 7400 was available with diesel or electric power. The machine shown was built in 1948, and is stripping anthracite in South Wales. In 1973, this machine was relocated to Estevan, Saskatchewan, Canada, where it worked for a further 20 years.

sented a massive jump in size, with its 85-yard bucket on a 275-foot boom. On the 8800, Marion had to redesign its traditional single-shaft walking crank system, so the massive weight of 6,000 tons could be supported on two walk shafts. Each had eccentrics with different throws, resulting in an oval path for the shoe motion. Peabody Coal Company purchased the one and only 8800, which was later upgraded to a 100-yard machine.

Bigger draglines followed in the 1960s, the decade of the big strippers. Peabody Coal purchased the only two Marion 8900s, one for work in Australia, the other for a coal mine in Indiana. These carried 130- and 145-yard buckets, although Indiana's 8900 was upgraded to a 155-yard bucket in 1993. Marion's largest dragline was the 150-yard 8950, the only one of which was purchased by Amax Coal Company in 1973, and put to work in Indiana.

The design of *Big Muskie* (Model 4250-W), the most famous of all draglines, gained Bucyrus-Erie Company the

The largest of Marion's first three draglines was the 7800, launched in 1942. At 30 cubic yards on a 185-foot boom, it took the title of the world's largest dragline. *JKH collection*

The Bucyrus-Erie 1150-B was the largest dragline built by the company when it went to work in 1942. Carrying a 20-yard bucket on a 200-foot boom, it had an operating weight of 1,265 tons. The 1150-B shown is loading iron ore into a portable crusher, which is discharging onto a conveyor. The location is the South Agnew Mine in Minnesota, and the year is 1949. *Bucyrus International*

The world's largest walking dragline in 1961 was this Rapier W1800. The machine pictured carries a 40-yard bucket on a 250-foot boom, and is working at a large open pit coal mine in South Wales operated by contractor G. Wimpey & Company. The last W1800 still working belongs to Estevan Coal Company, Saskatchewan, Canada.

Marion's largest-ever dragline was the one-and-only 8900. First scooping dirt in 1973, the 150-yard machine worked for Amax Coal Company at its Ayrshire Mine, Indiana. *JKH collection*

crowning glory of the largest bucket ever to swing from an excavator. In 1969, *Big Muskie*'s massive 220-cubic yard capacity and 310-foot boom walked away with the "biggest dragline" title, wresting it from Marion's 145-yard Model 8900. With an estimated operating weight of 15,000 tons, *Big Muskie* housed 32 D.C. generators, powering 10 hoist motors, 8 drag motors, and 10 swing motors for a total of 48,500 horsepower. The unique hydraulic propelling system held 20,000 gallons of hydraulic oil to operate 95 hydraulic pumps. In propel mode, four massive vertical jacks lifted the base clear of the ground. Then, with the machine supported on its shoes, four horizontal jacks pushed it backward on sliders.

When *Big Muskie* went to work at the Muskingum Mine of the Central Ohio Coal Company, its size was

just the latest on a rapidly ascending curve. Manufacturers predicted the curve to continue, as no one even 10 years before had contemplated a machine of such gigantic proportions as the 220-yard machine. So manufacturers continued to design larger machines, and 1,000-yard machines were discussed, but nothing larger was ever put to work. *Big Muskie* was shut down in June 1991, because of weak markets for high-sulfur coal. At the time of writing, plans are afoot to preserve *Big Muskie* as a public interpretive site.

After a hiatus of some 13 years, the rush to coal mining in the 1970s prompted Ransomes & Rapier Ltd. to reenter the dragline business in 1975. It came out with a redesigned line of machines, and built several of the W700 and W2000 models. The new line represented a departure for Rapier in that a cable-supported conventional boom was utilized instead of the cantilever type. The 14-yard class W700 was available with diesel or electric power, while the W2000 carried up to 45 cubic yards. In 1988, the manufacturing rights of Rapier walking draglines were purchased by Bucyrus Europe, an offshoot of Bucyrus-Erie (now Bucyrus International). Today, Bucyrus still offers the W2000 Rapier-designed model in its dragline roster.

From its inception, Page Engineering Company produced a steady stream of walking draglines in its Chicago plant. Specializing only in draglines and dragline buckets, Page never produced a super-sized record-breaking machine, but its draglines in the small- and medium-size ranges found a respectable marketshare. The 621- and 625-series diesel-powered machines, featuring Page's own low-revving diesel engines, were very popular in the 1940s. In a typical installation, two diesels running at 450 rpm were utilized. One, a five-cylinder 550-horsepower engine, powered the hoist and drag functions, while another 240-horsepower three-cylinder engine, mounted on a raised deck at roof level, drove a generator to power two electric swing motors. These two slow-revving engines, especially when lugging down under load, emitted an unforgettable sound!

Page modernized its draglines in the mid-1950s, and started to build its 700-series. The Model 752 was the most popular and swung a standard 42-yard bucket. Many of these found homes in midwestern coal mines and in Florida phosphate fields. The largest dragline built by Page was the Model 757 delivered in 1983 to Obed Mountain Coal Ltd. near Hinton, Alberta, and

A big jump in size occurred in 1963 when Marion unveiled its 8800 monster dragline. The 8800 weighed in at 6,000 tons, and carried an 85-yard bucket on a 275-foot boom, comfortably taking the "world's largest" title. The 8800 was later increased to 100 cubic yards. *Eric Orlemann collection*

A midrange dragline from the Bucyrus-Erie (now Bucyrus International, Inc.) line is the 1300-W. The example shown here is working at the Sheerness Mine in central Alberta, Canada. It has a 260-foot boom and carries a 46-yard bucket. It started work in its present location in 1995, having been moved from Arkansas, and rebuilt from its former configuration of 28 yards on 325 feet of boom.

The greatest dragline by any scale is the Bucyrus-Erie 4250-W, known as *Big Muskie*. It swings a full 220-cubic yard bucket weighing 550 tons, on the end of a 310-foot boom, the biggest bucket on any dragline. This picture was taken at the launching ceremony in 1969 at the Muskingum Mine of the Central Ohio Coal Company. *Bucyrus International*

In 1975, Rapier came out with a redesigned line of walking draglines. Booms were of more conventional design, and represented a departure from Rapier's distinctive cantilever type used on its earlier draglines. The machine shown is the modern W2000 carrying a 44-yard bucket. It is stripping coal for C&K Coal Company near Clarion, Pennsylvania.

Big Muskie, the greatest and most famous dragline of all, is shown at work at the Muskingum Mine in Ohio. Wider than a football field, and almost 1 1/2 times the length, the machine weighs an estimated 15,000 tons. The propelling system consists of four shoes, each operated by a vertical hydraulic cylinder, which lift the machine's base entirely off the ground. *Big Muskie* was shut down and parked in 1991. *Bucyrus International*

This aerial shot of the *Big Muskie* erection site gives an indication of the enormous task involved in erecting the biggest-ever dragline. During erection, the wide revolving frame was rotated periodically, so that extreme locations on the deck could be brought within the range of the derrick crane. *Bucyrus International*

operated now by Luscar Ltd. Weighing 4,500 tons, it carries a 75-cubic yard bucket.

In 1988, Page Engineering Company was purchased by Harnischfeger Corporation (P&H), providing Harnischfeger with a range of draglines to supplement its popular shovels. The first P&H dragline was sold to British Coal Opencast for work in northeast England. It was an updated version of the Model 757, commissioned in 1991. P&H has since redesigned its draglines, and assembled the

Page Engineering Company specialized in draglines and dragline buckets. It produced a steady stream of draglines out of its Chicago plant. This Model 627, built in 1946, carries a 13-yard bucket on a 160-foot boom. It is working at the Muskingum Mine in Ohio.

first of its new 9000-series machines in Australia. The Model 9020 went to work in 1996 at the Bulga Coal operation in New South Wales. It swings a 115-yard bucket on a boom 320 feet long. P&H also offers its 9160 model, which can swing buckets of up to 160 cubic yards.

As large draglines continue to sell, there is a possibility that the *Big Muskie*'s 220-yard size record held for almost three decades could be broken. Black Thunder Mine in Wyoming put a new 160-yard Bucyrus-Erie 2570-WS dragline with a 360-foot boom to work in 1993. In 1994, Fording Coal Ltd., at its Genesee Mine in Alberta, started up a Marion 8750 with its 106-yard bucket on a 420-foot boom—the world's largest.

The first walking dragline was built in 1913, and except for a few machines built in the former Soviet Union, the walk-

161

The most popular of Page's 700-series draglines was this 752LR with a standard bucket of 42 cubic yards. *JKH collection*

The largest dragline Page built is this Model 757 working at Obed Mountain Coal Company, near Hinton, Alberta, Canada. In operation since 1983, it carries 75 cubic yards on a 291-foot boom, and weighs 4,500 tons.

ing draglines for the entire world market, have come from only four manufacturers. These are (1) the Monighan-designed machines that became Bucyrus-Erie's line in 1932, (2) the Page Engineering machines that were acquired by P&H in 1988, (3) the draglines built by Ransomes & Rapier Ltd., acquired by Bucyrus in 1988, and (4) the Marion machines, built since 1939.

In 1997, the Marion Power Shovel Company was purchased by Bucyrus International, Inc., reducing the already small number of suppliers to just two (plus those still built in the former Soviet Union) to supply the world's entire walking dragline needs.

A diesel-powered Page 625 carries a 10-yard bucket on a 150-foot boom. Page built its own diesel engines, specially designed for dragline duty. This machine is equipped with two diesel engines, one above the other. The lower one powers the main draw works, while the one upstairs powers the swing. *JKH collection*

Bucyrus-Erie put this 2570-WS monster dragline to work in 1993 at the Black Thunder Mine in Wyoming. Named *Ursa Major*, it carries a bucket of 160 cubic yards on a 360-foot boom. The structure on top of the house covers the air filtering system, so important on these large machines to keep dust from interfering with the electrics. *Bucyrus International*

The latest dragline to be completed by Harnischfeger Corporation is this P&H 9020 sold to Bulga Coal Company in Australia. It swings a 115-yard bucket on a 320-foot boom. Harnischfeger brought itself into the dragline business in 1988 when it purchased the assets of Page Engineering Company. The original Page designs were greatly revised, so the modern-day P&H bears little resemblance to the former Page machines. *Harnischfeger Corporation*

The Marion 8750 at Fording Coal's Genesee operations near Edmonton, Alberta, Canada, swings the longest boom ever installed on a dragline. At 420 feet, the boom carries a bucket of 106 cubic yards. An unusual feature of this machine is its 16 swing motors of 500 horsepower each. Starting work in 1994, the machine uncovers coal for power generation by the City of Edmonton. *Fording Coal Ltd.*

This strange-looking dragline was designed in the former Soviet Union and is working in Russia. The part-cable, part-tubular boom is a design typically adopted by the Russians. The dragline's hydraulic walking system, utilizing two rams working in synchronous motion, is also a unique Russian design. The machine illustrated is a Model Esh 15-90, carrying a 20-cubic yard bucket on a 295-foot boom. *JKH collection*

Chapter Ten

CONTINUOUS EXCAVATORS

Continuous excavators, as the name implies, move earth or mineral in one continuous stream. This is in contrast to all other types of earthmoving machines which operate in cycles such as excavators that dig, swing, and dump; bulldozers that must back up after each push; and haulers that must return empty after each load.

Continuous excavators come in many varieties, from the small ditching machines seen on subdivision projects, to the giant bucket wheel excavators, including some of the largest self-propelled machines ever constructed. Several of these giants are working in Germany, and can excavate over 300,000 tons of material per day. That output exceeds the capability of any other single machine yet built.

The bucket wheel excavator, moving vast amounts of material in a short time, is the cheapest method of moving earth when used in appropriate conditions. Its scope can be extended if it is used in conjunction with a system of conveyors, or a constant stream of trucks.

This chapter covers elevating graders, surface miners, bucket chain excavators, and the largest types of bucket wheel excavators. Ditching machines are described in Chapter 11.

Elevating Graders

This early form of continuous excavator was most popular for building roads. Most of the grader manufacturers, such as Russell (later Caterpillar), Austin-Western, and Adams, produced these machines. Originally elevating graders were pulled by teams of horses, and later by steam traction engine or crawler tractor. The elevating grader consisted of a cutting blade or disk, which directed the material onto a moving belt suspended laterally from the frame. The conveyor was powered by chain or gear drive from the wheels, or in later versions, a separate power unit was fitted. The discharged material could be loaded into wagons running alongside, or formed into windrows for compaction into a road base.

The earliest form of continuous excavator was the elevating grader. The 1917 Model A Russell pictured is owned by the Historical Construction Equipment Association, and has been beautifully restored. Its working motions are driven from the wheels by chains, and control is through the hand wheels.

Later elevating graders carried their own power units for the conveyor drive, but manpower muscle was still needed for most of the controls. The Adams No. 11 shown here was made from 1932 to 1946.

165

The Russell Grader Manufacturing Company was taken over by Caterpillar in 1928, and the graders became Caterpillar machines. The picture shows a restored Caterpillar No. 42 elevating grader, built in 1936, working on a county road job in 1985. It is owned by Bill Graham of Graham Brothers Contracting.

Another view of the 1936 Caterpillar No. 42 elevating grader, showing the cutting edge. On this machine, a power unit powers the conveyor and most of the controls through mechanical drives and jaw clutches.

This is a Model BV belt loader developed by Euclid in 1940. It found many successful applications in the 1940s when it was pulled by the largest crawler tractors of the day. With improved technology and a powerful diesel engine in the 150–190-horsepower class, the belt loader had a far greater output than the earlier elevating graders.

Probably the earliest elevating grader was the machine built by the New Era Manufacturing Company in 1866. In 1887, the Austin Manufacturing Company purchased the New Era company, and by 1898, the former wood-constructed machine was redesigned to steel construction. Both the Austin Manufacturing Company and the Western Wheeled Scraper Company made a line of elevating graders that continued after these two companies merged into the Austin-Western Company in 1934. The Russell Grader Manufacturing Company also made these machines in several sizes. Later, Caterpillar adopted the machines after it took over Russell in 1928. The J.D. Adams Company, having initially marketed the Stroud Elevating Graders (built since 1904), produced its own machines from 1930 to 1946.

By the mid-1940s, most grader manufacturers had discontinued the elevating types in favor of nimble motor scrapers and regular graders with greater capability. Although their technology is obsolete today, elevating graders built roads efficiently, as the dirt moved straight from ditch to embankment over the shortest distance. However, sometimes the roots and topsoil went in the fill as well!

Surface Miners (Continuous Excavators)

A type of machine developed by several manufacturers is the surface miner, also known by various trade names. These self-propelled machines operate in a similar manner to the old elevating grader. They consist of a cutting wheel or blade, which directs the material onto a conveyor belt for loading trucks traveling alongside. Capable of extremely high output, surface miners seldom work with enough trucks to achieve their maximum output! Their ability to peel off thin layers of material makes surface miners useful in mining thin coal seams, or separating partings from the mineral.

In 1940, Euclid produced the BV loader, which was probably the first continuous excavator, but its development was interrupted by World War II. However, it was exhibited at the 1948 Chicago Road Show, and it attracted much attention. Designed to be pulled by the largest crawler tractors of the day, the BV loader consisted of a blade that simply cut the material and directed it onto its conveyor belt. The belt was driven by a Cummins 150-horsepower engine or optional GM 190-horsepower engine, and the machine was mounted on a pair of nonpowered crawler tracks. The tractor operator controlled its cutting depth hydraulically.

The Euclid BV loader enjoyed considerable success on the big dirtmoving jobs of the era, such as the Garrison Dam in North Dakota. The Ohio Turnpike job utilized 19 units. The last BV loader was built in 1956, its popularity having waned due to competition from the vastly improved motor scraper.

While Euclid was under ownership of the White Motor Corporation in 1969, it took another shot at the belt loader concept. The substantially larger "Super BV" had a 635-horsepower GM engine to drive the conveyor, and four nonpowered crawlers to support the machine. Only two of these units were built, one of which worked on the San Luis Dam in California.

P&H Harnischfeger offered its Model C-30A belt loader in the late 1950s. Designed to be pulled by a crawler tractor of 150 horsepower or more, it was mounted on large rubber tires, and its controls were operated by cable from the double-drum winch on the tractor. The conveyor was powered by a P&H 120-horsepower diesel engine.

From its line of pavement profilers, CMI Corporation of Oklahoma City, Oklahoma, developed some surface miners for coal loading operations in the mid-1970s. The machines featured a centrally mounted cutting drum whose powerful milling action could dig hard coal, without ripping or blasting. The larger CMI machines utilized engines that produced up to 750 horsepower to drive the cutter, plus a 208-horsepower engine for propelling. They were mounted on three crawler tracks, the single front track steering the machine.

Another type of continuous excavator developed by CMI was the Autovator 1000. This spectacular machine was driven by two 425-horsepower diesel engines and propelled on eight hydrostatically driven crawler track assemblies. The 90-ton machine could dig at speeds up to 240 feet per minute, and excavate at rates up to 6,000 cubic yards per hour. The Autovator sliced material from a face at one side of the machine, and loaded it from a discharge

The Euclid Super BV loader was a totally different machine to the one shown in the previous picture. This bird's-eye view shows the impressive machine in the factory. It was mounted on four crawlers, and carried a 635-horsepower engine. Two of these were put to work in 1969 on the San Luis Dam job in California. *Eric Orlemann collection*

Harnischfeger entered the continuous excavator market with this P&H C-30A in the late 1950s. Required to be pulled by a tractor in the 150-horsepower class, it was controlled by cables from a double-drum winch on the tractor. It carried a 120-horsepower diesel engine to power the conveyor.

CMI Corporation developed a line of continuous excavators in the 1970s, including some of the most powerful of their type ever produced. The PR-1200 shown here has two diesel engines totaling over 1,000 horsepower. These machines are mounted on three crawler tracks, and carry a centrally mounted cutting wheel. *CMI Corporation*

Another type of continuous excavator is the "Autovator" developed by CMI Corporation. This spectacular machine runs on eight crawler tracks, and can load material at rates up to 6,000 cubic yards per hour. The 90-ton giant is powered by two 425-horsepower diesel engines. *CMI Corporation*

A close-up view of the CMI "Autovator." This machine is equipped with two cutting edges to enable the machine to attack the cutting face from both directions, without having to turn around. It also has two operator's cabs, one for each direction of travel. *CMI Corporation*

The Barber-Greene principle of continuous excavation consists of a 16-foot-diameter digging wheel designed to cut material from a face on one side of a crawler-mounted machine. Known as the WL-50, this 116-ton excavator is powered by a Caterpillar 575-horsepower engine.

This Barber-Greene WL-50 stripping soil at a Wyoming surface coal mine is making the dirt fly. With its long conveyor, high discharge, and high output, it takes a lot of 120- to 150-ton trucks to keep the WL-50 digging.

The Holland Loader cuts and loads large volumes of material by sheer brute force. Developed in 1971, the Holland Loader utilizes two large crawler tractors to push the cutting edge through the bank to be excavated. The one shown is cutting a vertical face utilizing a pair of 520-horsepower Fiat-Allis HD-41 tractors. In addition to the tractors, there is a 525-horsepower engine driving the conveyor, for a total of 1,565 horsepower on the outfit. *Holland Loader Company*

conveyor at the other side. Two separate cutting edges facing opposite directions allowed the machine to dig in both directions without turning around, and two cabs were installed to let the operator always face the travel direction.

The Barber-Greene WL-50 Excavator, like the Autovator, also cut a slice of material from a working face on one side and discharged it on the other side. However, a 16-foot-diameter wheel with buckets around its circumference provided the WL-50's dig-

ging action. The discharge conveyor was 31 feet long enabling it to load 150-ton trucks. Powered by a Caterpillar 575-horsepower diesel engine, the WL-50 weighed 116 tons, and was propelled on three hydro-statically powered crawler tracks.

Beginning in 1971, Barber-Greene built several WL-50s. Typically, these excavators worked on large earth-moving jobs filling bottom-dump wagons, or on salvaging soil in surface mining operations. McNally-Pitts-

This view shows the vertical face being excavated by this Holland Loader being pulled by a Caterpillar D9H tractor. The loader carries a 525-horsepower engine to power the conveyor, and there is another D9H pushing at the rear. The entire outfit is controlled by one operator. *Holland Loader Company*

Another version of the Holland Loader takes a horizontal cut, as shown in this picture. The largest Holland Loader was recently pulled by two Caterpillar D11N tractors which, combined with the loader's own power unit, provide a massive 2,065 horsepower. *Holland Loader Company*

burg took over the rights of the WL-50 in the mid-1980s. Then, in 1990, the rights passed to Svedala Bulk Materials Handling when the latter purchased McNally Systems of Pittsburg, Kansas. Svedala still manufactures parts and provides service for the WL-50.

The Holland Loader, with its 15-foot-high cutting blade and 8-foot-wide main conveyor, is another machine able to cut a vertical slice of material. The entire machine is suspended on a frame, supported between two large crawler tractors, which provide the cutting and propelling power. The frame can be raised or lowered hydraulically. The sheer brute force of the tractors and the 525 horsepower of the engine driving the conveyor combined to produce the ability to load up to 7,000 cubic yards per hour.

In 1971, Holland Construction Company of Billings, Montana, first built the loaders for its own use, and later the company began building them for sale. Typically, Holland Loaders are coupled between two of the largest crawler tractors available: first Caterpillar D9Gs, then D9Hs or Fiat-Allis HD-41s. In 1997, two Caterpillar D11Ns were in use on the East Side Reservoir job in California. In this configuration, the combined power of the two tractors and the conveyor engine runs to a massive 2,065 horsepower! The Holland is offered in vertical or horizontal cut configurations. Over 70 Holland Loaders have been built to date for use on major earthmoving jobs around the world.

Wirtgen GmbH of Bonn, Germany, has been making road milling machines for more than 30 years, and has become the market leader of this type of equipment. Based on similar design principles, the company introduced the Wirtgen Surface Miner in 1980. The machine consists of a centrally mounted drum with cutting teeth, and a 180-degree swinging rear-mounted conveyor. It is propelled on three or four tracks, depending on the model size. The milling action of the cutting drum enables it to cut through hard material. The present range of Wirtgen Surface Miners consists of four models from the 600-horsepower 2100SM at 44 tons to the massive 4200SM at 1,600 horsepower and 193 tons. Over 60 of these machines have been built to date, and many of these have found their way into surface mines in North America.

The Huron Manufacturing Company of Huron, South Dakota, was established in 1963, initially to build curb and gutter machines. Huron developed a continuous coal loader called the Easi-Miner and announced it to the industry in 1976. Like the Wirtgen just described, the Easi-Miner is propelled on four crawlers, has its cutting drum mounted centrally within the main frame, and discharged to the side or rear. Four models of Easi-Miners are offered. The largest is the Model 1224. So far 19 units have been built. The 1224 weighs 140 tons and is powered by a 1,200 horsepower Cummins engine.

In 1985, Rahco International, formerly R.A. Hanson Company, of Spokane, Washington, produced the first CME-12 continuous excavator prototype. This twin-crawler machine can excavate a 12-foot-wide path with a rotating cutter head at one end, and a discharge conveyor at the other. It can excavate thin coal seams with the cutting head at ground level, but since the cutting head is mounted on a boom, it can be raised to cut up to 14 feet high. A 475-horsepower Caterpillar diesel engine provides its power.

Another continuous coal excavator was offered for a short time by Unit Rig of Tulsa, Oklahoma, now a division of Terex Corporation. Unit Rig purchased the manufacturing rights from Satterwhite International, Inc., and tested it in 1975. Called the "Unimatic," the machine utilized a 12-foot-diameter cutting drum fitted

R.A. Hanson Company offers the CME-12 continuous excavator. This carries its cutting wheel at the front, and is capable of digging a 12-foot-wide path. It can also excavate a face up to 14 feet high by raising the wheel on its support arms. Power comes from a Caterpillar 475-horsepower diesel engine. *R.A. Hanson Company*

The Wirtgen Surface Miner was introduced on the market by the German company in 1980. One of its line of four machines, ranging up to 1,600 horsepower, this 750-horsepower Model 300SM is shown loading coal in a Canadian surface mine.

Huron Manufacturing Company brought out its Easi-Miner in 1976. The top-of-the-line model was the heavyweight Model 1224, with 1,200 horsepower and a 140-ton operating weight. *JKH collection*

171

The prototype Unit Rig "Unimatic" continuous excavator is shown under test in 1975. This machine incorporates a 12-foot-diameter cutting wheel employing electric drive, while the machine is propelled on four hydrostatically driven wheels. *Unit Rig*

Here, the "Unimatic" from Unit Rig is ready for work at the Navajo Mine, New Mexico, in 1975. This big 1,200-horsepower excavator weighed 125 tons, and could cut a path 15 feet wide.

This is the Krupp KSM 2000, developed jointly by the German firm and the Russian Institute of Mining. The prototype machine completed successful tests in 1996 at the Taldinskij Mine in Russia. The machine is outfitted with diesel power of 1,340 horsepower, and tips the scales at 220 tons. *Krupp Canada*

with buckets and teeth and driven electrically by AC motors. Mounted on four large steerable, hydrostatically driven rubber tires, the Unimatic weighed 125 tons. Diesel engines pumping out 1,200 horsepower supplied electric power generation for the wheel drive, and power for the hydrostatic propulsion.

The line of Surface Miners made by Krupp Fordertechnik GmbH of Germany includes the largest continuous excavator yet produced. First available in 1988, these machines consist of a rotating wheel at the front of the machine, similar to the Rahco and Unit Rig machines. Material is discharged to the rear via a conveyor that can swing through an arc of 200 degrees. Mounted on a pair of crawler tracks, the entire upper frame pivots at the rear, so the digging wheel can be raised and lowered by two hydraulic cylinders attached to the front of the crawler frame.

The record-beating KSM 4000 machine was tested in 1991 and 1992 at a Wyoming coal mine. With 3,100 horsepower, the machine weighed 419 tons, and was designed with a nominal capacity of over 5,000 cubic yards per hour. More recently, Krupp and the Russian Institute of Mining have jointly developed a prototype of the smaller KSM 2000. Of similar design to its larger brother, the KSM 2000 is outfitted with diesel engines producing 1,340 horsepower. In June 1996, the machine completed successful performance tests and was handed over to the Taldinskij Mine in Russia.

Bucket Chain Excavators

The bucket chain excavator consists of a series of buckets attached to an endless chain that can be raised and lowered over the working face. The buckets excavate the material, lifting it upward to dump into a hopper, which empties onto a conveyor. Most machines travel on rail tracks laid on top of and parallel to the working face. The machine digs as it moves slowly from one end of the face to the other. So the longer the working face, the more efficient the operation, as the rails must be repositioned after each pass.

Bucket chain and bucket wheel excavators are probably the earliest types of excavating machines ever built. Their origins go back to ancient times. Leonardo da Vinci had sketches of a bucket excavator in the sixteenth century. Over the decades, many different types and designs have been drawn up, but it is unclear if any of these were actually built. The earliest confirmed multibucket excavators were ladder types that were used on

This British bucket chain excavator was designed and built by Stothert & Pitt Ltd. It is mining clay for use in cement manufacture, an application very suitable for a bucket chain excavator, where the full face of clay can be blended to improve the product sent to the processing plant.

One of the first bucket chain excavators was this steam-powered machine from LMG in 1882. This rail-mounted machine could dig above as well as below its grade level. *O&K*

The German firm of Lubecker-Maschinenbau-Gesellschaft (LMG) was a leader in bucket chain excavators in the early part of this century, although as early as 1911, it was absorbed into the Orenstein & Koppel (O&K) organization. Giant steam machines were built, including this one in 1909, with a digging depth of 72 feet, and a capability of 1,300 cubic yards per hour. *O&K*

This Steenbrugge bucket chain excavator, shown working in central England, was built in Belgium. Instead of transporting the excavated material by the usual method of conveyor, this machine pulverizes the clay and, with the addition of water, pumps the material in the form of a slurry to its destination.

Bucket wheel excavators were developed some 50 years after the first bucket chain machines. O&K/LMG built its first in 1934. This 1937 machine from the same company has an output of 3,500 cubic yards per hour. It is working in the German lignite coal fields near Cologne. *JKH collection*

In 1908, British engineer A.R. Grossmith designed one of the first bucket wheel excavators, and put it to work in the ironstone mines at Corby, England. Although the principle was sound, this early machine, shown under repair with its digging wheel removed, was not a success.

water-borne eighteenth-century dredgers. Used to lift mud from shipping channels, they were driven by animals, manpower, or even by windmills.

The advent of the steam engine permitted dredgers to be built in more substantial proportions, enabling them to attack tougher material. One of the earliest recorded was a steam dredge working in 1796 in the Port of Sunderland, England. Many modern-day ports were initially constructed, and later dredged, by large ladder dredgers in the early 1800s.

The first documented application of a bucket chain excavator for use on land was by a French contractor, Alphonse Couvreux, in 1859. Couvreux used some of his first excavators in the construction of the Ardennes railway. From 1863 to 1868, seven Couvreux excavators moved almost eight million cubic yards of earth in the

construction of the Suez Canal. A scale model of the 1859 Couvreux excavator is in the Museum of Technology in Paris. Bucket chain excavators by Couvreux, and machines built by Weyher & Richemond and Buette, were also used on the Panama Canal during the unsuccessful French attempt by Ferdinand de Lesseps beginning in 1879.

In 1877, Lubecker-Maschinenbau-Gesellschaft (LMG) of Germany made its first bucket dredger, which had an output of 40 cubic yards per hour. Then LMG produced its first bucket chain excavator for use on land in 1882. Steam-driven and rail-mounted, it was adaptable for digging above and below grade level. LMG rapidly introduced a vast range of improved models, which found use in canal excavation in Europe and in surface mining around 1900. As early as 1909, LMG built a 335-horsepower machine with a digging depth of 72 feet and an output 1,300 cubic yards per hour. The machines were very successful, and two of the Type B bucket chain excavators built in 1887 were still operating in Germany as late as 1957. In 1911, Orenstein & Koppel (O&K), founded in 1876, bought a majority interest in LMG, and continued the bucket chain excavators.

Over the decades, large bucket chain excavators were very popular in clay pits, where the full face of material must be blended for brickmaking, etc. They are used in the German coal fields to mine lignite, and at the vast Yallourn open pit coal mine in Victoria, Australia. Although very few bucket chain excavators are built today, they still have their uses. An application has been found in stockpiling and reclaiming work in bulk materials. The original LMG/O&K machines are now available from Krupp Fordertechnik GmbH, established in 1993 when O&K and Krupp merged together as subsidiaries of Hoesch-Krupp. Other machines have been built in Belgium (Boom and Steenbrugge), England

The first of the giant bucket wheel excavators was billed as the largest mobile land machine in the world when it was erected in 1955. The monster machine weighs 6,100 tons and, mounted on 18 crawler tracks, measures over two football fields in length. Designed by O&K, this machine led the way to machines of even greater capacity. *JKH collection*

(Stothert and Pitt Ltd.), the former Soviet Union, and other eastern European countries.

Bucket Wheel Excavators

Like the bucket chain excavator, the bucket wheel excavator (BWE) originated in Europe, although the BWE was developed much later. It is essentially an extension of the chain excavator, except that a wheel fitted with digging buckets around its circumference rotates at the end of the boom. Bucket wheel machines are usually connected to an elaborate system of conveyors, or a belt wagon (mobile conveyor), which can transport the material considerable distances, although BWEs can also be arranged to load trucks.

A British engineer, A.R. Grossmith, put one of the first BWEs to work in 1908 in the ironstone fields near Corby, England. Although earlier attempts had been made, surprisingly, the first BWEs did not appear until about 50 years after the first bucket chain excavator. Many patents were granted, and some experiments were conducted, but the technology of the day could not produce a reliable machine. Even the Grossmith machine was unsuccessful, and was soon converted to a shovel. The late development of the BWE was due to the difficulty of transferring the material from wheel to conveyor, lack of reliable material to build a conveyor, and the fact that a chain with attached buckets was easier to construct.

After the initial attempts, BWE development continued in Germany, with one of the first machines built by Humboldt in 1919. The first successful BWE appeared in 1925 at the Luise Mine of Braunkohlenwerke, in Germany, where it was used in reclaiming stockpiles. In 1926, ATG Leipzig purchased manufacturing rights to the Humboldt machines and expanded the BWE program. By

1938, ATG had delivered its 50th machine.

Buckau-Wolf AG built a crawler-mounted BWE in 1938. Established some 10 years earlier, and with ancestor companies dating back to 1838, Buckau-Wolf had built bucket chain excavators dating back to the nineteenth century. In the 1950s, its range was expanded with many sizes and types of BWE and bucket chain machines sold worldwide.

O&K/LMG built their first BWE in 1934. The following year, a machine with an output of 3,500 cubic yards per hour appeared, and in 1937, the first crawler-mounted BWE was created.

In 1955, a major breakthrough occurred when O&K erected the first of the giant BWEs at the vast open pit coal mine of Rheinische Braunkohlenwerke AG., Cologne, Germany. Billed as the largest mobile land machine in the world, this monster weighed 6,120 tons, and could excavate more than 5,000 cubic yards per hour. Mounted on 18 crawler tracks, including its belt wagon, it was the length of more than two football fields. Over the subsequent two decades, this same mining company ordered many more monster BWEs, including the largest ever built.

Size records for BWEs (based on operating weight) were broken in 1956 (8,200 tons), 1975 (13,400 tons), and 1977 (14,500 tons). The last machine is the largest built to date. It can dig to the height of a 16-story building, and has 18 eight-yard buckets mounted on a wheel 71 feet in diameter. It moves overburden at rates of over 300,000 cubic yards each working day, and its power comes from a multitude of electric motors totaling 18,700 horsepower.

Because of the vast amount of expertise and technology required to build the large bucket wheels, two of

The German firm of Krupp delivered its first bucket wheel excavator in 1948, and gained much experience in this technology over the subsequent decades. One of the largest Krupp machines is shown here working for the German coal company Rheinbraun in its Hambach Mine. This larger-than-life monster weighs just over 14,500 tons, and can excavate up to 314,000 cubic yards of earth per day. *Krupp Fordertechnik*

the leading German manufacturers formed a joint arrangement in the 1960s called the Bucketwheel Export Union. This group, consisting of Krupp and O&K, combined their forces and expertise to build the giant machines for export around the world. Krupp had delivered their first BWE in 1948, and by 1972 had sold more than 100 machines.

Other German companies came into the BWE market and achieved substantial success. Demag-Lauchhammer carried on the pioneering work done by Mitteldeutsche Stahlwerke AG, and produced many vari-

eties of BWEs over the years. Hermann Surken built many BWEs for special purposes such as tunneling and clay extraction for brickmaking from 1956. Weserhutte AG also built a large variety of smaller machines. In 1980, Weserhutte became a member of the PWH Group, and was known as PHB Weserhutte. Later it was associated with O&K, and following the merger with Krupp in 1993, it became part of Krupp Fordertechnik.

Several other European countries developed BWEs, such as the former GDR, now part of the Federal Republic of Germany (Takraf), Czechoslovakia (Unex),

This is the largest bucket wheel excavator working today, and one of the largest mobile land machines ever created! After taking just under 2 1/2 years to erect, it went to work in 1991. Towering to the height of a 30-story building, it weighs almost 14,900 tons, and can move up to 314,000 cubic yards of material per day. This enormous machine was built by O&K for use by Rheinbraun in its Hambach Mine. In 1992, Krupp purchased the rights to O&K's bucket wheel excavators, and the expertise of both companies has combined to form Krupp Fordertechnik. *Krupp Fordertechnik*

The newest giant bucket wheel excavator operated by Rheinbraun is this MAN/Takraf machine, starting in late 1995. Like its sister machines built by O&K and Krupp, the MAN/Takraf has a capacity of 314,000 cubic yards per hour. Note the operator's cab suspended at the end of the long boom. These giant bucket wheel machines move on no less than 15 crawler tracks, each one measuring 49 feet long by 12 feet wide. *Yvon LeCadre*

and the former Soviet Union. In Scotland, Mavor & Coulson Ltd. launched the Mavor E10 diesel-powered BWE, a small portable machine mounted on four wheels, in 1967. A crawler-mounted machine soon followed. In the 1970s, these machines were marketed by Anderson Strathclyde Ltd. In Austria, Voest-Alpine Bergtechnik makes many varieties of continuous excavating machines, including surface miners, belt wagons, cross-pit spreaders, and BWEs.

The manufacturers of the large BWEs such as O&K, Krupp, and Weserhutte also developed a line of smaller, "off-the-shelf" machines beginning in the mid-1960s. These are of a standard design as opposed to the large machines, which are specified for a particular application. Although known as "compact excavators," these BWEs range to quite large dimensions and weights. The O&K S-630, for example, has an output of up to 3,900 cubic yards per hour and weighs about 370 tons. Compact excavators are mounted on two crawler

tracks, and their discharge boom swings independently of the wheel boom.

Bucket Wheel Excavators— Application in North America

Several of the European BWEs have operated in North America. One of the Demag-Lauchhammer machines was used on the Oroville Dam construction in California. Built in 1962, this two-crawler machine had an operating weight of 670 tons, and worked in conjunction with a crawler-mounted belt wagon to feed a conveyor. When this contract was completed, the entire outfit was moved to the Centralia Coal Mine, Washington. There it successfully

Another Krupp machine is this type Sch Rs 250, installed in a surface coal mine in the north of England by contractor Derek Crouch in 1960. The machine is taking the upper clay layer, up to 40 feet high, and feeding it onto a round-the-pit conveyor system to dump via a spreader onto spoils, where the coal has been removed. Below, draglines are removing the lower strata to expose the coal, as much as 180 feet deep.

This is the discharge end of the conveyor system fed by the bucket wheel excavator in the previous picture. A movable "tripper" traveling on rails picks up the material and transfers it to the crawler-mounted slewable spreader. *JKH collection*

moved five million cubic yards per year at rates up to 1,200 cubic yards per hour.

From 1964, another Demag-Lauchhammer BWE operated at the Glen Harold Mine in North Dakota, belonging to Truax-Traer Coal Company (later Consol). Built by McDowell-Wellman Engineering Company of Cleveland, Ohio, this machine had an operating weight of almost 3,000 tons. Unfortunately, it only had a short stay in North Dakota, after encountering unforeseen boulders in the overburden. It was then moved to the Norris Mine in Illinois, but this mine was closed in the late 1970s, and the BWE scrapped.

A notable Krupp machine to operate in the United States was the machine put in service by Peabody Coal Company at its Northern Illinois Mine in 1963. Mounted on a standard "shovel base" of eight crawler tracks built by

Marion Power Shovel Company, this 3,600-ton machine was equipped with an independent swinging discharge conveyor. It stood on the uncovered coal in the bottom of the pit, excavated from the top of the high wall, and discharged the material onto the spoil pile across the pit. This type of BWE is referred to as a cross-pit bucket wheel excavator. The machine is self-contained, and no other machine is needed to discharge the material.

Because the very hard shale caused a high rate of bucket tooth wear, Peabody soon moved its Krupp machine to the River King Mine, Illinois, where conditions were more amenable to a BWE.

Successful BWEs were designed and built by the United Electric Coal Companies (now Freeman-United Coal Mining Company) for use at their mines in Illinois. Under the guidance of their president, Frank Kolbe, a series of six cross-pit BWEs was built beginning in 1944. All were built on old stripping shovel bases, utilizing four crawler assemblies, each with two crawler tracks to level and steer the machine. The resulting BWEs were five times as productive as the shovels they replaced! In 1959, the largest of the Kolbe "wheels," as they became known, was built. The W4 had an enormous capability of 2 million cubic yards per month. The massive Kolbe W4 weighed 2,100 tons, carried a 27-foot diameter digging wheel, with ten 2 1/2-cubic yard buckets, and could tackle a face height over 10 stories high. The distance from the digging buckets to the end of the discharge conveyor measured 420 feet, but the material landed a further 25 feet away after shooting off the end of the conveyor. The 60-inch discharge belt ran at an unprecedented 1,225 feet per minute, beating previous world-record conveyor speeds.

On the Kolbe BWEs, the discharge boom and wheel boom always remain in the same vertical plane as the machine rotates from side to side during digging. Cross-pit BWEs usually remove the upper, softer overburden from the working face, casting it on top of the previous spoil pile. A stripping shovel working in the same pit as the wheel removes the remainder of the material, casting it into the adjacent worked-out pit where the coal has been removed.

After the launch of the W4 in 1959, United Electric Coal announced the sale of the plans and patents for the Kolbe wheel to Bucyrus-Erie Company, which continued to develop this type of cross-pit BWE. Bucyrus-Erie built the 810-ton Model 684-WX for the contractors working on the 40-million-yard San Luis Dam job in California. This crawler-mounted machine was used to load 100-ton bottom-dumping wagons at a rate of 4,500 cubic yards per hour, when supply of wagons permitted. When this project was completed, the 684-WX was purchased by Great Canadian Oil Sands (now Suncor) for work in the tar sands in Alberta.

This Voest-Alpine bucket wheel excavator, made in Austria, is working at Texas Utilities Mining Company's Winfield South Mine in Texas. It carries a 40-foot-diameter digging wheel, and the machine weighs 1,375 tons. This machine works in conjunction with a 1,100-foot-long cross-pit spreader.

Made in Scotland, this mobile wheel-mounted excavator was built by Mavor & Coulson Ltd. in 1967, and is typical of many similar small bucket wheel excavators produced by various manufacturers. The Mavor excavators, including crawler versions, were marketed by Anderson Strathclyde Ltd. in the 1970s. *JKH collection*

Bucyrus-Erie built several other large BWEs whose design was similar to that of the Kolbe wheels. The largest went to work in 1986 at the Captain Mine of Arch Coal Inc. The 5872-WX excavator is mounted on the lower works of a Marion 5860, an 80-yard shovel purchased secondhand for the purpose. The 40-foot-diameter wheel has 12 buckets of 2.14 cubic yards each. This immense excavator has a 259-foot maximum cutting radius, 442-foot dumping radius, an operating weight of 3,500 tons, and overall length of more than two football fields. The Marion 6360, the largest stripping shovel ever built, was assigned to work with the 5872-WX wheel. When this shovel was destroyed by fire, a 105-yard Marion 5900 took over the duty.

Another American-designed line of BWEs was built by Mechanical Excavators Inc. (MX) of Los Ange-

The leading bucket wheel excavator manufacturers offer what they call "compact excavators." Unlike the monster bucket wheels designed for a specific mine, these off-the-shelf machines are made to a standard specification. However, they often reach large proportions. The Krupp C-700 illustrated has a 25-foot-diameter wheel and an operating weight of 404 tons. *JKH collection*

This large "compact excavator" is Model S-630 from O&K. It has a maximum output of 3,900 cubic yards per hour and weighs 370 tons.

This slewable discharge spreader, manufactured by Mitsubishi, handles the material from the conveyor system fed by the O&K bucket wheel machine shown in the previous picture.

Seen here at the Centralia Coal Mine in Washington is a Demag-Lauchhammer bucket wheel excavator, built in the United States by McDowell-Wellman Engineering Co. Seen here undergoing repairs, the 670-ton machine excavated overburden at the rate of 1,200 cubic yards per hour, and fed it onto the mobile stacker seen in the background.

Another spectacular machine from Demag-Lauchhammer was this bucket wheel owned by Consolidation Coal Company, shown here after completing its work at the Norris Mine in Illinois. Built by McDowell-Wellman, it had an operating weight of 3,000 tons.

les, which acquired the construction rights from Bill Mittry of Mittry Construction Company in 1960. These compact-type machines were mounted on wheels or crawler tracks. Their claim to fame was their angled digging wheel, allowing the material to flow straight onto the belt. This eliminated the usual discharge chute. After placing many MX machines of different sizes in North America, and in several overseas countries, Mechanical Excavators Inc. was sold to American Hoist & Derrick Co. in 1982.

In the massive tar sands operations in northern Alberta, Canada, both major operators, Syncrude and Suncor, included bucket wheel excavators in their mining plans from day one. Syncrude used bucket wheels to rehandle the tar sand from stockpiles thrown up by large draglines. Incidentally, Syncrude probably has amassed the world's greatest concentration of earthmoving equipment at one location. At Suncor, wheels have been used for both overburden and tar sand removal. Both O&K and Krupp have supplied BWEs to the tar sands.

Two cross-pit systems, employed by Texas Utilities Mining Company in its coal mines, utilize BWEs to feed crawler-mounted cross-pit spreaders (XPS) of spectacular dimensions. These systems are used to strip the upper levels of overburden and discharge it onto the spoil piles, well clear of the pit. Draglines remove the remaining overburden to expose the coal. In the earlier system, built by Demag in 1986, a pair of compact BWEs working on different bench levels feed separate receiving hoppers of the cross-pit spreader. This consists of a main conveyor, running on a 680-foot-long

A close-up view of the Kolbe W4 bucket wheel excavator. The machine was built on the lower works of a retired stripping shovel, which was built in 1929 and is shown in chapter 8. The operator's cab is mounted atop the tower, almost 100 feet above the ground. The W4 was the largest of six bucket wheel excavators built by the company.

LEFT: This is one of the cross-pit bucket wheel machines built by the United Electric Coal Companies (now Freeman-United Coal Mining Company). The one illustrated was known as the W4 Kolbe wheel, named after the company's president, Frank Kolbe. It started work at the Cuba Mine in Illinois in 1959, and could excavate at the tremendous rate of two million cubic yards of overburden per month. Unlike the machines in the previous two pictures, this "cross-pit" wheel excavator had its discharge boom fixed in the same plane as the digging boom.

boom, suspended by cables from a high gantry. The combined system is designed to move 7,800 cubic yards per hour.

In 1991, the second Texas system was installed. Manufactured by Voest-Alpine of Austria, it consists of a single BWE feeding a crawler-mounted cross-pit spreader with a discharge boom 834 feet long, which is the equivalent of 2 1/2 football fields. It is among the longest mobile booms in the world, and is suspended by cables from a gantry 246 feet (25 stories) high. Designed to move 20 million cubic yards of overburden per year, the machine travels on three pairs of crawler tracks, each 13 feet wide and 46 feet long. A Voest-Alpine BWE weighing 1,375 tons feeds the spreader. From the wheel's cutting teeth to discharge end of the mobile spreader, the excavated material travels 1,300 feet—nearly one-quarter of a mile. Amazing!

This is a Model 684-WX bucket wheel built by Bucyrus-Erie Company. It is shown working in the Alberta tar sands for Great Canadian Oil Sands (now Suncor). The 684-WX has a 30-foot-diameter digging wheel, and an operating weight of 812 tons. *Bucyrus International*

One of the first Bucyrus-Erie bucket wheel excavators was this Model 954-WX. Like the Kolbe machines, this one was built on the base of a retired stripping shovel, a 950-B. This lumbering mass of 1,180 tons could cut to a height of 75 feet. The wheel excavator removes the top layer of glacial till material, while the lower, harder material is cast aside by the stripping shovel, shown in the background. *Bucyrus International*

This is the digging end of the 954-WX wheel excavator shown in the previous picture. The sticky material requires buckets with chain backs to dislodge the contents. Also note the two rotating wipers, which ensure that the material dropping on the plate is directed onto the conveyor that carries it away. *Bucyrus-International*

The largest-ever bucket wheel excavator built by Bucyrus-Erie was this Model 5872-WX, installed at the Captain Mine of Arch Coal Inc. in Illinois. First going to work in 1986, this cross-pit machine has a 40-foot-diameter wheel, and moves the excavated material, from the digging face to the dump, a distance of 700 feet! It is built on the lower works of a retired Marion 5860 stripping shovel. *Eric Orlemann*

Another U.S. manufacturer of bucket wheel excavators was Mechanical Excavators of Los Angeles, California, established in 1960. After many successful installations of its excavators, the company was sold to American Hoist & Derrick Company in 1982. The machine shown is the Model 3000E, located at the Belle Ayr Mine in Wyoming, in 1981. It is owned by Amax Coal Company.

This is the midsection of a huge cross-pit excavator and spreader system employed by Texas Utilities Mining Company at its Big Brown Mine in Texas. Designed and built by Demag, the system consists of a pair of bucket wheel excavators, positioned on different-level benches, and a crawler-mounted spreader that receives the material from the excavators and discharges it across the pit.

These are the two Demag wheel excavators that feed the massive cross-pit spreader in the previous picture. Each excavator has its own discharge conveyor, and all equipment moves forward on crawler tracks as the excavated face advances.

This view shows the excavated material streaming off the 680-foot-long boom of the Demag cross-pit spreader shown in the previous two pictures. Installed in 1986, the system can handle up to 7,800 cubic yards per hour. This is the second-longest freely suspended boom ever used on an excavating machine.

Texas Utilities topped its record of owning the world's longest excavating boom when it ordered its second cross-pit excavator-spreader system with a freely suspended boom 834 feet long, the longest ever used on an excavating machine. Designed by Voest-Alpine of Austria to remove 20 million cubic yards per year, the cross-pit spreader is fed by a single bucket wheel excavator (shown earlier in this chapter). From the wheel of the excavator to the discharge point beyond the conveyor, the material moves a staggering quarter-mile!

The massive structure of the Voest-Alpine cross-pit spreader can be grasped from this view showing a haul road passing beneath the machine. Starting work in 1991 at the Winfield South Mine in Texas, the machine weighs 4,800 tons in operation, not counting the wheel excavator. *Voest-Alpine*

Chapter Eleven

TRENCHING MACHINES

There are two types of trenching machines, also known as trenchers or ditchers: wheel and ladder. The wheel ditcher carries a wheel with a series of buckets fixed to its circumference. The rotating wheel is lowered into the ground, and the action of the buckets digs the trench. As each loaded bucket reaches its highest point on the wheel, the material empties onto a conveyor via a chute. The conveyor, running laterally through the wheel, can be set to dump either side. The machine is propelled on its crawler tracks, which force the rotating wheel into the earth to carve the trench. Recently, powerful ditchers fitted with special teeth have been developed to mill through hard rocky material without blasting.

Ladder ditchers are similar to wheel ditchers except that the buckets are attached to an endless chain called a "ladder." The ladder assembly is lowered into the ditch using a hoisting arrangement, and the buckets discharge onto a lateral conveyor in the same way as the wheel ditcher. The ladder ditcher is capable of digging a deeper trench than a wheel type, but it has more moving parts, and thus, operating cost is higher.

In the past, ditchers were a common sight on all sewer and pipe jobs, as well as on housing and subdivision projects. Although they are not seen as frequently today, they are still being made by manufacturers who have specialized in this kind of equipment. Ditcher work has been eroded by the inexpensive tractor backhoe, as well as plowing-in pipelines using powerful crawler tractors with cable plowing equipment. But the large wheel ditcher is still "king" on the big cross-country pipeline jobs.

Gar Wood/Buckeye Ditchers
(Origin of the Ditcher)

In 1893, James B. Hill claimed to have built the first ditching machine at Bowling Green, Ohio, while working at the Bowling Green Foundry and Machine Company. He secured a patent the following year and, after building seven machines, Hill took over the operation of a machine shop at Deshler, Ohio. There, he continued to

Van Buren, Heck & Marvin Company built this steam-powered ditcher in 1902. The machine was built the same year the company commenced manufacture in Findlay, Ohio. Four years later, the company changed its name to the Buckeye Traction Ditcher Company. The No. 88 is now preserved at the Hancock Historical Museum, Findlay. *Mae Huston Local History Resource Center, Hancock Historical Museum*

A 10-horsepower Buckeye wheel ditcher dating from 1913 is shown at work during a convention of the Historical Construction Equipment Association in 1995 in Bowling Green, Ohio.

manufacture the ditchers. Two years later, Hill moved to Carey, Ohio, and became associated with Van Buren Foundry and Machine Company, who built his ditchers on a royalty basis.

In 1902, the Van Buren Foundry and Machine Company merged with Heck & Marvin Company of Findlay, Ohio. The new company, Van Buren, Heck & Marvin Company, was established to build the ditchers in Findlay. In 1906, the company name was changed to Buckeye Traction Ditcher Company to reflect the popularity of the machine. At that time, the largest ditchers being built were steam driven, and capable of digging a trench 54 inches wide by 12 feet deep. By 1919, giant steam ditchers were leaving the works weighing more than 70 tons, and measuring 55 feet in length. The largest could dig a triangular ditch 12 feet wide at the top, tapering to 1 foot at the bottom, and 6 feet deep. Mounted on massive 8-foot-wide crawler tracks, these machines were excellent for digging drainage ditches in swampy ground; and in remote areas too, because the machine came equipped with living accommodations for the crew, including bedroom, kitchen, living room, bath, and electric lighting!

Buckeye developed many sizes and types of ditching machines throughout the 1920s and 1930s. By 1943, the range included ten wheel ditchers and six ladder ditchers. The largest wheel could dig a trench 4 feet wide by 8 feet deep at rates of up to 10 feet per minute, depending on the material. The largest ladder ditcher could reach down 24 feet, and dig a 4-foot wide trench at 7 feet per minute.

In 1947, the Buckeye Traction Ditcher Company was purchased by Gar Wood Industries, who continued the Buckeye products. In 1971, Gar Wood became a division of Sargent Industries, and ditcher production was transferred from Findlay to Wayne, Michigan. However, by this time ditcher sales were diminishing, and the machines were produced only a short time under Sargent's control. The Wayne plant closed down in 1972 when production ended.

Cleveland Ditchers

Another prominent ditcher manufacturer is Cleveland Trencher Company, which still makes ditchers today at Cleveland, Ohio. The company originated in 1921, when A.J. Penote Company of Cleveland built a small wheel ditcher for its own use in Detroit. Following many inquiries after this successful machine, the company decided to manufacture and sell it, and the Cleveland Trencher Company was established in 1923.

Over the years, a wide range of wheel ditchers was marketed, including many to the armed forces in World War II for tough overseas work. The JS-series, which incorporated wheel side shift and tilt, permitted flush

Some of Buckeye's large wheel ditchers retained a somewhat archaic design up to the 1950s. This Model 301, built in 1949, employs hand-powered, tiller-wheel steering, reminiscent of an old traction engine.

In 1947, the Buckeye Traction Ditcher Company was purchased by Gar Wood Industries. The Model 306 wheel ditcher, shown here, was built from 1950 to 1954.

This Buckeye Model 120 ladder ditcher, dating from the early 1940s, was fitted with a 60-horsepower diesel engine. It could dig 11 1/2 feet deep and weighed 11 1/2 tons.

The Cleveland Trencher Company was established in 1923. Here is one of the company's first machines, "The Baby Digger," built in 1924. *The Cleveland Trencher Company*

The action of a Cleveland JS-36 wheel ditcher gains avid attention from onlookers, young and old, in this street scene. The JS-36 was one of Cleveland's most popular ditchers, as it could side-shift its boom to avoid obstacles or dig flush to walls. *The Cleveland Trencher Company*

A modern Cleveland ditcher, this Model 7648, is en route to its first job. Equipped with hydrostatic drive providing infinitely variable crawl speeds, the 7648 can dig 7 feet 6 inches deep, and weighs 23 tons. Its power comes from a Caterpillar 150-horsepower diesel. *The Cleveland Trencher Company*

digging against parallel structures, and added the capability of digging around obstacles. The tilt feature allowed the machine to travel across a steep slope while still cutting a vertical ditch. The big 400W digs nine feet deep, and up to 6 feet wide.

From 1968 to 1984, Cleveland was owned by American Hoist & Derrick Co. of St. Paul, Minnesota. Because of American's dominant crane lines, the trencher line was overshadowed and not supported by senior management. Sales declined, and in 1984, Cleveland was purchased by a management team formed in 1980 to operate the Cleveland division autonomously. But the depressed 1980s did not favor Cleveland and, in 1987, the company was rescued by Mr. Metin Aydin, who purchased it outright. Today, the machines continue to be built in the original Cleveland, Ohio, plant.

Parsons Ditchers

The Parsons Company of Newton, Iowa, was also a leading force in the ditcher business. In 1905, George W. Parsons made his first production model, a ladder ditcher. As early as 1906, a ladder ditcher capable of digging a ditch 12 feet deep and 2 feet wide was produced. Over the next quarter century, Parsons not only became famous for its large ladder machines but it also made a line of wheel ditchers from the smallest to the largest then built.

Parsons was purchased by Koehring Company in 1929, becoming part of the National Equipment Corporation (NEC), which was formed by an amalgamation of several construction equipment companies. Although NEC was dissolved in 1931, Parsons remained a division of Koehring. More varieties of ditchers followed, including the giant Model 355, billed as the world's biggest capacity ladder trencher of its time (1964 to 1974). It could dig a trench 25 feet deep and up to 6 feet wide.

In 1976, Koehring divided and sold Parsons to two companies. The Seaman Company purchased the small, rubber-tired end of the line, and soon expanded the range by adding more small "compact" rubber-tired trenchers. Today, trenchers under the Parsons name are manufactured and sold by Seaman-Maxon, Inc. of Milwaukee, Wisconsin, which purchased the rights and assets of the small Parsons line in 1992.

The other company involved in Koehring's sale of Parsons was Trenchliner, which purchased the rights to manufacture the large Parsons wheel and ladder ditchers. Trenchliner, taking its corporate name from the former

The Parsons 310 was a big ladder ditcher that could dig a trench almost 20 feet deep in widths from 2 to 5 feet. Operating weight was 22 tons, and power came from a 117-horsepower diesel engine.

Down in the ditch dug by this Model 400W, the largest Cleveland ditcher. Shown with the trapezoidal ditch attachment, the 400W can dig a ditch 9 feet deep and up to 6 feet wide. It has an operating weight of 35 tons, and is powered by a Caterpillar 175-horsepower diesel. (See the photograph of the Jetco version on page 194.) *The Cleveland Trencher Company*

From 1930, Parsons ditchers were made under license in the United Kingdom by John Allen & Sons (Oxford) Ltd. The picture shows an Allen 12-18 ditcher in use by the British Army in the early 1950s.

Right down the middle of a residential street goes this Parsons 355, leaving behind a magnificent sewer trench! Even the bottom is curved to receive the pipe. The ladder on this machine is equipped with longitudinal rotating picks to trim the trench to a wider than normal dimension. Note also the parallel discharge conveyor for filling trucks ahead of the machine, minimizing disruption to the street. The Model 355, Parsons' largest ladder trencher, could dig to 25 feet deep. *Kukla Trenchers*

A Parsons 255 Trenchliner at work for an Oklahoma contractor in 1965. The 255 could dig 15 feet deep, and carried an 80-horsepower engine. It was introduced in 1961. *Kukla Trenchers*

The first Barber-Greene ditcher was the Model 44 vertical-boom type introduced in 1923. Able to dig a trench 18 inches wide and up to 5 feet deep, the 44-series ditchers were so successful that, with upgrades, they remained in production until 1957. Shown here, with its boom in the raised position, is a machine from the early 1950s. *JKH collection*

trade name of its large trenchers, was set up in Austin, Texas. However, this company only survived until 1980, when the product line was acquired by Michael Kukla International. Today, Kukla continues to build a line of cable plows and rubber-tired chain trenchers, but the last of the big Parsons trenchers left the factory in 1984. Kukla, however, continues to offer service and parts supply to the Parsons machines still in the field.

Barber-Greene Ditchers

The Barber-Greene Company of Aurora, Illinois, famous for its paving machines, jumped into the ditcher business early. Co-founded by Harry Barber and William B. Greene in 1916, the Barber-Greene Company invented many machines for the road builder in the 1920s and 1930s. In 1923, the company produced the first vertical-boom ladder ditcher, the Model 44. The machine had the obvious advantage of cutting a clean vertical trench from start to finish, minimizing hand work at each end. The following year, the 44-A came out with a patented automatic spring release drive sprocket, which protected the machinery when it hit an obstacle in the trench. Booms to dig ditches up to 7 feet deep were available. This ditcher caught on very quickly, and by 1926, the company claimed it sold more than any other make of machine. Through further upgrades, the 44-series ditchers remained in Barber-Greene's line until 1957.

Barber-Greene developed hydrostatic drive on its crawler models, permitting infinite crowd control and allowing crowding to match the speed of the digging wheel. The big Model 777 wheel ditcher, built from 1960 to 1966, and its successor the TA-77, were the largest Barber-Greene ditchers. The TA-77 could dig up to 8 1/2 feet deep and weighed 33 tons.

In 1987, Barber-Greene became a division of Astec Industries, Inc. In 1991, Astec sold the rights of Barber-Greene's paving products to Caterpillar. But Astec

retained the ditchers, since it already owned another trencher company, Trencor-Jetco, Inc. (now Trencor, Inc.), purchased in 1988. The Barber-Greene ditchers continue to be manufactured as the BG-series in the Trencor line.

Capitol Trenchers

Capitol Trencher Corporation of San Dimas, California, made an extensive range of machines. Capitol had the bases covered from the 7 1/2-ton Model 450 with a digging depth to 4 feet to the 90-ton Model 1050 large wheel ditcher with a depth capability to 10 feet. Capitol Trenchers featured hydrostatic crawler drive, and the machines could be equipped with either ladder, wheel, or trapezoidal ditch digging attachments.

The Capitol trencher designs are now incorporated in the line offered by Trencor, Inc. of Grapevine, Texas, which purchased Capitol in 1994.

Trencor-Jetco

The Jiffy Excavator Tooth Company (Jetco) was established in 1945 in Alhambra, California, and made a variety of trenching machines and attachments. In 1960, the company moved to Dallas, Texas, and became known as Dallas-Jetco. In 1984, Dallas-Jetco was purchased by Trencor, Inc., another trencher company, established in 1981 as the Trencher Corporation of America (Trencor). The merger of the two companies was a natural fit, as Jetco specialized in the manufacture of wheel trenchers, and Trencor designed and built the chain-type trenchers for cutting through hard rock. The new company was known as Trencor Jetco.

In 1988, Astec Industries, Inc., purchased Trencor Jetco, and merged the line with the Barber-Greene ditchers purchased a year earlier. The two lines resulted in a vast range of wheel and chain trenchers, as well as other specialized continuous excavators. More recently, the Capitol Trencher line was added in 1994, providing an even wider range of machines. That same year, the company, still owned by Astec, changed its name to Trencor, Inc.

In 1997, Trencor was offering a line of 39 machines, including some of the largest trenchers ever built. The range covers wheel types from 17 1/2 tons to 118 tons weight, with depth capability up to 10 feet and chain (ladder) types from 7 1/2 to 265 tons. The top-of-the-line machine is the massive Model 1860HD chain type, with a maximum digging depth of 35 feet. It is the world's largest production-model trenching machine, and uses one 1,200-horsepower engine for the digging chain, and another 300-horsepower engine to power the tracks and conveyors.

Contractor-Built Ditchers

In the 1970s and 1980s, some of the large specialist pipeline contractors couldn't find a trencher on the mar-

A Barber-Greene TA-65, owned by C.M.& G. Contractors Ltd., is working on an Alberta oilfield project. The 22-ton TA-65 was introduced in 1967. It can dig 7 feet 6 inches deep, and is powered by a Caterpillar 160-horsepower diesel.

Barber-Greene's largest ditcher, the TA-77, can dig up to 8 feet 6 inches deep, and weighs 33 tons. The hydrostatic drive provides the machine with infinitely variable propel speeds up to 72 feet per minute. *C.R.C. Evans Ltd.*

This Model 630SW (pictured) is one of a line of ditchers formerly made by Barber-Greene, and currently sold as the upgraded BG-series in the extensive line of trenchers manufactured by Trencor, Inc. This BG-630 is equipped with a 117-horsepower engine, and boasts a side-shiftable wheel assembly. *Trencor, Inc.*

This is the kind of work done by Dallas-Jetco Inc. prior to the company's takeover by Trencor in 1984. The machine is a Cleveland 400W wheel ditcher, which has been rebuilt by Jetco. Since its establishment in 1945, Jetco provided a rebuild service to the trencher industry and provided teeth and entire wheel assemblies for many makes of machines. *Trencor, Inc.*

This 40-ton ditcher from Trencor is fitted with a "rocksaw" wheel. Rocksaws are used to dig narrow trenches in solid rock for fiber optic cable installation, utility line placement, etc. The Model 960HD is powered by a 325-horsepower engine. *Trencor, Inc.*

This specialized machine was made by Jetco, Inc. It is known as an "offset rock wheel" and is used to dig ledges in coral around sea walls to form marinas. It digs a path 6 feet wide up to 6 feet deep. It is mounted on an International TD-25 tractor with a 170-horsepower engine. *Trencor, Inc.*

ket big enough for the projects they were tackling, so they built their own machines. One such machine was the Banister Model 710 wheel ditcher, designed and built by Banister Pipelines of Edmonton, Alberta. Banister built its first wheel ditcher in 1965, the Model 508, designed to cut through frozen ground, and developed the technology in the 1970s that led to some of the largest ditchers ever built. In 1972, the prototype Model 710 was tested in frozen ground. Still in use today, it weighs 115 tons, and is capable of digging a ditch 7 feet wide and 10 feet deep. The 710 wheel has 18 buckets, each of 1-yard capacity, and its power of 1,120 horsepower is provided by two Caterpillar diesel engines. In certain unfrozen conditions, it can achieve a very high production rate of up to 20 feet of trench per minute.

Five of the Model 710 ditchers have been built to date, and are in use by Banister. The machines are popular in the north, where their power cuts through permafrost on some of the toughest pipeline jobs. In 1978,

Banister built an even larger ditcher, known as the Model 812, almost twice the size of the 710. Designed to dig 12 feet deep, this monster ditcher weighed 240 tons, measured 76 feet long, and was over two stories high. However, after successful field trials, it was dismantled when the project for which it was designed was canceled.

The Henuset "Polar Bear" built by Henuset Pipeline Services Ltd. of Calgary, Alberta, was another giant ditcher that was released in the mid-1980s. Based on a Caterpillar D9H undercarriage and equipped with a pair of turbo-charged GM V12 engines producing 2,200 horsepower, the Polar Bear outfit tipped the scales at 168 tons. The machine could dig a trench 7 feet wide by 11 feet deep at high speed.

Small Ditching Machines

At the opposite end of the scale, many manufacturers make small ditching machines, some so small the operator walks behind them. In 1949, Edwin

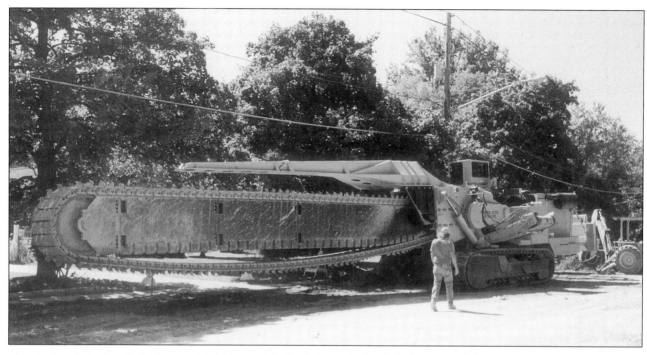

Showing its massive length, this Trencor Model 1660HD is fitted with a digging chain for use in solid rock. The machine can dig to more than 25 feet deep. To power this massive chain, a diesel engine of 750 horsepower is necessary. Machine weight is approximately 120 tons. *Trencor, Inc.*

Trencor, Inc., produces the world's largest ditching machine, the 265-ton Model 1860HD. This awesome unit is shown digging a trench 32 feet deep in solid rock for Key Enterprises, Odessa, Texas. The digging chain is powered by a 1,200-horsepower engine, while a separate 300-horsepower engine operates all other machine functions. *Trencor, Inc.*

Contractor-designed giant ditchers have been developed for special heavy-duty applications, such as digging through perma-frost. Here is the Banister 710, designed and built by Banister Equipment Co. of Edmonton, Alberta. It measures 56 feet long, and carries Caterpillar diesel engines totaling 1,230 horsepower. *Banister Equipment*

Malzahn designed and built the first of these machines, which have become known as "compact trenchers." Later, he went on to establish the Charles Machine Works and their famous "Ditch Witch" line. Other pioneers in this field include ARPS Corporation of New Holstein, Wisconsin, which made a chain ditcher that could be attached to a farm tractor, and later built self-propelled machines. The Davis Manufacturing Company of Wichita, Kansas, made its small line of "Task Force" crawler machines, which were acquired by Case in 1968.

"The Diggin' Dutchman" say the advertisements from Vermeer Manufacturing Company of Pella, Iowa. The company made its name in the "compact ditcher" industry, but has recently expanded into the larger machine market. They now offer ladder-type ditchers up to the T-1455, with 10-foot digging depth, operating weight of 90 tons, and 675 horsepower Caterpillar power.

Other Ditching Machine Manufacturers

As an epilogue to ditcher history, large wheel and ladder ditchers built by companies, who only pursued this business for a short time, must be mentioned. The Austin Machinery Corporation made large trenchers in the 1920s and 1930s. Harnischfeger made P&H ditchers from 1915 to 1933. The Bucyrus Company built large ladder ditchers for several years beginning in 1915. The steam-powered Class 72 could dig down 17 feet. It weighed 37 tons, and measured over 53 feet long with the ladder raised.

A view of the 115-ton Banister 710 giant wheel ditcher in action. Five of these giant ditchers have been built, and are in use by Banister Pipelines. *Banister Equipment*

Although the modern backhoe has taken away much of the work formerly done by ditching machines, the ditcher is still "king" of the big ditch. Here, the Henuset Polar Bear starts to cut into a 23-mile-long trench for a 42-inch water pipe in central Alberta, Canada, in 1982. The Polar Bear can dig 6 feet wide by 10 feet deep, and is powered by a pair of GM V12 engines. The outfit tips the scales at 168 tons. *Henuset Pipelines*

The Austin Machinery Corporation, Muskegon, Michigan, made trenching machines in the 1920s and 1930s. The picture shows a Model 105 ladder ditcher, powered by a Waukesha diesel engine.

The Bucyrus Company made some large steam-powered ditchers beginning in 1915. The big Class 72 shown here weighs 40 tons, and is digging a trench 17 feet deep with a standard ladder. An extension was offered to dig up to 20 feet. *Bucyrus International*

Chapter Twelve

HYDRAULIC EXCAVATORS

In recent years, hydraulic excavators have probably become the most familiar of all earthmoving machines. They can be seen at work on every kind of construction job from road maintenance, trenching, and foundation work to mass excavation on major industrial sites, as well as in quarries and surface mining operations. Today, they are made in every industrialized country by hundreds of manufacturers around the world.

Hydraulic excavators have largely replaced the old cable-operated excavator, except in the very largest sizes. Hydraulic units are less expensive to buy, easier to operate, travel faster, and have positive action in all movements instead of relying on gravity to provide some of the digging forces.

Although the backhoe and shovel fronts are the most common for hydraulic excavators, a vast array of attachments is available for all makes and sizes, which has increased the machine's usefulness. Attachments include hydraulic clamshells, log grapples, rakes, rippers, shearers, packers, lifting hooks, and hydraulic hammers.

Evolution of the Hydraulic Excavator

Strictly speaking, hydraulic excavators were first used in the last century, but those early attempts used water instead of oil to transmit the power, and were not a success. Two railroad-type hydraulic shovels were built by unrelated Armstrongs. The earliest was in 1882 by the British firm, Sir W.G. Armstrong & Company, and was used to construct the Hull docks in England. In 1914, the other machine was tested by Frank H. Armstrong, a mechanical engineer for the Penn Iron Mining Company in the United States. On both machines, the hoisting power was provided by a hydraulic cylinder operating a set of multiplying sheaves.

The Kilgore Machine Company of Minneapolis, Minnesota, designed another hydraulic shovel, patented in 1897. This machine used direct-acting cylinders, dispensing with all ropes and chains. Reportedly, only five of these machines were built, including one shipped to Mexico.

Today's hydraulic excavator has a relatively recent history, having been developed almost simultaneously in

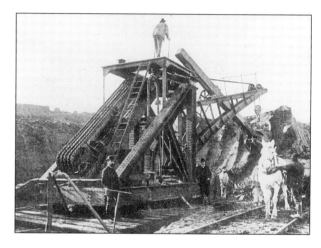

The earliest hydraulically powered excavator was this machine built by the British firm, Sir W.G. Armstrong & Company in 1882. It is shown working on the construction of a dock at Hull, England. It used water to power its hydraulic cylinders. *JKH collection*

One of the earliest "modern-day" excavators to use an oil hydraulic system was the "Gradall." Invented by Ray Ferwerda, the rights to manufacture were purchased by the Warner & Swasey Company in 1946. This early Gradall is truck-mounted. Still produced today by the Gradall Company, Gradalls have always featured a telescopic boom with bucket rotation capability.

A G-600 crawler-mounted Gradall of 1960s vintage. With its telescopic boom and bucket rotation as well as wrist action, the Gradall can simulate the movements of the human hand. The machine shown is equipped with a ripper tooth to assist a drainage trench through hard rock.

Another early entrant into the hydraulic excavator field was the Milwaukee Hydraulics Corporation. This company first produced the "Hydrocrane" in 1946, the rights of which were then purchased by Bucyrus-Erie in 1948. The H-5 machine shown is an early Bucyrus-Erie "Hydrohoe" version. Note the cable reeving and hydraulic pistons at the rear for use when the machine is set up as a "Hydrocrane." *Bucyrus International*

Italy, France, and the United States in the late 1940s. Carlo and Mario Bruneri produced a prototype wheeled-hydraulic excavator at Turin, Italy, in 1948. After several further prototypes, lack of financial resources caused the Bruneri brothers to relinquish their patent rights to a French company, SICAM in 1954. That same year, SICAM produced a small truck-mounted excavator known as the Yumbo S25. Interest in the new machine increased, and further wheeled and crawler models were developed. SICAM also made licensing arrangements in the early 1960s with Drott in the United States, TUSA in Spain, Mitsubishi in Japan, and Priestman in Britain.

In France, Poclain produced a truck-mounted loader in 1948, and built its first hydraulic excavator in 1951. From that time, the company prospered, and

became a world leader in hydraulic machines by the end of the 1960s.

In the United States, contractor Ray Ferwerda of Cleveland, Ohio, invented a fully hydraulic telescoping-boom excavator, and mounted it on a truck. This machine became known as the famous "Gradall" excavator. The famous excavator's manufacturing rights were purchased by the Warner & Swasey Company in 1946. With its bucket wrist and rotational movement, the Gradall can simulate the movements of the human hand. Today, Gradalls are built at the New Philadelphia, Ohio, works of the Gradall Company.

The Milwaukee Hydraulics Corporation was another U.S. company that made an early entry into the hydraulic field when it launched the H-2 Hydrocrane in

This is a Model TU Poclain's first excavator, produced in 1951. First designed to be towed behind a farm tractor and driven from the tractor's power take-off, the TU was soon equipped with its own motive power, as this three-wheel version testifies. *JKH collection*

An advanced excavator of the 1950s, this Poclain Model TYA is shown equipped with a hydraulic clamshell. A TYA was Poclain's primary exhibit at the Bauma equipment show in Munich, Germany, in 1958. *JKH collection*

1946. Bucyrus-Erie purchased this company in 1948, and further developed the Hydrocrane into the H-3 and H-5 Hydrohoes. These machines and their derivatives remained in the B-E line until 1981.

With the advent of the early hydraulic excavators in Italy, France, and the United States, the foundation was laid for what would become a complete revolution of the excavator industry. The 1950s were the pioneering years, when many manufacturers ventured into making this new type of machine. It was relatively simple to manufacture compared to previous cable-operated machines. It needed only a power unit, hydraulic pumps and valves, and hydraulic rams to power the excavator's movements. However, unreliable hydraulic systems, unable to withstand the rigors of the excavation site, slowed development, and the hydraulic machines were thought by many to be just a passing phase. The perseverance of the manufacturers, however, gradually remedied the problems.

The 1960s were the developing years, when hydraulic excavators rapidly increased in size, and many more manufacturers entered the field. Their popularity increased with the evolution of reliable hydraulic systems, utilizing higher hydraulic pressures, initially successful in the early Poclain and other machines in Europe. In the 1960s, many staunch cable excavator manufacturers entered the field, but most found it difficult to compete, as their engineering was steeped in cable shovel design. It took some manufacturers many years to forsake features like jaw clutch steering and tumbler-type excavator track shoes, and use instead hydraulic motors in each crawler frame, and tractor-type crawlers. Some manufacturers made a brief entry, and then abandoned hydraulics altogether. Also, North American manufacturers tended to employ low hydraulic pressures, which had severe limitations as excavators increased in size.

By the late 1960s, hydraulic excavators had graduated into a major force in the excavating industry. The decade ended with Poclain's EC-1000 machine boasting a record-beating 10-cubic yard bucket capacity. This machine was observed by the existing cable excavator manufacturers with some apprehension. For here was a machine encroaching well into territory thought to be the sole domain of cable machines. The concerns of the competition were well founded, as by the end of the next decade, much larger hydraulic mining shovels and backhoes were well established and selling in large numbers

What a show stopper! This giant Poclain EC-1000 was shown at the Paris Expomat, France, in 1970. Equipped with three GM engines, 10-yard bucket, and 150-ton operating weight, it was far bigger than any previous hydraulic excavator. Many visitors to the show wondered if such a large backhoe could possibly find any use!

The Poclain EC-1000 in action at a British opencast coal site operated by Miller Mining. The three-engined, 150-ton machine pioneered the use of hydraulic excavators in the mining field, and heralded the much larger and more sophisticated machines of today.

Following through with its large excavators, Poclain replaced the three-engined EC-1000 with the heavier and more powerful 1000CK in 1975. However, the 1000CK obtained its power from two engines instead of three. The machine shown is loading a Terex 33-15 electric-drive truck at a southern British Columbia, Canada, coal mine in 1979.

by just a few dominant manufacturers. By 1980, the O&K RH-300 excavator, a machine with a bucket capacity of 30 cubic yards, three times the size of the Poclain EC-1000, was already at work.

As all those in the construction industry know, recent years have witnessed the dominance of hydraulic excavators from Japan. The Japanese excavator dominance in the Western world can be segmented into three distinct phases. In the 1960s, the Japanese established their hydraulic excavator industry by manufacturing designs from established U.S. and European firms under license (e.g., Sumitomo-Link-Belt, Komatsu-Bucyrus, Kobelco-P&H, Yumbo-Mitsubishi). Having learned how to build and market a successful machine, the Japanese

then entered the second phase of their development by designing their own machines and severing ties with Western manufacturers. Further development took place, with Japanese-exported machines gaining a reliable reputation and selling at very competitive prices. More recently, we have seen an influx of Korean-built excavators such as Hyundai, Samsung, Daewoo, and Halla taking their technology from Japan.

We are now into the third phase, in which the Japanese have established their own factories in foreign countries, making machines for local markets. This cuts down shipping costs and avoids import duties, which had become a major issue in Europe. Today, nearly all the major excavator manufacturers in the Western world are building excava-

One of the new excavators offered by Case for the North American market, but designed by Sumitomo of Japan. This 9050 is excavating for a new mine development in central Alberta, Canada, in 1995.

Orenstein & Koppel (O&K) produced its first hydraulic excavator in 1961 in the shape of the 1/2-yard RH-5. This machine was so successful that over 20,000 were eventually sold. This early RH-6, built on similar lines to the RH-5, shows the public that shovels as well as backhoes were feasible on hydraulic machines.

tors to Japanese designs (e.g., Link-Belt, JCB, Deere, Case, Caterpillar). The industry has indeed turned "full circle."

Although Japanese excavators dominate in what could be termed the "construction-size" market, the giant "mining" class excavators are dominated by German manufacturers. Although challenged by Caterpillar and P&H in the United States and Hitachi in Japan, the largest hydraulic excavators today are of German origin.

A brief history of the industry giants, and descriptions of some pioneering machines and companies, follows in this chapter.

Case/Poclain Hydraulic Excavators

Georges Bataille, founder of Poclain, produced a truck-mounted loader in France during 1948, and built his first hydraulic excavator in 1951, the Model TU. Experience gained over the next decade produced the successful Model TY45 in 1960, of which over 30,000 were eventually sold. The TY45 brought Poclain worldwide attention, resulting in many new models of both crawler and wheeled excavators introduced throughout the 1960s.

The Poclain EC-1000, a 10-yard excavator, made headlines in 1970. Equipped with three GM 8V71 diesel engines for a total of 840 horsepower, the machine weighed over 150 tons, and easily captured the title of the largest hydraulic excavator yet built. In 1975, the 1000CK replaced the EC-1000. Subsequent upgrades increased its weight to 210 tons, and power increased to 900 horsepower, obtained from two Cummins diesel engines.

In 1976, Tenneco became a major shareholder in Poclain. Over the next few years, Poclain excavators and Tenneco's existing Case/Drott excavators were merged into a single line. Poclain machines covered the larger end of the range, while the Case/Drott machines covered the small machine market. For a while, Poclain excavators were made at the Drott factory at Wausau, Wisconsin.

Beginning in the mid-1980s, the Case excavator line weathered some radical changes when the large mining excavators were discontinued. In 1984, the last 1000CK left the factory, after 59 had been produced. Case introduced the 88-series, a new line of smaller excavators at the 1987 Conexpo in Las Vegas, Nevada. The Models 688 and 888 excavators had operating weights of 15 and 18 tons.

In Europe, the 88-series has expanded to an eight-machine line-up, peaking at the Model 1488. In North

204

America, Case adopted another new line—the 90-series machines, introduced in 1992. These machines, which graduated to the B-series in 1994, are based on designs by Sumitomo of Japan, and comprise six models ranging in operating weights from 14 to 50 tons.

O&K Hydraulic Excavators

In 1908, Orenstein & Koppel (O&K), founded in 1876, made its first steam shovel and soon established itself as one of the leading German excavator manufacturers. O&K's switch from cable to hydraulic excavators occurred so quickly that it was almost abrupt. The 1/2-yard RH-5, first hydraulic machine, appeared in 1961, and more than 20,000 of them were sold. A rapidly expanding line of hydraulic excavators was developed, finding immediate acceptance.

In only 10 short years after its first hydraulic excavator, O&K launched the largest series-produced hydraulic excavator—the RH-60. This 124-ton machine was equipped with two Deutz diesel engines creating 760 horsepower, and an 8 1/2-cubic yard bucket in shovel configuration. The time was just right for the launch of such a large, diesel-powered hydraulic excavator. The nimble machine, not dependent on a trailing power cable, and easily dismantled and moved in modular units, found excellent use with contractors in the expanding surface coal mine industry, especially in the United Kingdom.

In 1976, the larger RH-75 followed the RH-60. Bucket size was increased to 10 cubic yards and weight increased to 150 tons. This machine was so successful that over 200 were sold in 27 countries before it was superseded by the RH-75C in 1986. Approximately 30 RH-75s were also manufactured in O&K's Canadian plant in Ontario, mainly for distribution in North America.

As early as 1979, O&K took a huge jump in size when it took title to the world's largest hydraulic excavator. With an operating weight of 535 tons and a 34-yard bucket, the RH-300 easily surpassed anything built up to that time. The RH-300 was powered by two Cummins KTA2300C diesel engines, each producing 1,210 horsepower. The first unit was purchased by contractors Northern Strip Mining Ltd. (NSM), which was already operating large fleets of RH-60s and RH-75s in British surface coal mines.

O&K's mining excavators have enjoyed increased sales growth since the launch of the 235-ton RH-120C in 1983, and 176-ton RH-90C in 1986. So far, 240 of these two models have been sold. A large shovel of new design, the RH-200, was introduced at the Bauma equipment show in Germany in 1989. Although somewhat lighter than the RH-300 at 512 tons, the RH-200 carries a similar-sized 34-yard bucket, and has a greater output capacity. The

The mining-size RH-60 was launched by O&K only 10 years after its first hydraulic machine. This advanced 124-ton machine took power from two Deutz engines, and could wield a clamshell-type shovel bucket of 8 1/2 cubic yards. The machine shown is owned by British contractor Northern Strip Mining Ltd.

The O&K RH-75 replaced the RH-60 in 1975. Bucket size was increased to 10 cubic yards and weight to 150 tons. Over 200 of the successful RH-75 were sold, including about 30 manufactured in O&K's Canadian plant. The machine in the picture, in backhoe configuration, is at a western Canadian coal mine.

At the Bauma equipment show in Munich, Germany, in 1989, O&K staged the launch of the RH-200, a massive 512-ton excavator carrying a standard bucket of 34 cubic yards. Over 50 of this model have been sold to date. The one illustrated works for British contractor Crouch Mining. *Peter Grimshaw*

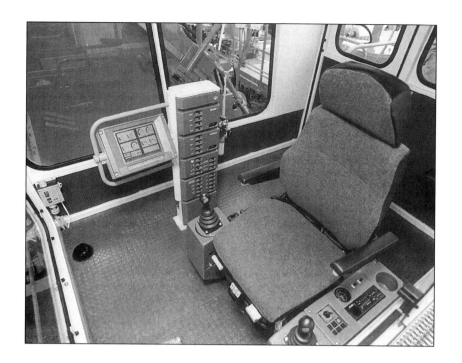

This O&K machine gives a good example of an operator's compartment on a modern hydraulic excavator. All digging functions are controlled by the two joystick controls. The machine status reporting functions are visually displayed on the operator's right. *O&K*

O&K's RH-400 took the title of the world's largest hydraulic excavator when it went to work in 1997 at the Syncrude tar sands operation in Alberta, Canada. The 900-ton giant carries a 55-cubic yard bucket for three-pass loading of 240-ton trucks. Shown before shipment at the O&K plant in Dortmund, Germany, the RH-400 stands fully assembled over the top of a 1/2-yard RH-5, O&K's first hydraulic excavator. *O&K*

The world's largest hydraulic excavator in 1979 was this RH-300 from O&K, representing a huge size increase above any machine then available. One of only two built, the machine shown was purchased by British contractor Northern Strip Mining Ltd. It weighed a massive 535 tons and could carry a 34-yard bucket. It was probably ahead of its time, as only recently has its size been exceeded. *David Wootton*

TriPower system, a distinguishing feature of O&K's large shovels, is a mechanical linkage that provides automatic bucket leveling through a trunnion system, which also amplifies the crowding force during hoisting.

O&K's crowning excavator achievement is the RH-400. This mammoth 900-ton hydraulic shovel has a 55-cubic yard bucket, and twin Cummins K2000E engines spinning out 3,400 horsepower. It claimed the world record size title, and is ready to challenge any cable shovel application. In 1997, the first one went to work at the Syncrude tar sands operation in Alberta. In late 1997, O&K's mining division, which includes its large hydraulic excavators, was purchased by Terex Corporation.

Demag Hydraulic Excavators

In 1925, the old-established German firm of Demag ventured into excavators when it acquired the complete excavator line from Carlshutte. Established in 1820, Carlshutte had been building steam shovels since the early part of the twentieth century. Demag expanded and updated its cable excavator line until after World War II, and then introduced the B504, the world's first all-hydraulic, crawler-mounted excavator in 1954. This 1/2-yard machine was remarkable in that it was the first to feature a 360-degree continuous swing and hydraulic crawler drive in the lower works. These features were ahead of their time, but are now standard on all machines.

Consolidation and expansion took place through the 1960s, as Demag rapidly replaced its cable excavators with hydraulic models. The H-41's introduction in 1968 enhanced Demag's excavator reputation. Although two

cable excavators were still offered up to 1982, the hydraulic excavators became the primary product.

Demag laid the foundation for today's giant hydraulic excavators when it launched the H-101 in 1972 and broke into the 100-ton-plus class. It carried a 6 1/2-yard shovel bucket, and was powered by a pair of Caterpillar diesels totaling 508 horsepower. Other large shovels and backhoes followed, including the 10-yard H-111 in 1976 and the 18-yard H-241 in 1978. The H-241 was Demag's first "super excavator," claiming the title of the world's largest, at 262 tons operating weight. This giant was powered by a single Cummins or GM diesel with over 1,300 horsepower. About 80 H-241s were sold worldwide by the time the model was upgraded to the 21-yard H-285 in 1986.

Also in 1986, the much-larger H485 went to work in Scotland for Coal Contractors Ltd., again claiming the title of the world's largest hydraulic excavator for Demag. This machine was powered by a single MTU diesel engine of 2,500 horsepower, weighed 620 tons, and carried a 34-yard bucket. The upgraded H485S version carries shovel buckets up to 44-yard capacity, weighs 690 tons, and has dual Cummins diesels totaling 3,000 horsepower.

Contractor T.A. Klemke & Son Construction Ltd. purchased the second H485 to add to its huge equipment fleet working under contract to Syncrude at the tar sands operations in northern Alberta, Canada. Then in 1995, Klemke put to work an even larger machine, the H485SP, and retained the distinction of operating the world's largest hydraulic excavator. The H485SP is heavier (750 tons), has larger bucket (46 yards), and more power (4,000 horsepower from two Caterpillar diesels) than the H485S. Although the first machine of this size was identified as the H685SP, Demag has decided that future machines in this size class will retain the H485 model number.

In 1996, a joint venture was established between Mannesmann-Demag and Komatsu Ltd. to market the Demag excavators along with Komatsu's other lines. The following year, Komatsu formed a worldwide mining group, Komatsu Mining Systems, Inc., to concentrate on sales and support of the larger machines from this group, including Haulpak trucks.

Liebherr Hydraulic Excavators

In 1957, Liebherr entered the hydraulic excavator market with the wheeled Model L-300. Prior to this, the company was well known for its tower cranes, which it commenced manufacturing in 1949. The company, founded by Hans Liebherr, who had taken over the family construction business in 1938, prospered and expanded rapidly in the 1950s and 1960s. Many subsidiary companies were set up in foreign countries, including the Colmar factory in France in 1961, which

This is the machine that started it all. Demag's B504 was the world's first 360-degree, crawler-mounted hydraulic excavator when it came out in 1954. Surprisingly advanced for its day, the 1/2-yard machine featured rotating joints on its front end instead of flexible hoses. *Demag Komatsu GmbH*

eventually became the world center for hydraulic excavators. In 1970, Liebherr opened its Newport News, Virginia, factory to manufacture hydraulic excavators for the North American market.

Liebherr developed its 900-series excavators in the 1960s, with identifying prefix letters A (Wheeled) or R (Crawler). From the small R901 through to the R961, the largest in 1968, the top end of the line has progressively pushed upward in size through the R971, R981, and R991. Introduced in 1977, the R991's operating weight of 180 tons and standard rock bucket of 10 yards firmly positioned Liebherr in the large mining market for hydraulic excavators.

The R991, with dual Cummins engines totaling 720 horsepower, was upgraded to the R994 around 1985, with a weight increase to 227 tons. A single Cummins diesel of 1,050 horsepower powered the first R994. Weight and power were subsequently increased to 244 tons and 1,273 horsepower. Over 200 units of the R991 and R994 have been sold to date. Since 1995, the R996 has spearheaded Liebherr's drive for the world's mining excavator market. This monster machine weighs over 600 tons, has a standard 36-yard shovel bucket, and is powered by two Cummins engines with a combined output of 3,000 horsepower.

Hitachi Hydraulic Excavators

Hitachi has been one of the few Japanese manufacturers to challenge the "mining" excavator market, and it certainly has made its mark. The parent company of Hitachi Construction Machinery Company Ltd. was established in 1910 and built its first excavator, an electric cable-operated mining shovel, in 1939. However, it was not until 1965 that Hitachi unveiled its first

By 1976, Demag's flagship machine had grown to the 10-cubic yard H-111. The machine illustrated is owned by Hepburnia Coal Company, Grampian, Pennsylvania. With rapid design progress being made in the 1970s, the H-111 was superseded by the H-121 in 1978.

Demag launched its record-beating H-241 in 1978, the first one going to Benjamin Coal Company, Troutville, Pennsylvania. Seen here loading Caterpillar 777 trucks with its 18-yard rock bucket, the H-241 is powered with a single 1,300-horsepower diesel engine, and weighs 262 tons.

Demag's H-485S carries buckets up to 44 cubic yards and tips the scales at 690 tons. Powered by twin Cummins diesels totaling 3,000 horsepower, it is seen here loading a Komatsu 930E, 320-ton hauler at Asarco's Ray Mine, Arizona. Both machines in the picture are marketed today by Komatsu Mining Systems.

Demag's current largest excavator is the H-485SP, the first of which went to work for Canadian contractor T.A. Klemke & Son in the Alberta tar sands. Powered by two Caterpillar diesels of up to 4,000 horsepower, the "SP" model weighs 750 tons and digs with a 46-yard bucket. *Transwest Dynequip*

Liebherr's first hydraulic excavator was this L-300 in 1957. From this was developed the popular 900-series in the 1960s. *Liebherr-France, Colmar*

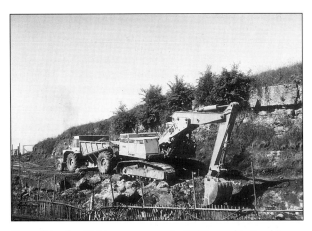

Top-of-the-line Liebherr excavator in 1968 was this 2-cubic yard 961 backhoe. Excavating the footings for a railway bridge in northern England, the 961 shown weighs 36 tons.

Liebherr's largest excavator in the mid-1980s was this 227-ton Model R994, powered by a single 1,273-horsepower engine. The 994 shown here with a 15-yard bucket is owned by the Clay Colliery Company in England. *Peter Grimshaw*

hydraulic excavator, the 3/8-yard UH03, the first to be developed using Japan's own excavator technology.

From this humble beginning, Hitachi used its UH-series machines, weighing up to 80 tons, to rapidly penetrate world markets. Hitachi's eighth-generation excavators, each one improved and upgraded from the previous, helped the company break into the mining excavator field in 1979. Including all sizes, Hitachi excavator sales had reached 20,000 units by 1973, and just seven years later, sales had reached 50,000 units. By 1983, sales had reached 70,000 units.

The 10-yard UH801 was Hitachi's first mining hydraulic excavator. It produced 800 horsepower from dual Cummins diesels, and weighed 173 tons. This machine and the smaller 100-ton UH501, introduced in 1984, validated Hitachi as a builder of reliable mining excavators. The EX-series was launched in 1987, consisting initially of the EX1000, EX1800, and EX3500, with standard shovels of 7-, 15-, and 24-cubic yards. In 1991, the EX3500 was upgraded to the Super EX3500-2 with a pair of Cummins diesels rated at 1,684 horsepower and

weighing 364 tons. The intermediate EX2500, unveiled at the 1996 Las Vegas Minexpo show, fits into the 18-yard class with an operating weight of 263 tons. The most recent, and largest, Hitachi excavator is the EX5500, announced in 1997. This 35-yard shovel weights 570 tons and carries two Cummins diesel engines that provide 1,250 horsepower.

Caterpillar Hydraulic Excavators

In 1972, Caterpillar unveiled its first hydraulic excavator—the Model 225. It was followed by the 235, 245, and 215, in 1973, 1974, and 1976. These four models, and their subsequent derivatives, remained in the Caterpillar line for about two decades. Caterpillar has bolstered its excavator line along the way by merging with other established ranges of machines, such as Eder from Germany and Mitsubishi from Japan.

In 1992, Caterpillar began introducing the 300-series machines, which eventually replaced every previous model. By 1997, Caterpillar's 300-series had expanded to 15 basic models, from the 8-ton Model 307 to the 85-ton Model 375, covering bucket sizes from 1/4 yard to 7 cubic yards. At the Las Vegas Minexpo show in 1992, Caterpillar unveiled its first "mining" shovel, the 5130, weighing in at 193 tons. Bucket range on this machine is from 11 to 14 yards, and power comes from a 755-horsepower Caterpillar engine. In 1994, the 350-ton 5230 was announced, powered by a single Caterpillar diesel engine of 1,470 horsepower, and rock buckets ranging from 17 to 24 cubic yards. The 5130 was uprated to a "B" model in 1997 with a weight increase to just over 200 tons.

P&H Hydraulic Excavators

In 1964, the P&H company entered the hydraulic excavator market when it acquired rights to a small excavator designed by Cabot Corporation. From this model, P&H developed the popular H312 and H418, which remained in the line until 1976. From 1970 until 1974, P&H made hydraulic excavators under license from Germany's O&K, such as the 3-yard RH-25 shovel.

In 1979, P&H designed and built the Model 1200 hydraulic excavator in its German factory utilizing German technology. Weighing 177 tons, and carrying buckets of 13 cubic yards, the 1200 was the first of a line of hydraulic mining excavators that firmly placed P&H in the hydraulic heavyweight class. Since that entry, P&H has expanded its hydraulic line upward to the present-day 1550 and 2250, with operating weights of 226 and 372 tons. These machines are available with electric power or single diesel engine up to 1,800 horsepower.

In 1995, Liebherr introduced its current largest excavator, the 996 in the 600-ton class. Shown in backhoe configuration, the machine in the picture works for Thiess-BHP Coal, Australia. It carries a 36-yard bucket, and is powered by a pair of Cummins engines totaling 3,000 horsepower. *Liebherr-France, Colmar*

It was not until 1965 that Hitachi unveiled its first hydraulic excavator, this 3/8-yard UH03. It was the first to be developed using Japanese technology. *Hitachi Construction Machinery Canada Ltd.*

Other Hydraulic Excavator Developments in the United States

Koehring, a traditional cable excavator in Milwaukee, Wisconsin, was one of the first North American manufacturers to recognize the advantages of hydraulic machines. Its first hydraulic machine, the Model 505, introduced in 1963, was also the largest all-hydraulic machine in North America at that time. The 505 was available as a 2-yard backhoe, and also as a "Skooper," Koehring's trade name for its unconventional hydraulic face shovel.

Continued on page 216

The 800-horsepower UH801 was Hitachi's largest offering from its hydraulic excavator line when it was introduced in 1984. It is powered with two Cummins diesels and weighs in at 173 tons. Carrying a 10-yard bucket, this 801 is working in a coal mine near Naugatuk, West Virginia.

This EX3500 is an example of the modern "EX" range of excavators currently offered by Hitachi. The machine shown is carrying a 24-yard bucket, and has an operating weight of 364 tons. It is working at the Barrick Goldstrike Mine in Nevada in 1989.

This P&H 312 represents Harnischfeger's first entry into the hydraulic excavator field. Having purchased the excavator designs from Cabot Corporation in 1964, Harnischfeger came out with the Models 312 and 418, which remained in the company's line until 1976. The 312 is a 105-horsepower machine in the 17-ton class.

Harnischfeger entered the mining-size hydraulic market in 1979 with this Model 1200. Up in the 13-yard class, it weighed 177 tons. Pictured is one of five 1200s purchased by British contractor Simms.

Currently, Harnischfeger offers the 2250 series A as its largest hydraulic excavator at 372 tons. A single 2,000-horsepower diesel engine provides the power. The standard shovel size for the 2250 is 25 cubic yards. A backhoe version is also available. *Harnischfeger Corporation*

Caterpillar was a late entry into the hydraulic excavator market in 1972. The model was the 27-ton 225, one of which is shown here demonstrating its acrobatic capabilities. With its various upgrades, the 225 remained in Caterpillar's product line until 1991. *JKH collection*

Another popular excavator from Caterpillar's first series was the 235, introduced a year after Caterpillar's first excavator. With upgrades, it remained in production until 1993. The original series 235, one of which is shown here, was in the 44-ton weight class. *JKH collection*

This Caterpillar wheeled excavator Model 214 has its origins in the German excavator range made by Eder, which Caterpillar added to its line in 1983. The 214, shown here performing clamshell duty, is in the 17-ton class. *JKH collection*

Caterpillar's current largest hydraulic excavator is the 5230 mining shovel, announced in 1994. It is powered by a Caterpillar 1,470-horsepower engine, and can handle rock buckets from 17 to 24 cubic yards. Operating weight is just under 350 tons, making the 5230 the all-time heaviest machine Caterpillar has ever built. *Eric Orlemann*

In 1963, the Koehring Company unveiled the largest hydraulic excavator in North America. It was also the company's entry into the hydraulic excavator field. The machine was the Model 505 "Skooper" of unusual design. Its dipper was rated at 2 cubic yards.

Insley Manufacturing Corporation claimed the title to the world's largest hydraulic excavator when it announced the H-2250 in 1965. The backhoe bucket was sized at 2 1/4 cubic yards, and the machine weighed 46 tons. A 5-yard shovel version, the HL-5000, was also offered. *Ed Prodor*

Continued from page 211

Koehring's line broadened over the next two decades, both in number of models and in top-end size, reaching well into the mining excavator market with the models 1166, 1266, and 1466. The 1466, built from 1981 to 1986, was available as a 10-yard class shovel or 12-yard short stick backhoe. It weighed 154 tons, and was powered by a pair of Detroit or Cummins engines of up to 898 total horsepower.

Beginning in 1984, Koehring revamped its entire line of excavators, using the prefix 66 for its model designations. This line included certain models of Japanese IHI-design, a company Koehring had been associated with since the 1950s, when Koehring machines were made under license in Japan. The new 66-series was expanded to nine sizes, before being reduced in 1993 to three models of scrap handlers only.

Insley Manufacturing Corporation of Indianapolis, Indiana, was another early-American entrant into the hydraulic field, having built cable excavators since 1922. In 1963, it launched its first hydraulic machine, the H-100. The following year, the H-100 was replaced by the H-560, featuring a 5/8-yard backhoe. By 1971, Insley had built its last cable machine and fully changed over to hydraulic excavator manufacture.

In 1965, Insley launched the world's largest fully hydraulic backhoe—the H-2250, with a hoe bucket of 2 1/4 cubic yards and an operating weight of 46 tons. A shovel version, the 5-yard HL-5000, was also offered. In 1986, Insley was purchased by Badger Construction Equipment Company, and production moved to Winona, Minnesota. The Insley excavators were continued until 1996, when the last excavator, a Model H-3500D, left the factory.

The Badger Machine Company, incorporated in 1946, developed a tractor-mounted hydraulic backhoe called a "Hopto" (Hydraulically Operated Power Take-Off). From 1958 to 1977, Badger was owned by the Warner & Swasey Company, which developed the Hopto line of crawler and truck-mounted hydraulic excavators. The mammoth Hopto 1900 was America's largest hydraulic excavator when it was introduced in

The "Hopto" line of hydraulic excavators, originally developed by the Badger Machine Company in 1946, was built by the Warner & Swasey Company from 1958 to 1977. Model 500 shown here is a 17-ton class machine with a 112-horsepower diesel engine. *Badger Equipment Company*

The giant Warner & Swasey Hopto 1900 weighed over 100 tons and was America's largest hydraulic excavator when it was introduced in 1972. This massive piece of equipment was powered by two 308-horsepower GM engines, and incorporated no less than eight propel motors in its lower works. Standard bucket size was 8 cubic yards.

1972. This 100-ton, 4-yard machine came equipped with two GM 8V-71 diesels, each of 308 horsepower. The most amazing thing about this huge machine was its eight-motor propelling system. It boasted two hydraulic motors at all four corners of its crawler undercarriage, driving through spur gear and planetary reductions. Thus, the propelling arrangement consisted of four driving sprockets, with no less than 48 gears and pinions. That's a lot of hardware! The 1900 enjoyed a lengthy production run; the last one was shipped in 1990.

From 1977, the Hopto machines were made in Badger's own factory at Winona, Minnesota. The last one, a Model 900B, was shipped in 1991. Today, Badger continues to build its own line of Hydro-Scopic telescoping excavators.

Recognizing the increasing competitiveness of large hydraulic excavators against large cable excavators, Marion made a brave attempt to join its hydraulic excavator rivals. The result was one of the largest hydraulic excavators ever designed and built in North America. Weighing over 300 tons, the Model 3560 was offered in shovel or backhoe configuration, and could be powered by diesel engines or electric motors. Buckets ranged between 12 and 26 cubic yards. A total of eight 3560s were built between 1981 and 1989.

We have already seen that Bucyrus-Erie Company started to build the Hydrocrane and Hydrohoe machines back in the 1940s. In 1965, the company made a second hydraulic entry with the introduction of its full-hydraulic crawler excavator line with the 20-H. By 1970, this line was expanded to four basic sizes, up to the 3-yard 40-H. The 40-H was further stretched to the IPA (Improved Production Attachment) version in 1975 that featured a backhoe with special short stick and 5-yard bucket for coal loading. That same year, the 350-H was unveiled, the forerunner of a new line of advanced excavators with a high-pressure hydraulic system. By the end of the decade, this new line had superseded all previous models, and was topped by the 5 3/4-yard 500-H. A 10-yard shovel version, the 550-HS, was introduced in 1982. However, two years later Bucyrus-Erie announced it had sold its entire construction equipment business to Northwest Engineering Company (now Terex Corporation), and the hydraulic excavators were discontinued.

The famed cable excavator maker, Marion Power Shovel Company, made a brave attempt at a hydraulic machine in 1981. It was a large mining excavator with an operating weight of over 300 tons, one of the largest ever designed and built in North America. It was available with either diesel or electric power, and buckets ranging from 12 to 26 cubic yards, depending on the material. A 16-yard backhoe was also offered. The diesel version required two engines of 700 horsepower each. *JKH collection*

The Badger Equipment Company has been building its machines since 1977, when it purchased the rights from Warner & Swasey Co. The Hopto excavators continued until 1991. The 450 shown here, from Badger's current range, carries a 171-horsepower engine and weighs 18 tons. *Badger Equipment Company*

The 30-H was introduced in 1967 as a 1 3/4-yard excavator by Bucyrus-Erie Co. (now Bucyrus International, Inc.), another company famous for its cable excavators. The example shown is equipped with tractor-type crawlers, fit for use on long pipeline jobs. *Bucyrus International*

The "big one" in Bucyrus-Erie's hydraulic line from 1970 to 1979 was the 3-yard Model 40-H. From 1975, the 40-H was available as an "IPA" (Improved Production Attachment) version, boosting the hoe capacity to 5 cubic yards and operating weight to 61 tons. The 40-H IPA in the picture is loading a Ford tri-axle truck at a West Virginia coal mining operation of Grafton Coal Co. *Bucyrus International*

The largest hydraulic excavator from Bucyrus-Erie was the 500-H at 115 tons in operating weight, and a standard 5 3/4-yard bucket. Coming out in 1979, it headed up a line of new, advanced excavators that had been announced in 1975. However, all Bucyrus-Erie's hydraulic excavators were discontinued by 1985. *Bucyrus International*

GLOSSARY

The earthmoving industry has been grossly short of new words to describe its activities and machines. The result is that almost every word used to describe an activity, machine, or component has more than one meaning in the English language. The following are some of the common words used in the earthmoving industry:

Apron
The moveable front gate on a scraper bowl.

Backhoe
The front end of an excavator consisting of boom, stick, and dipper that is pulled toward the machine to collect its load. It may also refer to the entire excavator of this type. It is also known as hoe, backacter, or drag shovel.

Base Machine
A fully-revolving excavator without a front end.

Bench
A working level or the layer of material taken by an excavator making a cut or pit.

Bowl
Bucket or box on a scraper in which material is carried.

Crowd
The motion of a shovel that pushes the dipper stick into the bank.

Circle
The circular frame on a grader that carries the moldboard. It is mounted below the grader's main frame.

Dipper
The bucket of an excavator when equipped as a shovel or backhoe.

Dipper Stick
The arm or handle attached to a shovel dipper, which slides on a pivot in the boom.

Draw Works
The winch machinery fitted on a crane or cable-operated excavator.

Ejector
The moveable rear wall of a scraper bowl that ejects the load.

Excavator
A machine used for excavating where the digging cycle is usually performed from one spot without propelling. Includes shovel, backhoe, dragline, clamshell, skimmer, bucket wheel, and bucket chain types. Exceptions are continuous excavators and ditchers, which propel as they dig.

Front End
The attachment on the front of an excavator that does the digging. For example: shovel, backhoe, and dragline.

Full Trailer
A trailer that is fully supported by wheels at both ends.

GMW
Gross machine weight. Same as GVW.

GVW
Gross vehicle weight. This is the weight of a vehicle plus its load.

Handle
See Dipper Stick.

House
The structure on the revolving frame of an excavator that covers the machinery and incorporates the operator's cab.

Lower Works
All machinery and structural components below the swing circle on a revolving excavator.

Moldboard
The blade on a grader.

Open Pit Mine — A surface mine where a large pit or hole is dug in the ground; it consists of several benches.

Overburden — The material overlaying the mineral to be mined in a surface mine.

Partings — Bands of unwanted shale or clay within a coal seam.

Pass — Refers to one digging cycle, which consists of dig, transport, dump, and return.

Prime Mover — The mobile power unit on an earthmoving machine that is attached to a towed device, for example, a trailer or scraper.

Railroad Shovel — An excavator, usually steam-powered, that swings only its front end during the digging cycle. It can be mounted on rails or wheels.

Semitrailer — A trailer supported at one end on the fifth-wheel arrangement of a prime mover.

Shipper Shaft — The shaft located near the center of a shovel boom that supports the dipper stick slides.

Shovel — The front end of an excavator consisting of boom, dipper stick, and dipper which is forced away from the machine to collect its load. Can also refer to an entire excavator equipped with a shovel front end, consisting of a dipper, dipper stick, and boom.

Spoil — The material cast into piles by the excavator uncovering the mineral in a strip mine.

Strip Mine — A surface mine where long strips or cuts are removed to uncover the mineral. In the excavating process, the previous cut is back-filled with material from each successive new cut.

Stripping Shovel — A revolving crawler-mounted excavator with an extra-long boom, capable of casting the excavated material into piles instead of loading a truck.

Struck Load — It is the volume of a "water level" load, i.e., without heaping.

Surface Mine — Any type of mine that is open to daylight, as opposed to tunneling.

Swing Circle — The anti-friction bearing between the upper works and lower works on an excavator, usually consisting of rails and rollers.

Swing — The action of rotating or slewing an excavator or crane about its center point.

Tandem Truck — A truck having two driven rear axles and a single front axle (6x4).

Universal Excavator — An excavator capable of interchanging its front end.

Upper Works — All machinery and structural components above the swing circle on a revolving excavator.

INDEX